TPM Case Studies

TPM Case Studies

Edited by Nikkan Kogyo Shimbun

Factory Management Series
Productivity Press
Portland, Oregon

Compiled from *NKS Factory Management Journal*, originally published in Japanese by Nikkan Kogyo Shimbun.

Previously published in English in looseleaf form as *Total Productive Maintenance*, in the *Factory Management Notebook Series*, vol. 1, no. 4 (Productivity Press, 1991).

English translation copyright © 1995 by Productivity Press, Inc.

All rights reserved. No part of this book may be reproduced or utilized in any form or by any means, electronic or mechanical, including photocopying, recording, or by any information storage and retrieval system, without permission in writing from the publisher. Additional copies of this book are available from the publisher. Address all inquiries to:

Productivity Press, Inc.
P.O. Box 13390
Portland, OR 97213-0390
United States of America
Telephone: 503-235-0600
Telefax: 503-235-0909

Cover design by William Stanton
Text design and composition by Inari Information Services, Inc.
Printed and bound by Edwards Brothers in the United States of America

Library of Congress Cataloging-in-Publication Data

TPM case studies / edited by Nikkan Kogyo Shimbun.
    p. cm. -- (Factory management series)
  "Compiled from NKS factory management journal, originally published in Japanese by Nikkan Kogyo Shimbun" --T.p. verso.
  "Previously published in English in looseleaf form as Total productive maintenance, in the Factory management notebook series, vol. 1, no. 4"--T.p. verso.
  ISBN 1-56327-066-8
  1. Factory management. 2. Plant maintenance. 3. Total productive maintenance.
4. Factory management--Case studies. 5. Plant maintenance--Case studies. I. Nikkan Kōgyō Shinbunsha. II. Series. III. Series: Factory management notebook series : v. 1, no. 4.
TS155.T65   1995
658.2'02--dc20   94-31518
                                                                         CIP

98 97 96 95 94   10 9 8 7 6 5 4 3 2 1

CONTENTS

Publisher's Foreword	vii
Part I TPM: The Six Major Losses	**1**
The Toyota Production System (JIT) and TPM: Two Management Strategies	3
Gaining Perspective	3
JIT and TPM Cannot Be Separated	5
The Basic Ideas behind JIT and TPM	7
The Revolutionary Results of JIT and TPM	12
Using Perspective	14
Analyzing the Six Major Losses: Total Productive Maintenance	17
What Can We Expect from TPM?	17
Focusing on the Six Major Losses	19
The Introduction of a TPM Program	24
Using PM Analysis	25
The Definition of TPM and Individual Improvements	27
Focusing Improvement Activities on the Six Major Losses: Targets and Procedures	31
Eliminating Loss due to Failures	31
Eliminating Loss due to Setup Adjustments	38
Eliminating Loss due to Brief Stops	42
Eliminating Loss due to Speed Drops	46
Eliminating Loss due to Defects and Rework	49
Eliminating Loss due to Startups	50
Well-Conceived Machinery Results in Higher Productivity	51
Part II Reducing the Six Major Losses	**53**
Action against "Mistakes" to Reduce Equipment Loss: Improvements in Plant Structure	55
The Problems of Today's World	55
The Revaluation of TPM and the Future	56
Current Equipment Controls and Future Equipment Development	57
Taking Action against the Mistakes that Cause Loss	59
Taking Action against Loss due to Brief Stops	61
Taking Action against Loss due to Spontaneous Machine Failure	63
Taking Action against Loss due to Speed Drops	65
Taking Action against Loss due to Setup Adjustments	67
Taking Action against Loss due to Changing Consumable Parts	69
Taking Action against Loss due to Instable Precision	71

Increasing Human, Equipment, and Material Efficiency to Lower Failures:
Developing "TPM Eyes" — 73
    The Togo Seisakusyo TPM Program — 73
    Examples of Loss Reduction — 84

Improving Corporate Structure with TPM Activities:
100 Percent Participation — 93
    The NBC Corporation TPM Program — 93
    Examples of Loss Reduction — 108

Specialized Maintenance and Autonomous Maintenance in the
Process Industries: Sparking a Consciousness Revolution — 117
    TPM in the Process Industries — 117
    Examples of Loss Reduction — 135

Part III TPM Case Studies — 137

Overcoming the Six Major Losses: TPM Case Studies — 139

Improvements to Stop Breakage of Welding Robot Cable:
Loss due to Failures — 141

One-Touch Setups Using Common Fixtures for Sharpening Cutting Tools:
Loss due to Setups — 145

Shortening Setup Adjustment Time for Bend Reinforced Glass:
Loss due to Setups — 149

Cutting Clip Attachment Defects to 1/37th the Former Level:
Loss due to Brief Stops — 153

Overcoming Problems with Clogged Screws: Loss due to Brief Stops — 157

Eliminating Brief Stops at the Transfer Machine: Loss due to Brief Stops — 161

A 13 Percent Improvement by Updating the Machining Program:
Loss due to Speed Drops — 165

Maximizing Speed Efficiency for a Hydraulic Press:
Loss due to Speed Drops — 169

Reducing Machining Cycle Time for Special Pulleys:
Loss due to Speed Drops — 173

Countermeasures against Defects in Circularity with Cylindrical
Grinding Machines: Loss due to Defects — 177

Reducing Defects in Welding: Loss due to Defects — 181

Immediately Acceptable Quality for Machine Pressed Powder
Molded Products: Loss due to Startups — 185

PUBLISHER'S FOREWORD

Total Productive Maintenance (TPM) combines leading-edge maintenance practices with quality control concepts and small group activities to revolutionize plant maintenance. It is an innovative system for equipment management that optimizes effectiveness, eliminates breakdowns, and promotes autonomous operator maintenance through day-to-day activities. This is especially important in our increasingly automated manufacturing environment. In fact, TPM improves the productivity and efficiency of the total organization, not just its manufacturing facilities; we cannot settle for less ambitious goals in today's competitive environment.

Part I of this volume of the Factory Management Series, written by Seiichi Nakajima and other experts from the Japan Institute of Plant Maintenance, introduces TPM and its relationship to Just-in-Time manufacturing, and then discusses the six major losses in manufacturing. The reasons for these losses are analyzed through TPM techniques, and targets and procedures to deal with these problems are developed.

Part II takes you into the next steps of a TPM program, where action against mistakes and the six major losses is developed. Looking at programs from actual plants, improvements throughout the entire manufacturing environment are laid out, and plans for the future are formed. Part III concludes by following case studies in which workers develop TPM programs to combat recurring problems and improve plant, machine, and operator productivity and efficiency. Studying this volume will help you in your own TPM development program.

We are grateful to Nikkan Kogyo Shimbun and their *Factory Management* journal, and to those organizations that share their efforts in manufacturing improvement. Thanks also to Esmé McTighe for editing and production management, and to Michael Kelsey for translation, art and text integration, and page production. David Richardson designed the illustrations, and William Stanton created the cover design.

Norman Bodek
Publisher

TPM Case Studies

Part I

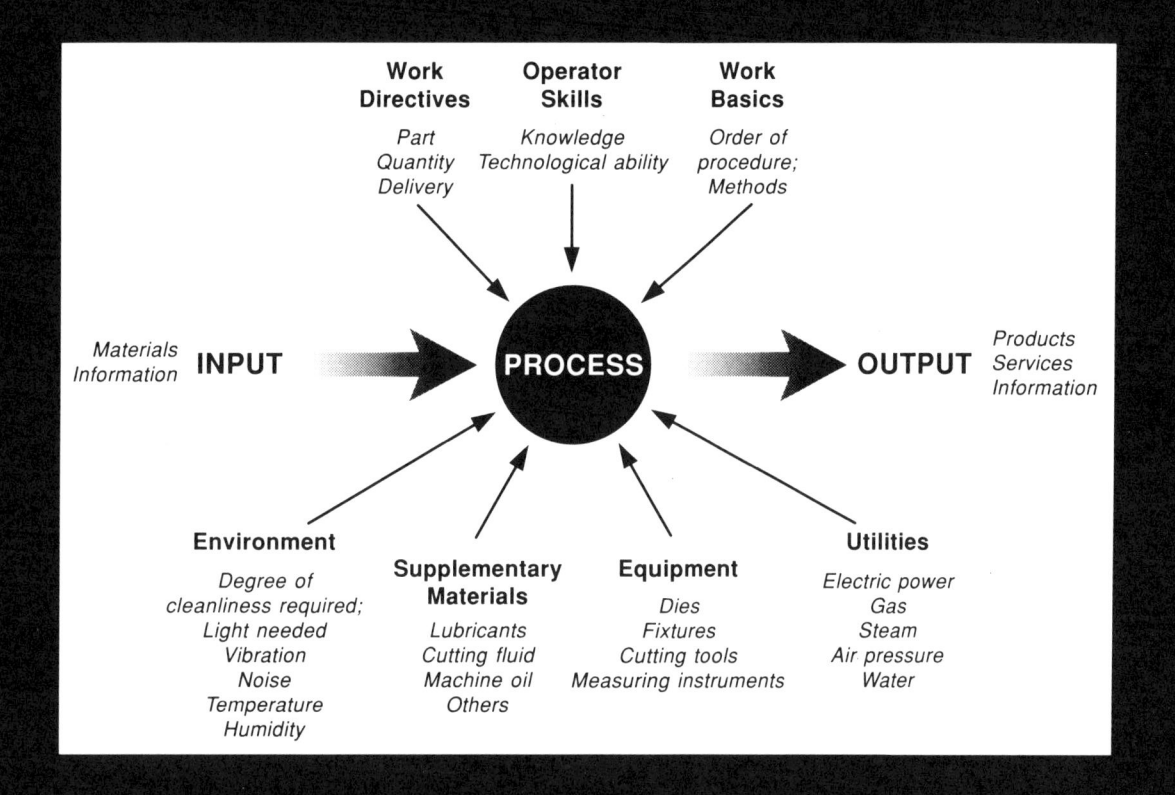

Inputs to Process

Work Directives
Part
Quantity
Delivery

Operator Skills
Knowledge
Technological ability

Work Basics
Order of procedure;
Methods

Materials / Information → **INPUT** → **PROCESS** → **OUTPUT** → Products / Services / Information

Environment
Degree of cleanliness required;
Light needed
Vibration
Noise
Temperature
Humidity

Supplementary Materials
Lubricants
Cutting fluid
Machine oil
Others

Equipment
Dies
Fixtures
Cutting tools
Measuring instruments

Utilities
Electric power
Gas
Steam
Air pressure
Water

TPM: The Six Major Losses

Two Management Strategies

The Toyota Production System (JIT) and TPM

By Seiichi Nakajima
President, Japan Institute for Plant Maintenance

Gaining Perspective

A number of external factors, such as trade friction, currency exchange problems, and the like, have come together in recent months to cloud the environment in which Japanese corporations—especially those in the manufacturing world—must operate. Those that wish to survive this period must change their corporate structure and devote more energy to developing local production systems.

The world has come to realize that the much-vaunted Japanese quality and productivity are direct reflections of its production system, and a good deal of attention has been paid recently by overseas concerns to this system—specifically, to the Toyota Production System and the idea of Total Quality Control (TQC). In the 1980s, there was a rapid increase in the number of experiments with these systems abroad. And recently, the idea of Total Productive Maintenance (TPM) also has begun to take the spotlight, and is coming under the scrutiny of overseas corporations.

The principles of the Toyota Production System and TQC are well known and in practice throughout Japan, but TPM is a comparative newcomer, building even now to a faster rate of incorporation by Japanese manufacturing concerns.

Mr. Taiichi Ohno, the father of the Toyota Production System, saw the ideas of "just-in-time" production and "autonomation" as being the two mainstays of his program, but abroad the system has come to be known primarily as the "Just-In-Time" production system, or, more frequently, simply as "JIT." We will bow, therefore, to this popular usage, and refer to the Toyota Production System simply as "JIT" in what follows.

Total Productive Maintenance, or TPM, has as its goal the maximizing of the overall productive rate; since its incep-

Figure 1 The Toyota Production System

```
Toyota Production System = Thorough elimination of waste
                (asking "why" five times)
    │
    ├─► Production in the Toyota System ──── Cross-trained employees
    │                                        Creation of flow
    │                                        Avoiding defects
    │
    ├─► "Just-in-Time" Production
    │       │
    │       ├─► Kanban (operational method)
    │       │     Necessary parts at the necessary times, only    (Eliminate inventory
    │       │     in necessary amounts                              completely)
    │       │
    │       ├─► Leveling of production (response to diversification)
    │       │        (Small lots and quick setup changes)
    │       │
    │       └─► Thorough implementation of standard work
    │              1. Cycle time
    │              2. Order of work performance
    │              3. Standard work in process
    │
    └─► Autonomation (line is stopped when a problem occurs)
            │
            ├─► Visual controls ──► (Signal lights (andon))
            │
            ├─► Operable rate (operates at any time when operation is desired)
            │        (Maintenance is assured)
            │        (Setup change time is cut)
            │
            └─► From work improvements to machinery improvements
```

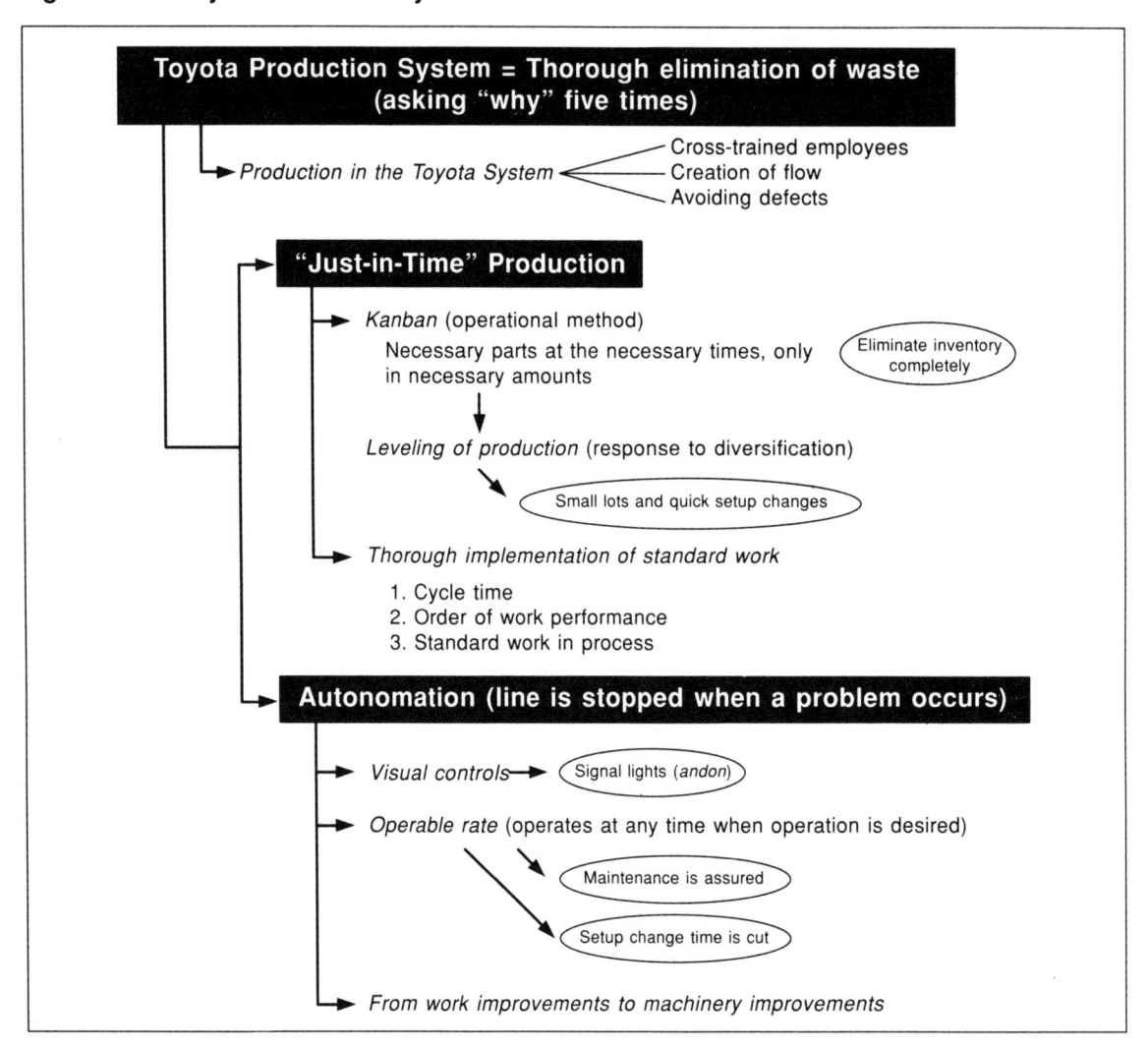

tion, it has been closely intertwined with JIT. In the balance of this article, we shall examine the relationships between these two ways of thinking, with the goal of gaining an essential understanding of each. By extension, we also should gain a good understanding of the types of basic corporate improvements that these systems should result in when they are introduced.

JIT and TPM Cannot Be Separated

Taiichi Ohno summed up the essence of the Toyota Production System—JIT—as shown in Figure 1. His primary emphasis was that the purpose of the system was to "thoroughly eliminate waste." Other goals were the creation of cross-trained operators, capable of handling more than one process; the creation of a production flow; and the creation of no defects. He stressed that the two pillars of support for this structure were "just-in-time production" on the one hand, and "autonomation" on the other.

On the operating level, the primary tool for the JIT system is the "kanban," a sheet of paper enclosed in a rectangular vinyl casing. This sheet of paper includes critical information concerning parts—parts pulling information, transporting directives, and production directives. All of this information is vital in producing the required part at the required time in the required amount, thus eliminating traditional problems such as overproduction, excessive transporting, and conventional inventory.

The Ford System, developed in the United States, was able to shorten production time and reduce costs simply by using conveyor belts for flow operations, but JIT was a more revolutionary approach. This system was designed for multiple model, small-lot production done by the flow method, and was epoch-making in its contributions to shortening production time and lowering costs to the minimum.

TPM got off the ground in Japan through the efforts of the Japan Institute for Plant Maintenance (JIPM), as a company-wide system for equipment control in plants with advanced automation programs. Its goals include the maximizing of overall equipment efficiency in multiple model, small-lot production systems so as to eliminate equipment failures, defects, and accidents; general improvements in quality and

Figure 2 TPM: A Definition and Its Characteristics

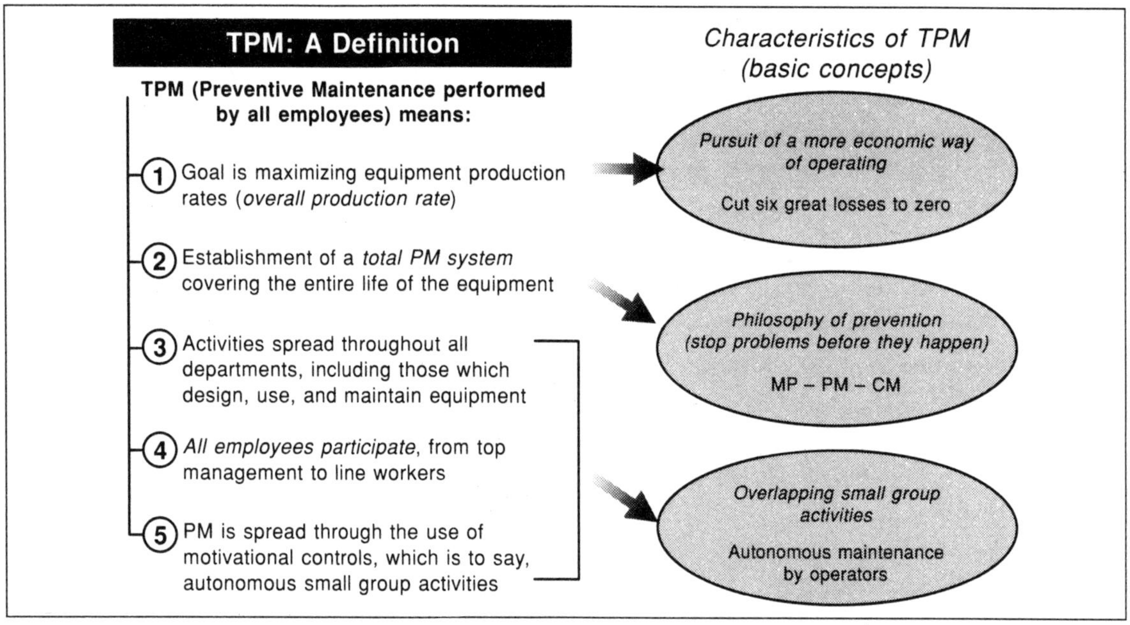

TPM: A Definition

TPM (Preventive Maintenance performed by all employees) means:

1. Goal is maximizing equipment production rates (*overall production rate*)
2. Establishment of a *total PM system* covering the entire life of the equipment
3. Activities spread throughout all departments, including those which design, use, and maintain equipment
4. *All employees participate*, from top management to line workers
5. PM is spread through the use of motivational controls, which is to say, autonomous small group activities

Characteristics of TPM (basic concepts)

- Pursuit of a more economic way of operating
  Cut six great losses to zero
- Philosophy of prevention (stop problems before they happen)
  MP – PM – CM
- Overlapping small group activities
  Autonomous maintenance by operators

productivity; and the creation of a more positive atmosphere in the workplace (see Figure 2).

The first company to implement a TPM program in Japan was Nippondenso, a member of the Toyota Group. In 1971, the JIPM officially recognized the outstanding fruits of this program by conferring the "Prize for PM Excellence in the Plant" (known more simply as the "PM Prize") on Nippondenso. As a member of the Toyota Group, it should go without saying that Nippondenso already had implemented the principles of JIT; the company also had received the Deming Award for Quality Control.

Toyota used the awarding of the PM Prize to Nippondenso as a focal point to encourage the other companies in the group to introduce TPM programs. They did, and a number of them were awarded the PM Prize. Companies outside the Toyota Group, of course, also introduced programs, and TPM became common in the machining and assembly industries, particularly in the device manufacturing field.

In the 17 years from 1971 to 1987, some 116 plants introduced and perfected TPM programs to the point where they were awarded the PM Prize. The trend has become particularly strong recently, with 15 or 16 firms a year winning the prize. Approximately 60 percent of these prize-winning firms are either members of the Toyota Group or are classified as "cooperating factories," meaning that they are among Toyota's principal vendors. This fact alone says volumes about the close—indeed, indissoluble—relationship between JIT and TPM.

We saw above that "autonomation" is one of the two major supports of JIT, but this has certain prerequisites. When production lines are to be operated simultaneously, they should always be in an operable condition, of 100 percent production potential. Constant maintenance is required to ensure this condition, and setup time also must be short. Among the goals of TPM are the total elimination of machine failures and setup preparation time, so it can be seen that the implementation of a successful TPM program is essential to JIT.

Conversely, TPM can result in significant effects in the implementation of fully automated, unmanned production systems in plants following the principles of JIT.

As we can see, then, JIT and TPM are closely interwoven, and provide mutual benefits for one another. It is generally preferable to introduce TPM after the incorporation of JIT, and to develop the two on a one-dimensional plane. It is best not to be too greedy and introduce JIT and TPM at the same time, though—introduce TPM after achieving a JIT-type production flow.

The Basic Ideas behind JIT and TPM

Mr. Ohno has defined industrial engineering (IE) as "company-wide manufacturing technology directly related to the management of the company," and the Toyota Production System, particularly "Toyota IE," as "profitable IE."

To borrow a phrase from the Ohno school, we might say that TPM is a form of company-wide manufacturing technology directly related to management, and focusing on the company's equipment. The bottom line is that TPM is "equipment IE," and we also can speak of "profitable TPM."

Thus, both JIT and TPM can be described as "company-wide manufacturing technology directly related to management." While each approach of course has its own individual characteristics, the basic ideas behind the two are similar.

The relationships between input and output in production are shown in the matrix depicted in Figure 3. Production input is made up of what we can call the "five M's"—men (personnel), machines, materials, methods, and money. Output is comprised of six factors: production volume (P), quality (Q), delivery (D), safety and environmental factors (S), and morale (M).

Controls for each of the output items are listed in the right-hand column of Figure 3. They include process controls, quality controls, cost controls, delivery controls, and the like.

JIT is a "company-wide manufacturing technology," and thus incorporates all input and output controls. Its focus can be characterized as being on the output side, though, with its aims being the maximum attainment of superior quality, low costs, and rapid deliveries.

TPM, on the other hand, is a company-wide manufacturing technology that focuses on equipment—which is on the

Figure 3 Input and Output in Production

Input / Output	Men (Personnel)	Machines	Materials	Control Methods
		Money		
Level of production (P)				Production controls
Quality (Q)				Quality controls
Cost (C)				Cost controls
Delivery (D)				Delivery controls
Safety and environmental factors (S)				Safety and environmental factors controls
Workers' morale (M)				Labor controls
Control Methods	Control of manpower	Equipment control	Materials control	Output / Input = Productivity

Purpose of plant activities

input side of our scale. Its goal is the "building in of quality at the equipment level," and by controlling the factors in the cause-and-effect chain, it strives to maximize output.

It is true, of course, that JIT does not ignore the input side in its quest for higher output. Indeed, the thorough elimination of waste on the input can help to maximize output, but it is still fair to say that TPM is, of the two, the input-oriented approach while JIT is output-oriented.

Mr. Ohno always maintained that the goal of the Toyota Production System was to increase production rates by the thorough elimination of all types of waste from the company. He identified seven types of waste:

- ✓ Overproduction
- ✓ Waiting
- ✓ Transporting
- ✓ Waste in machining itself
- ✓ Inventory
- ✓ Waste in movements
- ✓ The creation of defects

When it comes to this idea of the total elimination of waste, TPM is exactly the same as JIT. The first clause in the definition of TPM is the creation of "a corporate structure with maximum efficiency in the production system (overall production rate)." In short, the idea is to eliminate totally all loss created by equipment, in order to increase equipment efficiency. There are six major types of loss from equipment as identified by TPM:

- ✓ Loss from equipment failure
- ✓ Loss from setup adjustments
- ✓ Loss from brief stops
- ✓ Loss from speed drops
- ✓ Loss from process defects
- ✓ Loss from startups

These losses are of considerable concern throughout the manufacturing world, and the challenge is to identify and completely eliminate them.

It can be seen, then, that the idea of "zero loss" found in TPM is much the same as the idea of the thorough elimination of waste in JIT.

The basic idea behind TPM is "zero loss," but it must be realized that machine failures are the source for a number of the other losses, and the first step toward zero loss is thus the total elimination of failures. Failures cannot be eliminated through the use of the conventional type of after-the-fact maintenance, performed after a machine has failed—they must be prevented before they happen.

For this reason, the first goal of TPM is preventive maintenance (PM), performed to stop failures before they have the chance to occur. This is to machinery what preventive medicine is to human beings. Failures are "illnesses" to machines, and to stop them, we need to practice preventive medicine—this includes daily preventive measures, thorough diagnoses, and early treatment. The first important step in ensuring that machines are not stricken with disease is the performance of daily preventive activities (daily maintenance measures), specifically cleaning, lubrication, tightening, and inspection. These measures must be performed conscientiously, and they must be buttressed by periodic inspections, which correspond to complete physicals in the realm of human medicine. Early treatment (repair) also is required.

In addition to PM, TPM also stresses the need for corrective maintenance (CM), performed for the purpose of increasing overall reliability and maintainability. In addition, it calls for taking steps to ensure that new equipment will be maintenance free. This is known as "maintenance prevention," or "MP." All of these steps are part of what might be called the philosophy of prevention, aimed at preventing all types of loss before it happens.

Interestingly, Mr. Ohno said precisely the same thing regarding the Toyota Production System. He incorporated the ideas of preventive medicine into JIT under the slogan "prevention is more important than cure."

Maintenance, as we know, means the maintaining of all levels of functionality on any given piece of equipment, and obviously implies the stopping of failures before they occur. Mr. Ohno often said in personal conversations with this author that there was no need to speak of "preventive" maintenance when everyone should understand that *all* maintenance is preventive by nature.

The next feature of TPM is the fact that it is based on a very concrete approach, one we might refer to as "here-and-now-ism." In this respect, too, it has much in common with JIT. One of the goals of TPM is to keep the equipment as close as possible to its ideal state, which is the virtual epitome of "here-and-now-ism." In JIT, we often speak of "visual controls," an idea reflected in TPM by posting things in the "here and now," so that they can be immediately understood visually. For example, a "TPM Activity Board" should be posted in the workplace so that everyone will be able to comprehend immediately the state of the TPM program; tags are put on equipment at areas where problems occur; amounts and times of lubrication are posted at the lubrication areas on machines; the direction of rotation is posted on valves and rotating members of machines; pipes are color-coded for easy distinction, and other similar actions are taken to satisfy the need for knowledge based on here-and-now-ism in TPM.

In JIT, it is mandatory for "kanban" to be affixed to items which flow through the workplace, which is another example of here-and-now-ism. When a problem occurs on a line, a revolving red light is placed on the line at that location, and a call light ("andon") is hung from the ceiling to show what line is the source of the problem, so that the foreman or maintenance supervisor can rush to the spot when needed.

Shop floor improvements are not made from a desk, located somewhere totally out of the action. Both JIT and TPM stress the need for these activities to come from actual experience and observations conducted on the shop floor.

One more point in common between JIT and TPM is that both approaches favor participatory management which values the human element.

In JIT, the ideal form of production is one in which workers are cross trained to be able to fill a number of different jobs. Mr. Ohno used to say that enabling a single operator to acquire the technology needed to perform a wide range of production jobs was beneficial in the creation of a total system for the manufacturing workplace, a system in which the individual worker could play an important role. It was this knowledge, he said, that gave the worker some reason to work. Surely this is a form of participatory management which values the human element.

The major characteristic of TPM is known as "autonomous maintenance by operators." By "autonomous maintenance," we mean that operators all will maintain their own equipment, performing the preventive medical practices described above to ensure that their machines do not come down with some serious illness. The idea behind this approach is that the person actually using a machine is the one best qualified to perform the daily preventive measures—cleaning, lubricating, tightening, and inspecting—needed to keep it running properly.

The more automated a workplace becomes, the larger becomes the percentage of direct production that is carried out by the automated equipment. The jobs for the people in the workplace, at this stage, are switched to maintenance, to enable the automated equipment to continue to run efficiently. Tasks such as loading and offloading workpieces, or monitoring gages, should be done whenever possible by robots. Tasks which require knowledge and skill should be delegated to the human operators, who will then feel that their jobs have more meaning. This creation of "meaning" in work is one of the goals of TPM, and is one of the reasons behind the practice of autonomous maintenance performed by operators.

There is another interesting sidelight to TPM, in addition to its major contributions, which are the elimination of failures, defects, and accidents. Equipment and the work environment in shops where there are thriving TPM programs tend to be almost unbelievably clean, making them more conducive to human endeavor. In this sense, as well, TPM is the very epitome of participatory management which values the human element.

The Revolutionary Results of JIT and TPM

There is a very simple reason that both JIT and TPM programs began attracting attention, both in Japan and abroad—the firms which introduced these programs achieved what must be termed "revolutionary" results. Let us consider an example that shows the full scope of the revolutionary nature of these results.

The Toyota Production System (JIT) and TPM

Table 1 Comparative Effects in Companies Implementing the Toyota Production System

		Complete Implementation (8 companies)	Incomplete Implementation (18 companies)	Conventional Methods (37 companies)
LEAD TIME	Production time	3.75 days	12 days	17.6 days
	Total time	7.75	41.7	44
INVENTORY	Materials	4.2-day supply	11.2-day supply	17-day supply
	In-process work	3.2	11.2	16.3
	Products	2.1	8.9	14.6
CHANGING MODELS*	Average time per changeover	15.4 min.	52.5 min.	93 min.
	Number of changeovers per week	14.3 times per week	7.5 times per week	6.6 times per week
	Total time for week	87 min. per week	425 min. per week	404 min. per week
Percentage of number of control personnel		2.6 %	5.5%	4.7%

*Due to the use of different averaging practices by different companies, minutes per changeover times number of changeovers per week will not equal total minutes per week.

Table 1 shows the results of a study on the effects of progress controls, a study conducted by Professor Chitoku Kumaya of Nagoya University of Science and Technology.

As the table clearly reveals, companies which had fully implemented their JIT programs achieved results that could only be called revolutionary: inventory and lead time were cut to between 10 and 20 percent of former levels, changeover loss (setup time loss) was cut to one-fifth the former level, and the number of control personnel used was halved. One important fact shown by this table is that companies which had only incompletely implemented their JIT programs reported a 5 percent increase in changeover loss and a 20 percent increase in control personnel, despite the fact that there was only a small reduction in lead time. This is due to the fact that incomplete programs have not established a production base sufficient for reductions in changeover time, and in defects and failures. Herein lies the difference between companies which do not respect JIT and those which receive prizes in the field, according to the interpretation made by Professor Kumaya.

Like JIT, TPM also has had revolutionary results for companies which have implemented it. The PM Prize is awarded to companies which have achieved significant results with their TPM program. Quantifiable results for recent winners of this prize include a 1.5 increase in value-added productivity; drops to between 1/50 and 1/150 in the

Table 2 Examples of TPM Effects

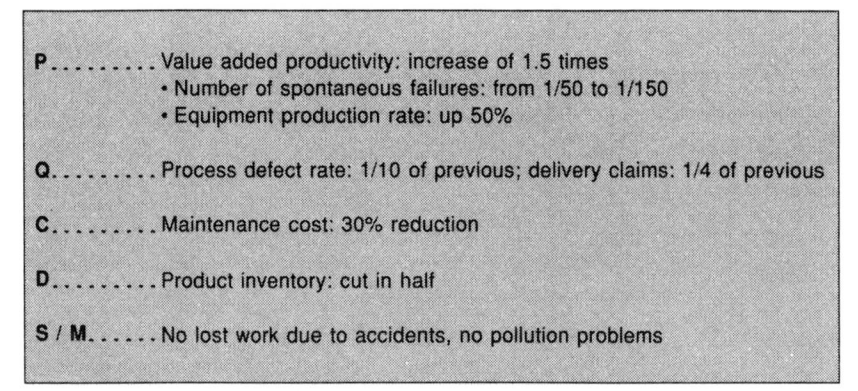

P........	Value added productivity: increase of 1.5 times • Number of spontaneous failures: from 1/50 to 1/150 • Equipment production rate: up 50%
Q........	Process defect rate: 1/10 of previous; delivery claims: 1/4 of previous
C........	Maintenance cost: 30% reduction
D........	Product inventory: cut in half
S / M.....	No lost work due to accidents, no pollution problems

number of instances of spontaneous equipment failure; drops to one-tenth of the former number of process defects, and other truly astounding results (see Table 2). In addition to these quantifiable results, there have been other, less tangible, results as well. Some examples include the creation of operators who are well-grounded in the basics of their equipment; projects to eliminate failures, defects, and accidents; and an overall improvement of the image of the company, which nearly always leads to new orders.

Using Perspective

The Toyota Production System is characterized as "company-wide manufacturing technology with direct links to management." It is widely known to have brought about revolutionary results in the optimization of quality, costs, and production lead time, and has been the focus of attention both in Japan and abroad. It has been the subject of many different experiments in many different industrial fields.

As we have seen, the Toyota Group has taken the lead in unifying JIT and TPM programs, getting from them revolutionary new mutual benefits.

Indeed, the need to add TPM to JIT has been recognized both in Japan and abroad in recent years, and more and more companies are turning to TPM.

I recently made my third trip to Brazil, where I conducted a "TPM Management Course" in two or three locations. During this time, I visited one company which was in the process of implementing a JIT program, and representatives from this company were enthusiastic in their desire to start TPM, now that they had JIT well underway. It struck me as remarkable at the time that, even in these far-off lands (far from Japan, that is), there was already a realization of the need to mate TPM to JIT.

As more and more Japanese companies become engaged in local production, the principal philosophies and methods of JIT can be logically expected to become even more global than they already are. At the same time, Professor Kumaya's research leads us to believe that companies which have not fully implemented the programs will experience a number of difficulties.

The JIPM is the official promotion body for TPM, and we have encouraged companies to add TPM to their JIT programs. In this way, it is clear, these companies can make further strides in shortening changeover operations, and in reducing defects and failures. The mutual benefits of the two programs will lead to revolutionary results that will be of interest throughout the world.

TPM is not just a Japanese approach. It needs to be instituted on a global basis, along with JIT, by all companies which hope to survive the economic hardships of the world to come.

Total Productive Maintenance

Analyzing the Six Major Losses

By Ichizoh Takagi
Japan Institute for Plant Maintenance

What Can We Expect from TPM?

The box on the following page presents a definition of Total Productive Maintenance (TPM). Keeping this definition in mind, we can list three primary benefits that a corporation might reasonably expect to attain through the introduction of a TPM program.

✓ Improved corporate structure

Changes in equipment and in the workplace in general will bring about concurrent changes in the attitudes, ideas, and actions of the people who work there. The result will be improvements in the general structure of the corporation.

✓ More productive equipment

One of the key features of TPM is the ferreting out and total elimination of the factors that impede productivity. The elimination of these problems will help to maximize productivity in the workplace.

✓ Better trained personnel

TPM requires a trained workforce. Employees must be brought to the level where they are able to maintain and improve the gains that have been made in productivity.

> ## TPM Is:
>
> 1. Aimed at creating a corporate structure with maximum efficiency in the production system (overall production rate).
> 2. A workshop architecture that allows the elimination of loss before it happens, through the total elimination of "disasters, defects, and machine failures" within the entire life cycle of the production system.
> 3. Applied to all departments in the corporate structure, including development, sales, and management as well as production.
> 4. The participation of all employees, from top management down to the line workers.
> 5. A means of achieving zero loss and zero defects through overlapping small group activities.

In brief, the creation of a workplace structure that will enable greater profits means more than simply strengthening the ability to make improvements. True progress will not be made until the workplace has increased its ability to maintain this higher level workplace structure.

What points, then, should we focus on in our TPM activities?

First, let us list some of the problems so often encountered in conventional improvement activities:

✓ Selection of topics is based on suggestions

✓ The assignment of responsibilities to the QC circle tends to discourage attempts at improvements which are technologically difficult

✓ Improvements are done for the sake of oral presentations at meetings, and are not standardized, making them impossible to maintain

✓ There is no support from control personnel or the technical staff

✓ Only simple topics are selected for implementation

✓ Lack of technology and techniques needed to maintain improvements often results in a complete loss of whatever was gained by them, causing a reversion back to the old way of doing things

✓ The activities shed no light on the real problems of the workplace

Now, keeping these problems firmly in mind, let us go on to examine the way that "loss" is understood in TPM, and the basic ideas behind improvements aimed at eliminating loss.

Focusing on the Six Major Losses

The idea behind TPM is to make equipment operate more efficiently by discovering and eliminating the major factors which prevent their efficient operation. Six major factors, called the "Six Major Losses," have been identified:

✓ Loss due to failures

✓ Loss due to setup adjustments

✓ Loss due to brief stops

✓ Loss due to speed drops

✓ Loss due to defects and rework

✓ Loss due to startups

There are other types of loss, in addition to the six listed above. These include control losses (related to the need to wait for parts, materials, tools, etc.) and planning losses (orders for a given product are cut off, the need for periodic repairs, etc.). Other losses come from the human factor, such as ineffectual operations, non-value added operations, and the like (see Figure 1).

Loss due to Failures

These are losses due to equipment breakdowns, which occur either spontaneously or chronically. They mean lost time and lost volume. To respond to loss due to failures, it is necessary to study what can be done to increase equipment reliability, and to study what type of maintainability is needed to minimize the amount of time it takes to bring the equipment back to working order once a failure has occurred.

20

Figure 1 The Structure of Chronic Loss

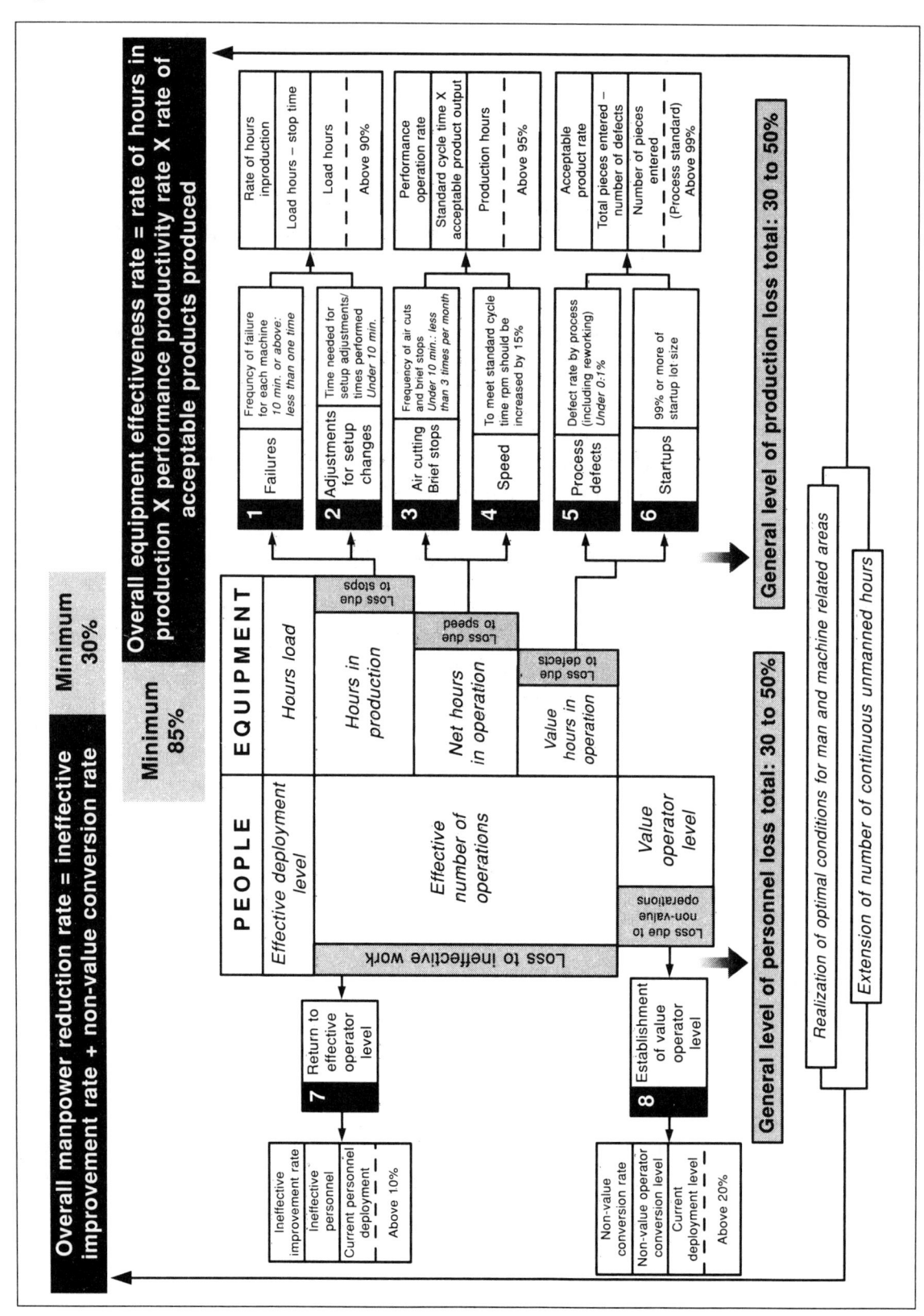

Analyzing the Six Major Losses

Spontaneous failures are relatively easy to monitor visually and then to take action against them, but frequently people forget the need to extend these measures to other, similar equipment so as to prevent the outbreak of comparable problems in the future.

Chronic loss is loss that happens with some frequency, and is often left to develop unchecked because of the difficulties inherent in trying solution after solution that just does not seem to work. Cases such as this require improvement heaped on improvement, which can cause one to lose sight of the way the equipment in question is supposed to be operating, thus even further complicating the issue. The first step, therefore, always should be to restore the equipment to its normal operating condition. Then, a thorough failure analysis must be made for every failure, to track the problem back to its true cause. At this point, it becomes possible to take truly effective countermeasures.

Conventional failure records have not done anything to trace the problem back to the failure mechanism, including the locations and parts of the machine where the failure has occurred. It is necessary to record more than just the fact that a failure has occurred—whether performing a full-blown analysis, one that gets at the actual physics of the problem, has really taken hold in the workplace without provoking the operators there, is a constant source of headaches for control personnel and the management team.

Loss due to Setup Adjustments

Setup adjustment loss is the lost time and defective parts that are involved when a piece of equipment is stopped and needed changes are performed to start the production of a different part properly.

The setup operation itself has always been a major topic treated in improvement activities, and a considerable degree of progress has been made in this arena. The industrial engineering approach is to divide setups into on-machine and off-machine setups, and to work to reduce the time needed for both types. These studies have resulted in significant time savings. The use of video equipment and similar methods also has resulted in suggestions that have brought about a certain level of improvement to the operation. But although the setups themselves might have been improved, the adjustment problem remains, as always, a major snag in the works.

The elimination of adjustment loss is a problem that is trying to deal with, and compared with the setup operation itself, the problems tend to be hidden. This makes the loss difficult at times to comprehend—which means they often go untreated. The best approach to the elimination of adjustment loss is to focus on the adjustment mechanism, finding a way to eliminate the time it requires.

Loss due to Brief Stops and Air Cuts

This refers to a situation different from those when a machine stops completely due to some internal failure. Here we are talking about very brief stops or air cuts (when the machine operates, but without a workpiece) due to some temporary problem.

For example, the machine might be cutting air while the workpiece is caught in the chute, or the misoperation of a sensor might cause a temporary stop. In cases such as this, removing the trapped workpiece or resetting the machine will bring it back to normal operation, which is a situation fundamentally different from a machine failure. But these minor problems often can impede the efficient operation of the equipment, and problems such as this are commonplace with automated equipment and transporting equipment in particular.

There has been a general tendency to overlook brief stops because they are so simple. Often they are caused by complex problems that are difficult to quantify, even if the problem can be laid out in a visible manner. This makes it hard to determine just what sort of overall affect the problem has on productivity.

The first step in the reduction of brief stops is to focus on the elimination of minute flaws in the equipment. The isolation and elimination of minute flaws that is a part of the initial cleaning stage in autonomous maintenance can be quite effective in dealing with this problem.

Loss due to Speed Drops

This loss represents the difference in the rated speed of the equipment in question and the actual speed at which it is being operated. It includes problems arising when operation at the designed speed results in quality or mechanical problems, forcing a speed reduction.

Generally speaking, there are many cases when operations continue without the operator being fully aware of the nature of the speed loss. Despite the fact that speed loss is the most significant contributor to overall efficiency decline of any of the six major losses, it is also the most difficult to evaluate properly.

This is often because the standard design speed itself is somewhat vague, or because the nature of the machinery makes it difficult to judge its speed. Improvements dealing with speed loss must at the very least begin with a good understanding of the maximum speed possible under current conditions, so it is necessary to clarify the conditions needed to enable this speed (deviations in workpieces, warmup operations for hydraulic devices, differences dependent on ambient temperatures, etc.).

Understanding the current conditions and devising ways to increase speed will contribute to the exposure of problems and increase the technological level of the workplace. The target for the difference between rated and actual speed always should be "0."

Loss due to Defects and Rework

This is volume and manhour loss caused by defects and the need to rework them. It is usually easy to deal with spontaneous defects, and they are not left to go unchecked. The causes of chronic defects, though, can be unexpectedly hard to pinpoint, making it difficult to institute countermeasures with the desired effects, and as a result, such defects are often ignored. Reworking requires manhours, and should be thought of as a chronic defect.

Loss due to Startups

This is the volume loss that can come at the start of production. It is the loss that occurs from the time that production is started until product quality has been stabilized, and its magnitude will vary depending on factors such as the stability of machining conditions, problems with fixtures or dies, and the abilities of individual operators. These losses tend to be hidden, and must be revealed for what they are so that steps can be taken to minimize them.

The improvement targets for the six major losses are listed in Table 1 on the next page.

Table 1 Improvement Targets for the Six Major Losses

Type of Loss	Target	Remarks
Loss due to failures	0	Must be at 0 for all equipment
Loss due to setup adjustments	Minimize	As brief as possible for all machines, and always under 10 min.
Loss due to speed drops	0	Difference between actual speed and design specification speed should be 0. Should strive to improve equipment so it can be operated at greater than rated speed.
Loss due to brief stops	0	Must be at 0 for all equipment
Loss due to defects and rework	0	Must be within tolerance range (for example, 100 to 300 ppm)
Loss due to startup	Minimize	

The Introduction of a TPM Program

The best way to go about introducing a TPM program is to select a machine as a test case; create a project team made up of production engineers, maintenance staff, and line control personnel; perform individual improvements to increase equipment efficiency; and indicate the effects of the program through a study of the quantifiable results it brings.

The machine selected to serve as the test case should be from a bottleneck process, which suffers from chronic loss and which seems capable of favorable response if subjected to an on-going improvement program for about three months. It is best to start by selecting a target from the most critical of the six major losses in that specific workplace.

Project teams should be designated for each target selected, performing individual improvements and striving for an overall increase in system effectiveness. At the same time, individual improvements performed by small group activities in the various workplaces should be continued. It is vital that those involved from the control perspective strive to discover, during the process of these individual improvements, exactly what factors have negative impacts on production efficiency. It is important to get an accurate idea of the loss involved, to take into consideration the progress of the autonomous maintenance program, to select appropriate targets for the overall program, and for control personnel to take leadership positions and the initiative in getting the program going. In order to keep the program going once it is underway, steps must be taken to increase the technological and skill levels of operators through autonomous maintenance programs, thereby developing operators who are well-grounded in maintenance.

Individual improvements are developed through the ideas described above, making it necessary to bring about qualitative results in a short period of time. But it still will be difficult to achieve results in the realm of chronic loss so simply. In most cases, physical-mechanism (PM) analysis must be applied to achieve results in the clearing up of chronic loss.

Using PM Analysis

PM analysis refers to the physical analysis of phenomena in order to uncover the mechanisms which cause them, and an application of the results to the factors which make up these mechanisms. These factors are known as the "4M's" (men, machines, materials, and methods).

The object of such analysis is chronic loss (especially loss due to defects, failures, and brief stops). This type of analysis is most effective when applied to problems where a number of conventional attempts at solutions have already proven ineffective.

The basic ideas behind PM analysis are as follows:

✓ All phenomena should be understood in the concrete context of the current workplace

✓ Phenomena should be viewed in terms of the physical principles behind the mechanisms which cause them

✓ It is necessary to understand the functions and structures of machining principles, the processes, and the equipment involved

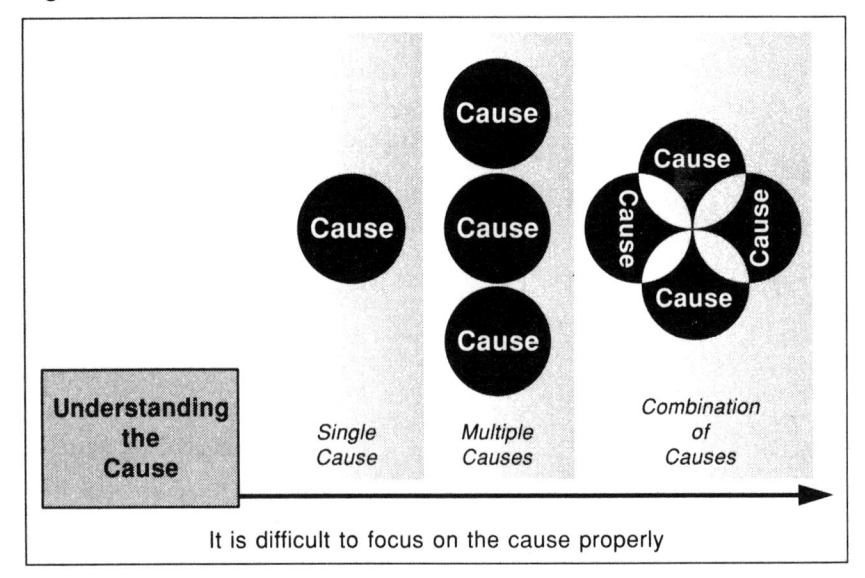

Figure 2 The Causes of Chronic Loss

It is difficult to focus on the cause properly

- Understanding the Cause
- Single Cause
- Multiple Causes
- Combination of Causes

✓ Detailed analysis of the interrelationships among the 4M's must be conducted

✓ All preconceptions and "critical indices" should be thrown out, allowing the problem to be viewed strictly from the standpoint of what logically appears out of place

Let us then consider some of the points that must be addressed when applying PM analysis to a chronic problem.

There are three basic patterns for all types of loss: first is loss with a single cause, second is loss with multiple causes, and third is loss with compound causes (see Figure 2). Nearly all spontaneous loss has a single cause, and though

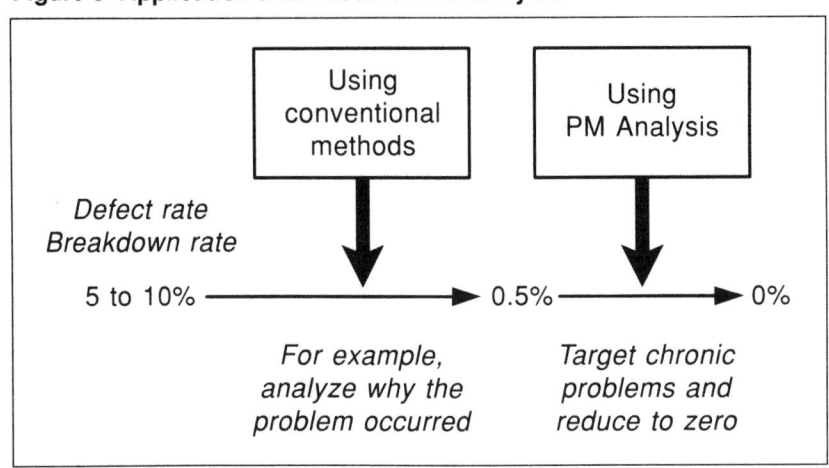

Figure 3 Application and Focus of PM Analysis

Defect rate
Breakdown rate

5 to 10% → 0.5% → 0%

Using conventional methods: For example, analyze why the problem occurred

Using PM Analysis: Target chronic problems and reduce to zero

Analyzing the Six Major Losses

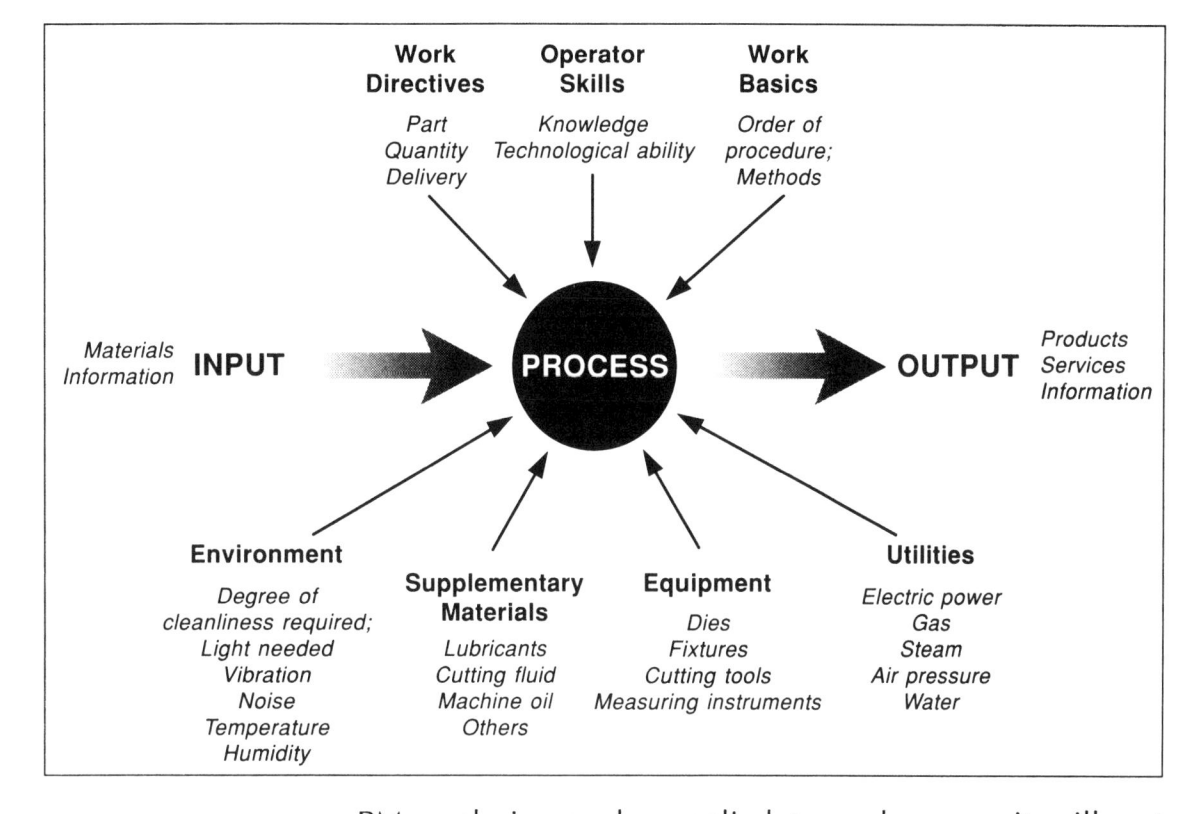

Figure 4 Model of a Single-Process Production System

```
                    Work         Operator        Work
                 Directives       Skills         Basics
                    Part        Knowledge      Order of
                  Quantity    Technological   procedure;
                  Delivery       ability       Methods
                       ↘           ↓           ↙
   Materials                                              Products
   Information  INPUT  ⟶    PROCESS    ⟶   OUTPUT   Services
                                                          Information
                       ↗           ↑           ↖
                 Environment   Supplementary  Equipment         Utilities
                 Degree of      Materials                     Electric power
              cleanliness required;  Lubricants    Dies          Gas
                Light needed    Cutting fluid    Fixtures       Steam
                  Vibration     Machine oil    Cutting tools   Air pressure
                    Noise         Others     Measuring instruments  Water
                 Temperature
                  Humidity
```

PM analysis can be applied to such cases, it will not necessarily be effective.

Chronic loss, on the other hand, generally has multiple or compound causes, and PM analysis can be applied effectively in these situations.

As can be seen, then, loss which occurs frequently can be analyzed by conventional methods, but for loss at a certain level (for example, 0.5 percent) of occurrence, it is more effective to use PM analysis (see Figure 3).

The Definition of TPM and Individual Improvements

Let us now consider the problems that tend to appear with improvements made in the conventional way and the individual improvements that are a part of the TPM program.

The first aspect of our definition of TPM is that it is "aimed at creating a corporate structure with maximum efficiency in the production system." What do we mean by "production system" in this context? To explain, we will consider the single-process production system outlined in Figure 4.

According to this model, the production system involves the input of raw materials to the process, where they are acted on by the factors noted in the figure, and output as final products, a service, or the like. The maximizing of productivity, then, involves the use of the smallest volume of input (including all factors) needed for the greatest volume of output. The concept of improvement activities, then, is not just the simple idea that utility use will increase because the topic selected was to lower the amount of raw materials used—a more complex way of thinking must be used to view all of the elements involved.

The second item in our definition of TPM involves "the entire life cycle of the production system." This means that TPM should be applied to the entire life cycle of the system, from planning and design to final discarding of factors, and not just to the operation and maintenance stages of the current production system architecture. Improvements, then, must be designed so that they will have an impact on the planning and design of new equipment, as well as have an effect on current equipment that can be maintained (see Figure 5). Further, the system should eliminate loss before it happens. The cutting of loss to zero is a basic philosophy of TPM, and one of its main characteristics is that the mechanisms designed to do this must be based on the actual workplace and the actual items that are handled there.

Figure 5 The Relationship between TPM and the Life Cycle of the Production System

LIFE CYCLE OF THE PRODUCTION SYSTEM	TPM ACTIVITIES
Planning and designs for production system	Design products to be easy to manufacture
Architecture of production system	Build in mechanisms that will prevent losses
Operation and maintenance of production system	Set conditions that will not lead to loss
	Set control conditions that will not cause losses
Abandoning production system	Improve production systems

(Information Feedback)

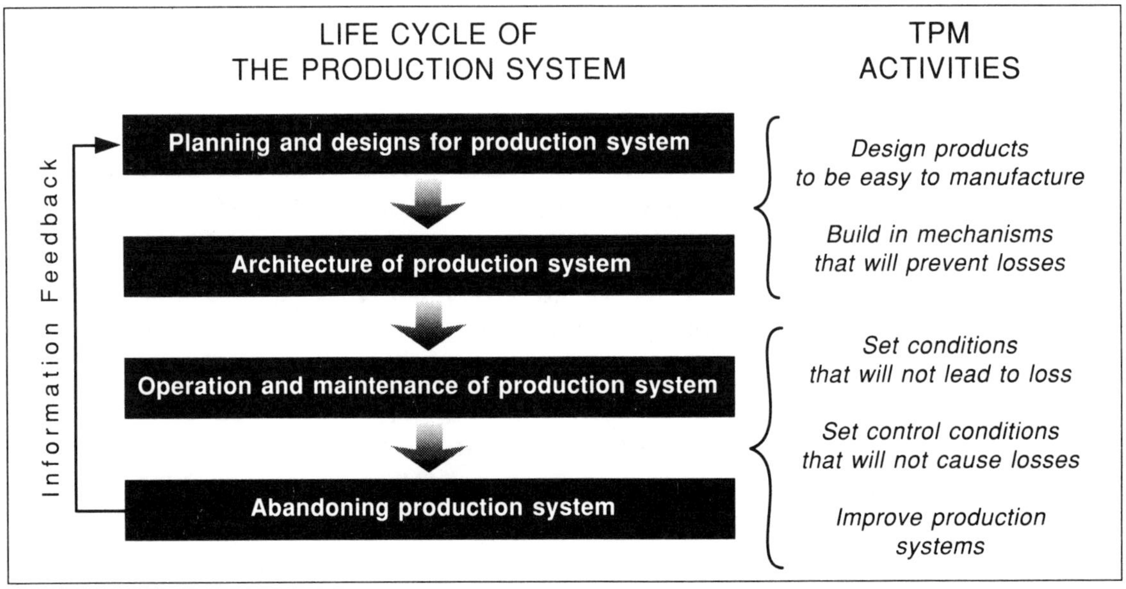

The third part of our TPM definition is that the program be "applied to all departments in the corporate structure." This means that TPM is more than activity carried out by the production departments.

The fourth part of the definition stressed "the participation of all employees, from top management down to the line workers." By this we mean that TPM should be a wide ranging program, encompassing all departments in the corporation, and that it thus requires the participation of all employees if it is to be successful.

The fifth part of the definition notes the need for "overlapping small group activities." This is another one of the major characteristics of TPM.

The idea of small group activities conventionally meant only those activities carried out by the first-line manufacturing personnel. In TPM, small group activities encompass every layer of the corporate structure, from top management on down. The major form of small group activity in TPM is autonomous maintenance, built around the activities of groups led by foremen and group leaders. Individual improvements, on the other hand, are performed mainly by small groups led by section and subsection heads. These middle managers will come to a better understanding of the functions and structure of their equipment through these improvement activities, which will give them more self confidence and make them more effective leaders of autonomous maintenance programs.

Achieving "maximum efficiency in the production system" is something that is easy to say, but hard to do. The reason that we have touched on the relationships between TPM and individual improvements here, though, is that the distillation of expertise accumulated by companies which have worked to achieve maximum efficiency is, basically, the definition of TPM.

Targets and Procedures

Focusing Improvement Activities on the Six Major Losses

By Takao Izumi
Japan Institute for Plant Maintenance

One of the main goals of Total Productive Maintenance (TPM) is the wholesale elimination of all factors that tend to obstruct equipment efficiency, in order to attain a higher overall rate of production efficiency. The improvement targets and level evaluations that are used for this purpose are included in Table 1.

Eliminating Loss due to Failures

Failures are one of the major reasons that machine efficiency deteriorates. To counter this problem, it is necessary to expose all hidden flaws, to stop the machinery on a planned basis before defects occur, and to deal with the flaws properly. This may seem so simple an approach as to be commonplace, but it is the basic rule behind the elimination of failures. There are five measures which must be taken in order to implement this simple rule:

Table 1 Levels of Evaluation for Improvement of Overall Equipment Effectiveness

Level / Target	Level 1	Level 2	Level 3	Level 4
1. Loss due to failures	1. Mixture of spontaneous and chronic loss 2. Basic maintenance greater than preventive maintenance 3. Excessive failure loss 4. Autonomous maintenance system not completed 5. Excessive deviation in service life of components 6. Weaknesses of equipment not clear	1. Spontaneous failures 2. Basic maintenance nearly equal to preventive maintenance 3. Excessive failure loss 4. Autonomous maintenance system nearly in place 5. Service life of components can be projected 6. Weaknesses of equipment becoming evident 7. Corrective maintenance implemented for the above	1. Time-based maintenance system implemented 2. Preventive maintenance greater than basic maintenance 3. Failure loss under 1% 4. Vigorous activities on the part of autonomous maintenance system 5. Service life of components lengthened	1. Condition-based maintenance system established 2. Preventive maintenance only 3. Failure loss from 0.1% to 0 4. Autonomous maintenance system being maintained through constant improvements 5. Service life of components can be predicted 6. Progress in reliability and maintenance design
2. Loss due to setups	1. Everything left up to operator with no controls 2. Excessive time variations due to confusions in operating conditions	1. Standards made for operation (distinctions made between off-line and on-line setups and procedures established for each) 2. Time variations exist 3. The next problem to be tackled is clarified	1. Work being done to convert in-line setups to off-line setups 2. Adjustment mechanisms and responses to them fully clarified	1. Full maintenance of optimal conditions, with setups under 10 min. 2. All products good without need for adjustments
3. Loss due to brief stops	1. No one notices scale of loss due to brief stops (because all is left up to operators) 2. Deviations in areas where loss occurs and in frequency lead to very vague understanding of conditions	1. Loss due to brief stops quantified and understood according to frequency and location of occurrence and volume of loss 2. Manifestations of loss have been classified and chain of events causing loss clarified, with measures based on trial and error being put into place	1. Problems inherent in losses due to brief stops have been focused on and countermeasures put into place, so that situation is now favorable	1. Loss due to brief stops is now zero (enabling unmanned operations)
4. Loss due to speed drops	1. Specifications of equipment not clear 2. No speed settings for different models and machines	1. Problems due to speed are focused on in terms of mechanical problems and quality problems 2. Speed settings (standards) made and maintained for each model 3. Only small variations in speed	1. Improvements being implemented on trial basis for problems as noted 2. Individual speed settings for each model, with clarifications made of problems and concerns regarding accuracy, particularly when it affects quality characteristics 3. Only small amount of speed loss	1. Machine operates according to specifications, with improvements allowing speeds at above specifications 2. Speeds set and standardized for all models, and maintained 3. Speed loss zero
5. Loss due to defects (includes starts and stops)	1. Chronic defects are left unchecked 2. Numerous actions are taken but with no results	1. Chronic defects are quantified in terms of type, frequency, and volume 2. Types and reasons for problems are analyzed and countermeasures under implementation	1. Problems regarding chronic defects are focused on and countermeasures implemented, with good results 2. Study made of in-process detection of defects on occurrence	1. Loss due to quality defects is from 0.1% to 0

- ✓ Establish basic conditions (clean, lubricate, tighten)
- ✓ Maintain basic operating conditions
- ✓ Restore all deteriorated functions to their original level
- ✓ Improve the design weaknesses of the machinery
- ✓ Strengthen operation and maintenance skills

Establish Basic Conditions

There are three components to the establishment of basic operating conditions: clean the machinery, lubricate the machinery, and tighten all bolts, nuts, and the like that need tightening. These seemingly simple activities can be of great help in stopping machine deterioration.

■ Cleaning

Machines always have been the bitter enemies of dirt and foreign matter. This is particularly true of their moving parts, hydraulic systems, and electrical control systems, where dirt and foreign matter can cause wear, leaks, operational defects, conductivity problems, and drops in accuracy.

Cleaning machines, then, of course helps to eliminate dirt and foreign matter, and can help expose hidden problems, such as wear, scratches, roughness, loose connections, shape deformations, leaks, cracks, abnormal temperatures, vibration, abnormal sound problems, and the like. We call these "hidden" problems because they are normally not apparent to us. This is why it is said that "cleaning is inspection."

■ Lubrication

Machines cannot operate contentedly without being lubricated. Slackness in lubrication can cause burnout and other machine failures. Coupled with wear and temperature increases, it can accelerate deterioration, thus giving rise to a number of other failures. There are many workplaces which have well-established policies regarding lubrications, but they are seldom, if ever, carried out.

■ Tightening

Connecting components, which are typified but not limited to bolts and nuts, can fall off or be damaged if they are not kept tight—this is a major cause of machine failure.

If only one bolt comes loose, this can cause vibration through the rest of the machine, resulting in the loosening of other bolts and leading to roughness in operation. This accelerates deterioration, and a number of problems can result before the operator is aware of their potential existence. There are generally a number of connecting components in machines, and each of them plays its own particular role. To ensure that all functions are properly satisfied, then, each bolt should be checked individually.

Maintain Proper Operating Conditions

In order for machines to continue to operate properly, their basic operating conditions must be established and maintained. For example, in the hydraulic system careful attention must be paid to temperature, volume of oil, pressure, the presence or absence of foreign matter, and degree of oxidation; in the electrical control system, the proper conditions must be established and rigorously maintained for ambient temperature, humidity, dust, vibration, magnetism, and other factors affecting operation. Further, individually dictated operating and load conditions must be established and maintained for each machine.

Ignoring operating conditions means that any attempts at improvement are useless, for operation accuracy and machining conditions will remain instable and such instabilities can still cause failures. Some conditions, it should be remembered, must be confirmed with the designer or the manufacturer of the machine involved.

Recovery from Deterioration

No matter how scrupulously you might maintain basic conditions and operating conditions, machines will ultimately deteriorate and fail. It is thus necessary to expose all deterioration and to recover properly from it. This entails proper checks and inspections, and preventive maintenance to eliminate problems and keep the operating conditions normal. But problems in machines are like cancers, spreading gradually from weak spots through the entire machine body, ultimately resulting in failure. Simply restoring the areas where failure took place, or revising just these areas, will still leave the machine open to failures caused by the gradual spreading of these cancers.

Thus, before considering any design changes, it is necessary first to return to the blueprints and thoroughly check all deteriorated locations in the machine, bringing the

Weak Point Improvement in Design

problems lurking in the shadows out into the light. This will help maintain an overall machine balance that preserves power and accuracy.

In cases where service life is short even though all basic conditions are being maintained, inspections, checks, and restoration actions will not be enough to prevent the generation of machine failures. Further, maintenance costs will become a major burden. In these cases, then, the most effective approach is to analyze the weak points in design, and to rectify these. Simple rebuilding should be avoided in such instances, though. Many such "rectifications" end in failure because they are made without regard to the basic structure of the machine, with no attention paid to the types of failures taking place or overall failure data—very often such reworking is nothing more than ideas gleaned from totally different machines, or from incomplete reading of catalogs.

If it appears that the life of the component parts of a piece of equipment is too short, it is necessary to determine whether this is due to design weaknesses or to other reasons, and then to get a firm grip on the true weakness so that a renovation plan can be formulated. There are several steps to follow in these cases:

- ✓ Come to a correct understanding of the circumstances surrounding the failure—what happened before and afterwards
- ✓ Check the structure of the machine and its functions
- ✓ Check the basic conditions, conditions of use, and whether proper recovery has been made from deterioration regarding related functions
- ✓ Clarify the chain of events that has caused the failure
- ✓ Search out the causes
- ✓ Devise a concrete proposal for improvement
- ✓ Implement the proposal
- ✓ Perform a follow-up study to determine whether or not the measure taken was the right one

Following these procedures can prolong service life of equipment. We call this "improvement maintenance."

Figure 1 Critical Points in Dealing with Failures

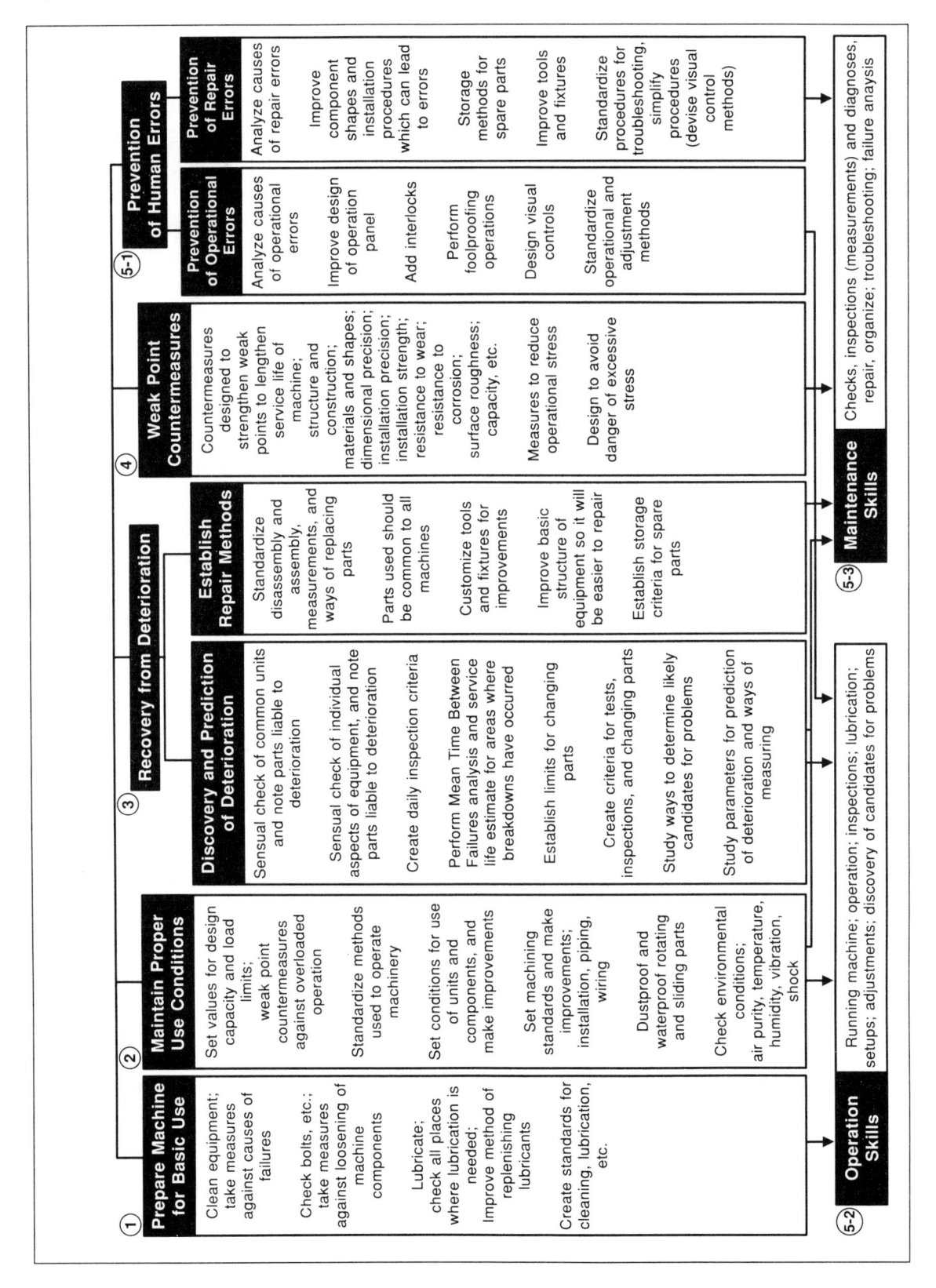

	① Prepare Machine for Basic Use	② Maintain Proper Use Conditions	③ Recovery from Deterioration		④ Weak Point Countermeasures	⑤-1 Prevention of Human Errors	
			Discovery and Prediction of Deterioration	Establish Repair Methods		Prevention of Operational Errors	Prevention of Repair Errors
	Clean equipment; take measures against causes of failures	Set values for design capacity and load limits; weak point countermeasures against overloaded operation	Sensual check of common units and note parts liable to deterioration	Standardize disassembly and assembly, measurements, and ways of replacing parts	Countermeasures designed to strengthen weak points to lengthen service life of machine; structure and construction; materials and shapes; dimensional precision; installation strength; resistance to wear; resistance to corrosion; surface roughness; capacity, etc.	Analyze causes of operational errors	Analyze causes of repair errors
	Check bolts, etc.; take measures against loosening of machine components	Standardize methods used to operate machinery	Sensual check of individual aspects of equipment, and note parts liable to deterioration	Parts used should be common to all machines		Improve design of operation panel	Improve component shapes and installation procedures which can lead to errors
	Lubricate; check all places where lubrication is needed; Improve method of replenishing lubricants	Set conditions for use of units and components, and make improvements	Create daily inspection criteria	Customize tools and fixtures for improvements		Add interlocks	Storage methods for spare parts
		Set machining standards and make improvements; installation, piping, wiring	Perform Mean Time Between Failures analysis and service life estimate for areas where breakdowns have occurred	Improve basic structure of equipment so it will be easier to repair		Perform foolproofing operations	Improve tools and fixtures
	Create standards for cleaning, lubrication, etc.	Dustproof and waterproof rotating and sliding parts	Establish limits for changing parts	Establish storage criteria for spare parts		Design visual controls	Standardize procedures for troubleshooting, simplify procedures (devise visual control methods)
		Check environmental conditions; air purity, temperature, humidity, vibration, shock	Create criteria for tests, inspections, and changing parts		Measures to reduce operational stress	Standardize operational and adjustment methods	
			Study ways to determine likely candidates for problems		Design to avoid danger of excessive stress		
			Study parameters for prediction of deterioration and ways of measuring				

⑤-2 **Operation Skills**: Running machine; operation; inspections; lubrication; setups; adjustments; discovery of candidates for problems

⑤-3 **Maintenance Skills**: Checks, inspections (measurements) and diagnoses, repair, organize; troubleshooting; failure anaysis

Increase Operation and Maintenance Skill Levels

It is not uncommon, when considering actions to take against failures, to be sidetracked into thinking only about the mechanical aspects of the problem, and to overlook the human factor. If an operator is in reality misoperating the machine, thinking all the while that his actions are the correct ones, the problems he can cause will be extremely difficult to solve. Thus it is important to determine what level of true skills in operation and maintenance the staff should have, and to provide them with the training and education needed to achieve this skill level.

None of these five steps can be mitigated—all must be assiduously implemented so that all hidden flaws can be brought to the surface and failures reduced to zero. This is the only short cut to the goal. The most important aspects of each of these measures have been included in Figure 1.

Attempting to perform these steps simultaneously, in a brief period of time, can prove to be very difficult. They have thus been organized into four different stages, as shown in Table 2, so that they can be implemented in a planned

Table 2 The Four Stages to Elimination of Defects

Goal	(1) Reduce deviations in intervals between failures	(2) Lengthen specific service life	(3) Restore deteriorations on a scheduled basis	(4) Predict service life
Major activities	✓ Restoration of deteriorations which had been left unchecked • Deal with hidden flaws ✓ Elimination of forced deterioration • Establishment of basic conditions • Clarification of and conformity to operating conditions	✓ Weak point improvements of design • Improvements in strength and accuracy • Selection of components which conform to conditions • Improvements to eliminate overloads ✓ Elimination of spontaneous failures • Improvement of operation and maintenance skill levels • Safeguards against operational errors • Safeguards against repair errors • Restoration of visual deteriorations	✓ Periodic restoration of deteriorations • Estimation of service life • Set standards for periodic checks and inspections • Set standards for periodic replacements • Improvements in maintainability ✓ Using five senses of operator to become aware of abnormal conditions indicating deterioration • Do problems exist or not? • What are symptoms? • How can symptoms be perceived?	✓ Predicting service life with diagnostic technology ✓ Technological analysis of areas prone to failure • Cross section analysis • Material fatigue analysis • Analysis of gear tooth surface • Ways to lengthen service life • Work from projection of service life to scheduled recoveries

Eliminating Loss due to Setup Adjustments

The tendency toward multiple model, small-lot production is intensifying these days, a fact which makes it all the more critical to shorten setup time, eliminate test machining, and be able to machine acceptable products straight out of the setup, without the need for adjustments.

Although there are those who believe that setup time has been cut right to the bone, there is still room for improvement in this area. This applies particularly to the realm of adjustment time, which now occupies from 50 to 60 percent at overall setup time. Many shops have mistakenly thought there is nothing that can be done about this problem, or that it is too difficult to address, and have tended to let it by without serious consideration.

Focal Points for Improvements to Setups

■ Off-line and on-line setups

An "off-line" (or "external") setup is one that is made while the equipment is still in operation. This requires that all preparations are completed prior to the setup itself (preparation of tools, specification of a location for the off-loaded fixtures, etc., and preparation of a useful work table), and that operations such as partial assembly, preheating, and the like be done ahead of time. An "on-line" ("internal") setup is one in which the machine must be stopped so that tools or fixtures can be changed, alignment and other operations performed, and the like. It is very important to determine which operations can be done off-line, and which can only be done as on-line setups.

■ Moving from on-line to off-line setups

The first step is to analyze what is being done as on-line setups, and address the question of how these operations can be moved to the off-line format.

There are four major methods that can be used to change on-line setups to off-line setups:

✓ Presetting

✓ Using common fixtures and a one-touch insertion method
✓ Performing adjustments off-line
✓ Use of an intermediary fixture

■ Studying on-line setup methods and shortening times

Let us consider, then, the use of fixtures for partial commonality, which will facilitate mounting of parts and help eliminate adjustments.

Measures that can be implemented from this perspective include the adoption of hydraulic clamping in place of the use of screws, or the reduction of the number of screws in use. If two people are used to do simultaneously a job normally done by one person, this greatly reduces time. This and other methods can be used to revaluate optimal personnel deployment and divide jobs in the most economic manner possible.

The Elimination of Adjustments

The drastic reduction of adjustment time needed to begin producing acceptable parts after a setup requires the careful consideration of a number of factors in order to determine which parts of a setup are avoidable and which are unavoidable. Factors which must be studied include the purpose of the adjustments, the reasons for the adjustments, the actual work performed in the course of the adjustments, and the effectiveness of the adjustments.

■ The purpose of the adjustments

First, analyze the purposes of the adjustments. Make it clear whether they are for positioning, alignment, measurements, timing, balance, or some other reason. Often an operator will notice in the course of doing this that two purposes can be met by one adjustment.

■ Break down the adjustments

Next, determine the procedures, methods, standards of judgment, number of times performed, and major points of the adjustments. Explore questions such as the differences between primary (rough) and secondary (finish) adjustments, the different methods used to fix workpieces to the fixtures, the stages of the adjustments, the reference surface (point), the function of the adjustments, methods used for measurements, methods used to move workpieces, inter-relationships between the individual points of adjustments (are they totally independent, or are they interrelated), and the like.

■ Determine what makes the adjustments necessary

After having broken down the individual adjustments for further analysis, it is necessary to uncover the reasons that the adjustments are necessary. This means checking each component task for each adjustment, and looking at the combined purpose of the entire operation as a unit, so that the reason for the adjustment will be clear.

■ Determine the physical principles of the adjustment

Now consider the adjustment in terms of the physical principles and rules that underlie it. What is the significance of these factors, seen purely from a logical standpoint?

■ Get at the causes

Study the possibility of the causes for the adjustment being rooted in a cumulation of errors, in a lack of rigidity, in a failure to meet standards, or in some mechanical insufficiency. Are the reasons the adjustment is necessary independent factors that can be treated individually, or are they a more complex interplay involving more than one factor?

■ Explore the potential

Determine whether or not the adjustment in question can be avoided.

The above was a brief discussion of effectiveness analysis for adjustments (see Table 3). Responses to unavoidable adjustments will be treated below (see also Figure 2).

■ Quantify

Quantify the process with numerical value standards at every opportunity. For areas where quantification seems desirable but not viable, study the possibility of different

Focusing Improvement Activities on the Six Major Losses

Table 3 Effectiveness Analysis of Adjustments

Steps	Purpose	Breakdown	Reasons necessary	Physical analysis	Causes	Study of potential
	Clarify reason for adjustment	Organize the stages in which adjustment is performed	Determine reasons adjustment is necessary under current system	Determine the nature of the adjustment as now performed from a logical standpoint	Determine the causes of the adjustment	Decide whether the adjustment is avoidable or unavoidable

methods of measurement that will enable quantification. If it is still not possible, change to substitute characteristics.

■ Define procedures

Establish the proper procedures for performing the operation, and enforce them rigidly.

Figure 2 Flow of Effectiveness Analysis for Adjustments

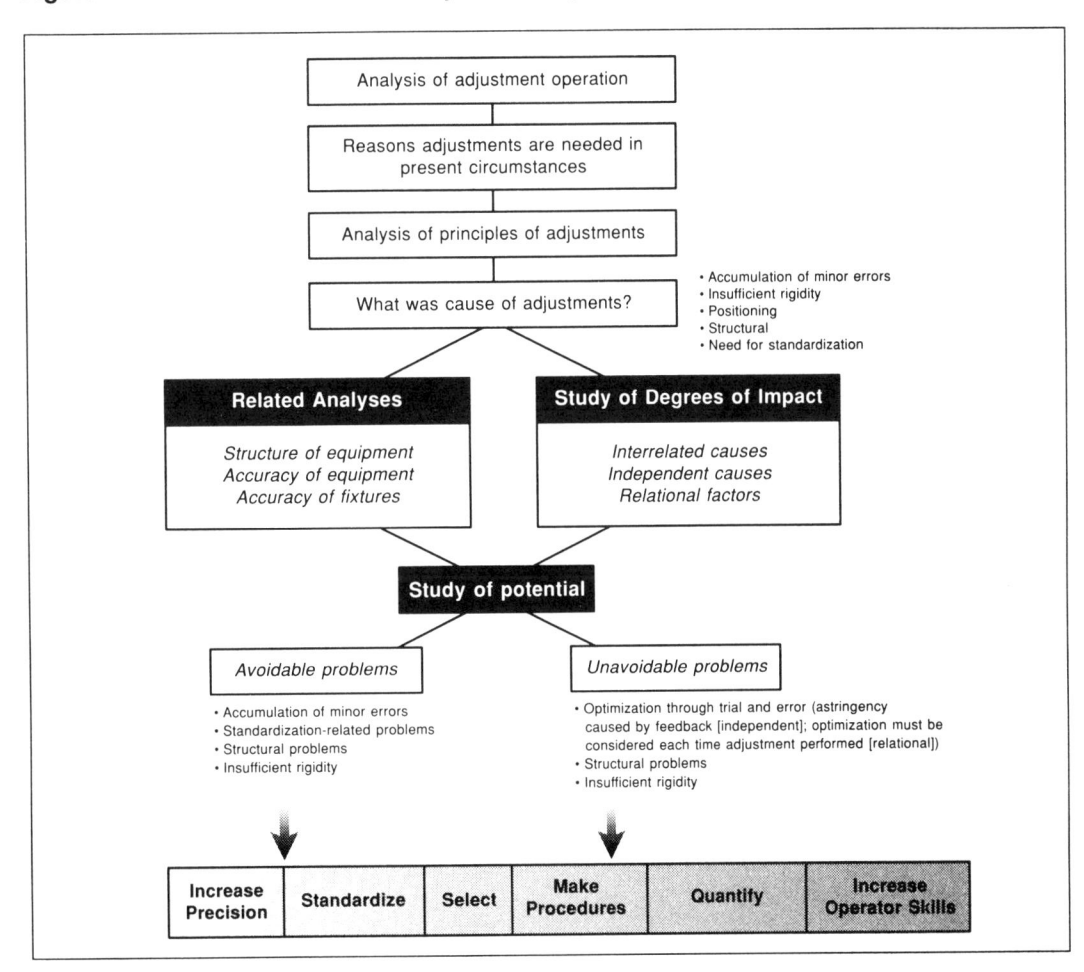

■ Increase operator skill levels

Follow an established set of procedures and use repetition to increase the skill level of the operators. Use repetition to make the operation totally automatic to the operator. Record the work procedures on tape, and play it on the plant public address system when the operation is being performed, if necessary.

Eliminating Loss due to Brief Stops

Brief stops can give rise to a number of major losses. These include, but are not limited to, the following:

- ✓ Drops in machine productivity ratios
- ✓ Restrictions in the number of machines an operator can efficiently oversee
- ✓ Quality-related defects
- ✓ Losses of energy
- ✓ Injuries to workers

Despite the presence of such significant losses, however, these problems often tend to go unchecked. There are three major reasons for this. First, because the frequency of individual problems tends to be low, the true magnitude of the overall loss involved is more often than not simply not noticed. Second, studies of the current situation tend to be shallow, and concerned only with immediately pressing problems, which results in "countermeasures" that are not very well thought out. Third, the problems often do not occur when a supervisor is looking for them, or if they do occur, they are quickly over, which means that the supervisor does not have an adequate opportunity for observation.

Table 4 contains a classification of brief stops and their major causes.

■ Correction of minor flaws

The first step in putting an end to this type of loss is to find all the small problems that occur with components and fixtures, as the result of problems with the movement surface of the workpiece, and to correct these problems. This

Table 4 Classification of Manifestations of Brief Stops and Their Causes

Type of Problem		Causes
Transport Related	1. Clogging 2. Catching 3. Enmeshing 4. Bridging 5. Insufficient parts 6. Inadequate feed 7. Excessive feed 8. Dropping 9. Insertion error	1. Materials or parts related causes (1) Dimensional defects (2) Visual or shape defects (3) Wrong parts mixed in with correct parts (4) Presence or absence of magnetism 2. Transporting or feed system related causes (1) Defective chute shape (shape, surface conditions, scratches, dirt, problems with joints) (2) Parts feeder related problems (amplitude, resonance, balance, optimal feed amount, installation conditions) (3) Posture control related problems (format, compatibility with parts, feed amount)
Assembly Related	1. Crushed or damaged 2. Overlapping 3. Chucking error 4. Timing 5. Defective assembly 6. Ejection error	3. Assembly related causes (1) Fixture precision (2) Assembly precision (3) Parts precision (4) Timing 4. Workplace control related causes (1) Errors in setup adjustments (2) Setting errors
Detection Related	1. Misoperation	5. Detection system related causes (1) Detection system itself (2) Method of mounting sensors, or positions of sensors (3) Proper sensing conditions (4) Adjustment defects (5) Timing (6) Conditions of use

requires a three-step approach that is different from the conventional way of approaching this problem. The steps are:

✓ Search for the manifestations of the problem with an understanding of the problem itself

✓ Look for problems arising from discrepancies between the way things *should* be and the way they actually *are*

✓ Watch for things which appear to be logically inconsistent or wrong

Applying these ideas will require more precision in observations and analyses, and make it necessary to be more accurate in measurements. The target for the correction of

Figure 3 Implementing PM Analysis

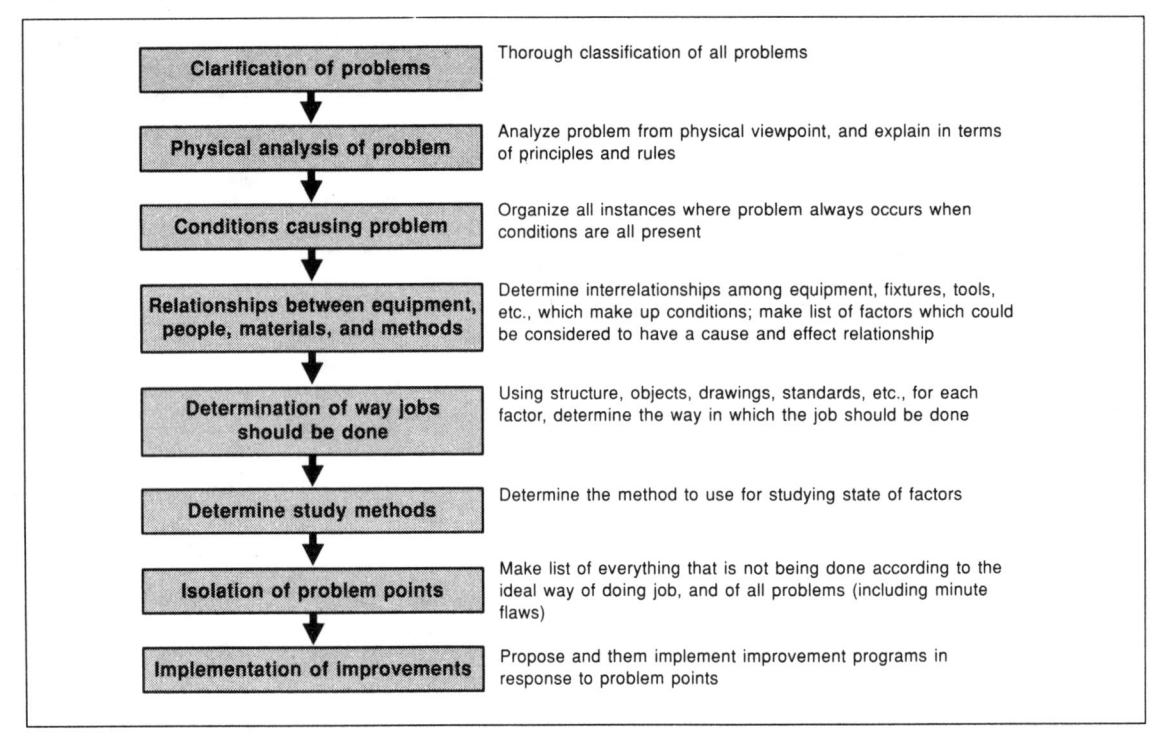

Clarification of problems	Thorough classification of all problems
Physical analysis of problem	Analyze problem from physical viewpoint, and explain in terms of principles and rules
Conditions causing problem	Organize all instances where problem always occurs when conditions are all present
Relationships between equipment, people, materials, and methods	Determine interrelationships among equipment, fixtures, tools, etc., which make up conditions; make list of factors which could be considered to have a cause and effect relationship
Determination of way jobs should be done	Using structure, objects, drawings, standards, etc., for each factor, determine the way in which the job should be done
Determine study methods	Determine the method to use for studying state of factors
Isolation of problem points	Make list of everything that is not being done according to the ideal way of doing job, and of all problems (including minute flaws)
Implementation of improvements	Propose and them implement improvement programs in response to problem points

minor flaws is to reduce to an absolute minimum fluctuations in the areas and frequencies of problems. This requires:

✓ Focusing on the causes of the problems

✓ Recognition of the differences or lack of differences between the manifestation of a problem now and the way it has manifested in the past

✓ Bringing to the surface all hidden flaws

■ Thorough implementation of the basic conditions

Adequate care must be given to cleaning, lubrication, and tightening—the basic conditions for machine operation—in the same way that attention is paid to counteractions against specific failures.

■ Thorough implementation of basic operating conditions

Many brief stops are the result of setup changes and adjustment operations. It may be necessary to reaffirm that setting adjustments are correct.

Focusing Improvement Activities on the Six Major Losses

Figure 4 Implementation of PM Analysis and Points of Concern

	STEP ONE	STEP TWO	STEP THREE	STEP FOUR	STEP FIVE	STEP SIX	STEP SEVEN	STEP EIGHT
PROCEDURES	Problem Shape in which it manifests itself as a problem	Physical Examination By "physical," we mean the principles of the objects involved	Conditions that Cause Problems Conditions are those factors that limit the problem to its actual manifestations	Relationships between Equipment, Materials, and Methods By "relationships," we mean the factors that link these elements	Determine the Way the Job Should Be Done	Determine the Way Study Should Be Done	Results and Evaluation of Study	Formulate and Implement Improvement Proposals
	Understand problem completely	Express the properly understood problem through a physical perspective	Clarify all conditions under which the problem can occur	Perform close analysis of the mechanism of the problem, including the elements which make it up	Study basics	Make up study plan	Results and evaluations for each factor	Standardize job

■ **Physical analysis of the problem**

In cases where the methods listed above have been followed to the letter and there are still problems with brief stops, it will be necessary to apply physical-mechanism (PM) analysis (see Figures 3 and 4).

■ **Determination of optimal conditions**

Revaluate the conditions for mounting parts and units and the conditions for machining, given the parts and fixtures currently in use, and work to optimize these. In many cases, the conditions currently in use are nothing more than extensions of the technology used in the past. These need to be studied through the use of experiments, and the trial and error method.

■ **Weak point analysis**

If the problem with brief stops is not solved even after the application of all the ideas described above, the problem is most likely connected to weak points in the design of the equipment, fixtures, and detection systems used. If this is the case, the structure of, materials used for, and shape of the parts must be studied from the design perspective; it is also necessary to look for design problems in the structure and shape of the fixtures used, and in the detection system (sensors and the system itself).

The procedures for improvements are indicated in Table 5, and also in Figure 5.

Eliminating Loss due to Speed Drops

The improvement of factors leading to speed losses is extremely critical in any attempt to increase overall equipment effectiveness, because of the great impact that speed has on effectiveness. Despite this urgency, however, these problems are very often overlooked, and there is little concern regarding them. The procedures to follow in addressing these problems are included in Table 6 (see page 48). Two of the most important considerations are as follows:

Table 5 The Approach to Improvements

	Concepts for Improvement	Objects for Improvement
Reliability of Use	Correction of minor flaws	Visual (scratches, wear) Dimensional (required dimensional accuracy, clearance) Operational (roughness, out of center)
Reliability of Use	Thorough implementation of workplace rules	Cleaning (dirt, roughness) Oil (dirt, wear) Bolts and screws (looseness)
Reliability of Use	Thorough implementation of basic job procedures	Correct operation procedures Setup operation (method of adjustment, setting) Way of looking at equipment (way of discovering problems)
Reliability of Use Reliability of Manufacturing	Determination of optimal conditions for job	Installation conditions (accuracy, position, oscillation, air pressure, vacuum, amplitude) Machining conditions (optimal feed level)
Reliability of Use Reliability of Manufacturing	Determination of optimal way to do job	Limits of required accuracy (part accuracy, installation accuracy) Conditions of use (optimal use range)
Reliability of Use	Study of weak points	Equipment matched to part shape (shape changes) Part selection (modifications from materials or functions) Study structure and system

Focusing Improvement Activities on the Six Major Losses 47

Figure 5 Improvement Procedures for Problems with Brief Stops

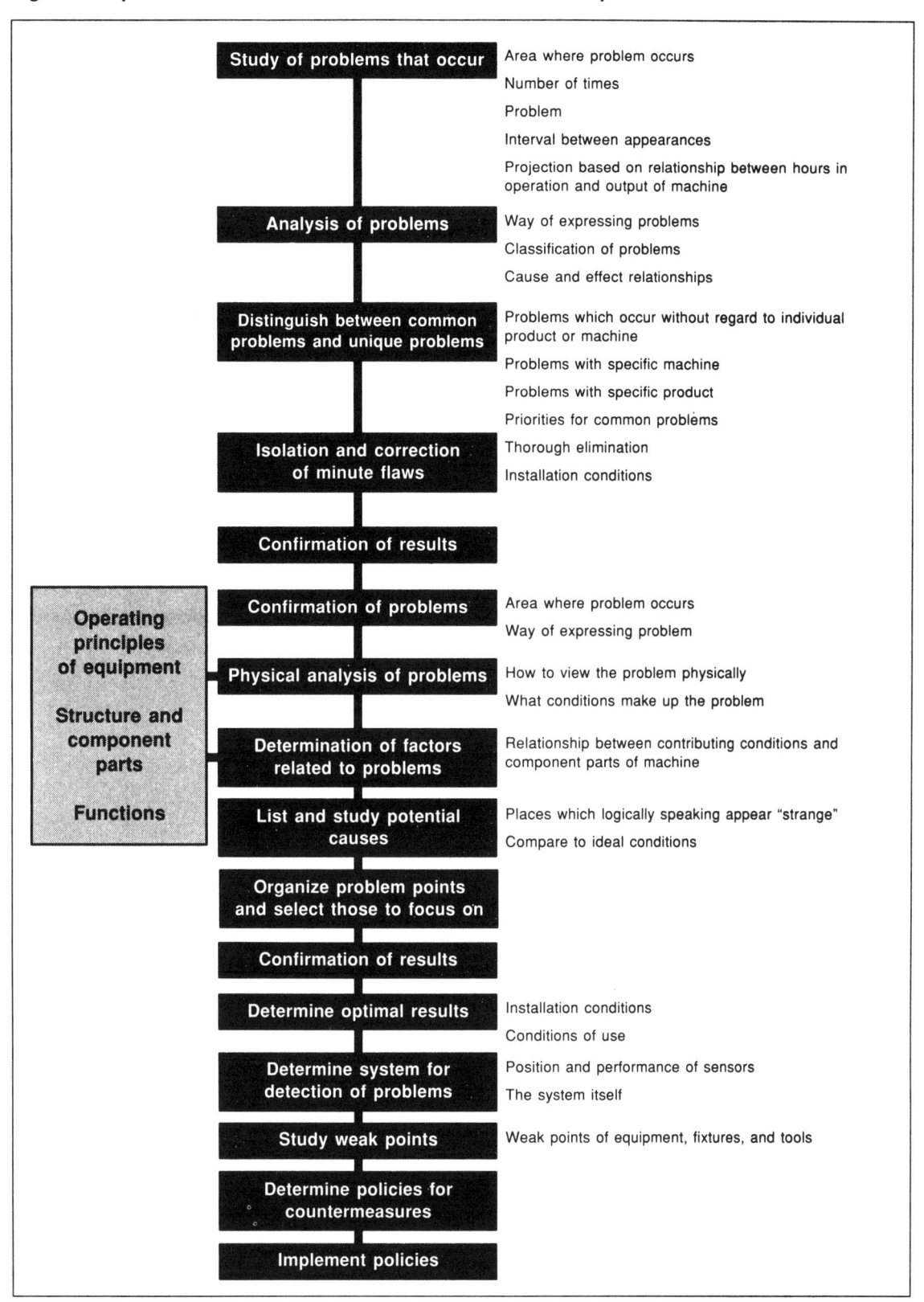

Study of problems that occur	Area where problem occurs Number of times Problem Interval between appearances Projection based on relationship between hours in operation and output of machine
Analysis of problems	Way of expressing problems Classification of problems Cause and effect relationships
Distinguish between common problems and unique problems	Problems which occur without regard to individual product or machine Problems with specific machine Problems with specific product Priorities for common problems
Isolation and correction of minute flaws	Thorough elimination Installation conditions
Confirmation of results	
Confirmation of problems	Area where problem occurs Way of expressing problem
Physical analysis of problems	How to view the problem physically What conditions make up the problem
Determination of factors related to problems	Relationship between contributing conditions and component parts of machine
List and study potential causes	Places which logically speaking appear "strange" Compare to ideal conditions
Organize problem points and select those to focus on	
Confirmation of results	
Determine optimal results	Installation conditions Conditions of use
Determine system for detection of problems	Position and performance of sensors The system itself
Study weak points	Weak points of equipment, fixtures, and tools
Determine policies for countermeasures	
Implement policies	

Feeding into the middle steps:
- Operating principles of equipment
- Structure and component parts
- Functions

Table 6 Procedures to Reclaim Speed

Current level adjustment	Speed Bottleneck process Downtime frequency Status of defect generation
Difference between specifications and current situation	What are specifications? Difference between specifications and current speed Speed differences between models
Study of problems from past	Has speed been increased? Classification of problems Measures taken against each type of problem Trends in defect rate Time line look at trends in speed Differences between this machine and similar machines
Study from perspective of machining principles	Problems from machining principles perspective Cutting conditions Machining conditions Theoretical value
Study from perspective of machine construction	Mechanisms Rated output and load rate Study of stress Moving parts Study of specifications of each component
Study of current situation	Machining time for each component task (chart out cycle) Loss time (idle time) Quality characteristics Accuracy check for each component Sensual check by operator
Organization of problem points	Organization of problems Comparisons with ideal settings Structure-related problems Accuracy-related problems Problems from machining principles perspective
Organization of anticipated problems	Mechanical Quality-related
Measures to counter anticipated problems	Relationship between anticipated problems and current situation Measures to counteract anticipated problems
Correction of problem areas	
Trial run	
Checking phenomena	Mechanical problems Quality-related problems
Analysis of problems, revaluation of cause and effect interactions, and measures taken to counter problems	Physical analysis of current problems Conditions which give rise to current problems Interrelated factors
Trial run	

- ✓ The specifications for the equipment are vague, and operators often are not sure of their limits.
- ✓ Operators mistakenly believe that the speeds described in the specifications cannot be attained, even though this is not the case; this leads to ignoring forced deterioration. Even though the shop has acquired the level of technology and controls needed to operate at full capacity, it does not apply this technology, and control personnel fail to notice that they are continually being plagued by problems of the past.

Eliminating Loss due to Defects and Rework

If defect rates are particularly high, the conventional approach based on critical point trends is acceptable, but if the goal is to reduce these problems to zero, then conventional ways of thinking must be changed. All causes of problems must be ferreted out, and countermeasures implemented for each of them. There are many factors which cause chronic defect problems, and the causes of problems vary, so there will be no real benefit to simply singling out a number of these causes for countermeasures and ignoring the rest. The following steps must be taken:

- ✓ Classify the manifestations of problems, and clarify their particulars
- ✓ Analyze these manifestations physically
- ✓ List all factors which can be thought to be connected in some way with the manifestations (do not do this by the degree of impact a cause might have—ignore contribution rates)
- ✓ Study each of the causes individually
- ✓ Correct any flaws found in any of the factors
- ✓ If possible, make corrections as a part of a unified whole

The truly important thing here is how the flaws are viewed. Flaws are all too frequently overlooked, for a variety of reasons—usually because the control personnel do not have the proper reference data needed to recognize a flaw as a flaw. Remember that quality problems can never be totally eliminated if minute flaws are not recognized for what they are and dealt with accordingly.

Table 7 Basic Properties Required of Machines

Basic Properties	Definition	Concrete Details	
Reliability	No drop in or total loss of functions	• Low frequency of failures • Low frequency of brief stops • Low frequency of defect generation	• Minimal adjustments • Stable machine cycle times • Easy to measure static and active accuracy
Maintainability	Easy to measure deterioration and to recover from it	• Quick discovery of area where failure took place • Easy to change parts and recover functions • Rapid confirmation time	• Rapid discovery of areas where deterioration took place • Easy to lubricate • Easy to overhaul
Autonomous maintainability	Maintenance activities such as cleaning, checking, and lubrication can be performed easily in a short period of time by machine operator	• Easy to clean, lubricate, and inspect • Chip collection performed simply • Source and ramifications of problems easy to spot	• Easy to find oil nipples • Easy to maintain quality level (easy to measure precision, etc.)
Operational ease	Proper operations can be performed quickly and accurately when operating machine or changing setups	• Easy to perform setup changes and adjustments • Easy to change cutting tool or grinding wheel and to make adjustments required by this operation	• Button operations are simple to perform (proper height, good position, right numbers, easy to operate shapes, distinctively colored, etc.) • Easy to move and to install
Energy conservation	Effectively uses natural resources in terms of energy, tool or grinding wheel, lubricants, and the like	• Low unit costs for energy and/or resources	• Allows the recycling of resources
Safety	Poses no direct threat to humans	• Requires few non-ordinary operations such as dealing with failures, brief stops, or quality problems • Moving and motive parts are not exposed	• Has few components which jut out or can be caught • Easy to move away from

Eliminating Loss due to Startups

Special problems arise with startups, when product dimensions can experience deviations or cycles are too long until a smooth production cycle is accomplished. Factors such as temperature changes in the operating oil of the hydraulic system or the lubricant, or thermal distortion of rotating areas and the like can influence these problems, but this is generally due to inadequate warmups. If the problem is serious enough to result in thermal distortions, a number of factors must be studied:

✓ Where do the problems occur, and to what degree?

✓ What impact do these problems have on the workpiece being machined?

✓ What is the minimal amount of warmup operation required?

✓ How does the passage of time affect the volume of thermal distortion at each location where it occurs (thermal distortion curve)?

✓ To what degree has the manufacturer of the machine provided for this problem?

✓ What must the user of the machine do, and how effective can these measures be?

Well-Conceived Machinery Results in Higher Productivity

Ultimately, the losses that have been discussed here must be dealt with thoroughly at the time the equipment is first introduced to the workplace. Each company must carry out its own maintenance prevention (MP) design activities, but these are most generally only partial in nature, and most companies need to institute programs that will allow them to view the problem from an overall organizational standpoint. Table 7 is a summary of all the information needed to enable improvements to be reflected in the design of the equipment, so that all equipment acquired will be well conceived.

Part II

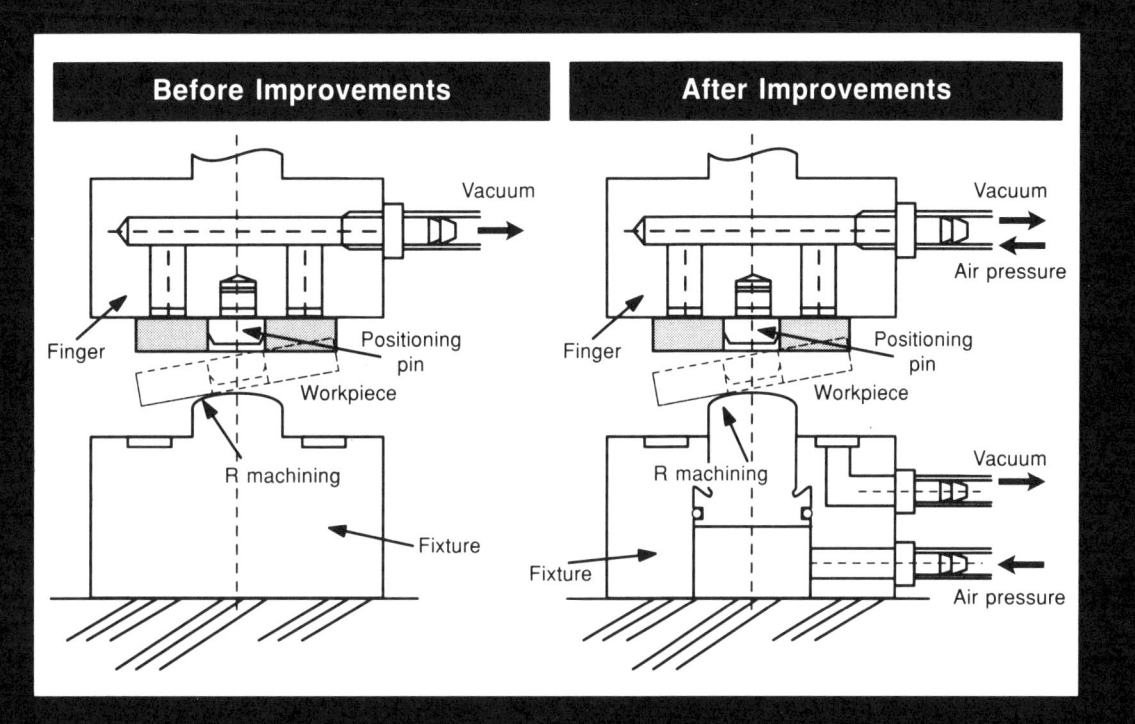

Before Improvements	After Improvements
Finger, Positioning pin, Workpiece, R machining, Fixture, Vacuum	Finger, Positioning pin, Workpiece, R machining, Fixture, Vacuum, Air pressure

Reducing the Six Major Losses

Improvements in Plant Structure
___

Action against "Mistakes" to Reduce Equipment Loss

By Tatsuo Takaku
Consultant Japan

The Problems of Today's World

There was a time in Japan when any mention of production in Japan was bound to begin an argument concerning the improvement and most efficient use of equipment. But a reconsideration of the equipment question just might be what is needed to bring about success in production without the danger of prohibitively high prices.

Revaluation of equipment, though, means much more than simply fooling around with what is available. It should go without saying that equipment now being used must be changed in a positive manner.

The age of "scrap and build" is now upon us. The conversion from equipment suitable for rapid growth and the large volume manufacturing of a relatively small number of models, to equipment suitable for slower growth rates and multiple model, small-lot production has begun. At the same time, we are faced with the need to work harder to implement fully unmanned production systems. Once, the term "FA" meant just "factory automation"; now, it signifies "flexible automation" as well. We need to work toward both of these goals.

Because the times are the way they are, now more than ever we need to add that extra effort to improve what have always been the problem points in our equipment, and to organize and quantify our efforts. Having done this, we can use the data we collect in the design of our next-generation equipment, thus coming ever closer to our goal of unmanned equipment that will require neither operator, nor maintenance man, nor setup man. This is the true key to gaining competitiveness in this challenging world.

The Revaluation of TPM and the Future

Some time already has passed since TPM was introduced to the industrial world, but the initial movement was one of TPM for a period of high growth. Now, problems have come to the fore regarding the nature of the systems and the methods used to implement the programs. For example, the transformation from maintenance programs for machines used for mass production, to those such as numerically controlled machines and machining centers, designed for small-lot production, has resulted in a shift in emphasis from mechanical structures to control systems. These new problems often tax the skills of maintenance personnel trained for the older realities.

A more serious problem, though, is the fact that the development of equipment that does not need maintenance has become a major priority, and the guidance of TPM is needed from the workplace for development of this. For this reason, the nature of the guidance provided from TPM also must change, to stress design problems (and this, too, should be centered on control systems).

Maintenance activities are shifting in emphasis from conventional preventive maintenance (PM) activities to total productive maintenance (TPM; this acronym is taken by many these days to mean "total production management"). This is, in itself, a desirable trend. However, contemporary plant management, centered around equipment, has become extremely sophisticated. This means doubts must arise regarding whether or not this shift can be accomplished by a management system that, with 100 percent participation, is more operator-heavy than in the past.

On the contrary, seen from the perspective of anticipatory-type management theory, the future will demand results at the planning, development, and—at the very least—production preparation stages. Companies which cannot or do not take rationalization back through all of these stages will have difficulty in surviving.

Current Equipment Controls and Future Equipment Development

One thing that becomes clear in addressing the question of what changes are likely to take place in our factories over the next two or three years is the fact that we cannot simply get rid of the equipment currently in use. Very likely this equipment will have its uses, and it should be treated well. It is possible, in fact, that this equipment eventually will find its way to the newly emerging industrial nations and to the consumer countries, and if this sort of return on investment is to take place, the equipment must be well controlled at this stage.

Figure 1 is a chart made from considerations of the types of improvements needed for equipment in order to bring a company into the position where it will have superior plants that excel all others in terms of the "Big Three" elements of quality, cost, and delivery (QCD). There are three major elements revealed here:

✓ The chronic problems block is comprised of items in the *effects* range

If the effects are not good, there is no way the plant will develop into a superior organization. Defects, increased costs, and late deliveries are true effects on finished products. Losses from materials costs, labor costs, and management costs, too, have defective equipment as one of their causes, and represent a major problem.

✓ There are twelve losses in the *cause* range that give rise to these chronic defects

Human intervention is required when a brief stop occurs. Spontaneous failures require fixing. Setups and their adjustments take too much time, and drive costs up. Or, instability

REDUCING THE SIX MAJOR LOSSES

Figure 1 Equipment Improvement Activities Necessary for the Superior Plant

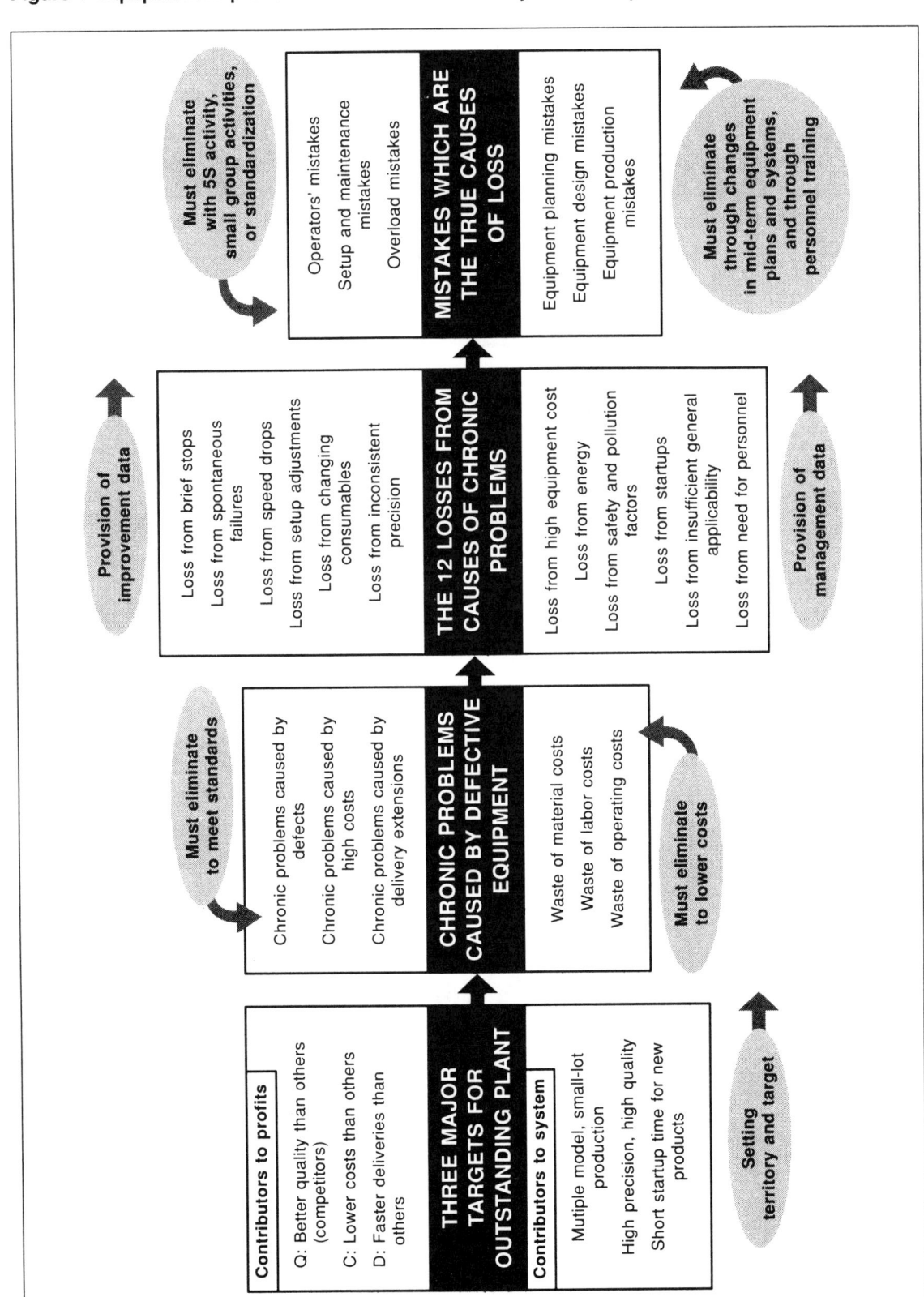

MISTAKES WHICH ARE THE TRUE CAUSES OF LOSS

- Operators' mistakes
- Setup and maintenance mistakes
- Overload mistakes
- Equipment planning mistakes
- Equipment design mistakes
- Equipment production mistakes

Must eliminate with 5S activity, small group activities, or standardization

Must eliminate through changes in mid-term equipment plans and systems, and through personnel training

THE 12 LOSSES FROM CAUSES OF CHRONIC PROBLEMS

- Loss from brief stops
- Loss from spontaneous failures
- Loss from speed drops
- Loss from setup adjustments
- Loss from changing consumables
- Loss from inconsistent precision
- Loss from high equipment cost
- Loss from energy
- Loss from safety and pollution factors
- Loss from startups
- Loss from insufficient general applicability
- Loss from need for personnel

Provision of improvement data

Provision of management data

CHRONIC PROBLEMS CAUSED BY DEFECTIVE EQUIPMENT

- Chronic problems caused by defects
- Chronic problems caused by high costs
- Chronic problems caused by delivery extensions
- Waste of material costs
- Waste of labor costs
- Waste of operating costs

Must eliminate to meet standards

Must eliminate to lower costs

THREE MAJOR TARGETS FOR OUTSTANDING PLANT

Contributors to profits
- Q: Better quality than others (competitors)
- C: Lower costs than others
- D: Faster deliveries than others

Contributors to system
- Mutiple model, small-lot production
- High precision, high quality
- Short startup time for new products

Setting territory and target

in precision gives rise to defects. These problems can be very difficult to fix, and they wreak havoc with the machinery, in the final analysis.

Equipment-related pollution can be harmful to the operator, and—if the equipment is not designed for general use, as it usually is not—can result in the need to purchase a new machine. This, too, increases product costs.

Suddenly, equipment which was supposed to be automated needs a maintenance man standing by at the ready at all times. "Unmanned" production is now "manned," and labor costs bring on a whole new set of losses.

✓ Many problems can ultimately be traced to birth defects

By "birth defects," we mean that mistakes were made in planning, design, or fabrication. Equipment that suffers from birth defects never can be set totally right, no matter how lovingly it might be pampered by the maintenance staff. Messing around with it is nothing more than a waste of time. Other types of mistakes are those made by operators, by the setup staff, and by the maintenance staff, when these people have not been adequately trained. These mistakes frequently lead to equipment failures. Additionally, failure to take factors such as process capacity adequately into account during the process planning stage can result in use overload, which can easily result in less than stable accuracy, thus giving rise to even more defects. There are far too many plants where these problems occur.

There are, then, many problems which can cause difficulties with equipment, but if full and flexible automation is to be achieved, currently available equipment must be used to its maximum capacity and in the proper way; accurate data must be gathered from this use, and anticipatory preventive maintenance activities must be stressed in the workshop. This is precisely what we mean when we speak of obligatory PM activities.

Taking Action against the Mistakes that Cause Loss

Until the mistakes that cause the losses associated with equipment are eliminated, it always will be necessary to keep PM personnel on the payroll; if these mistakes result in quality defects, materials costs and operating costs can leap to unprecedented highs as well.

There are two major types of actions that can be taken against such mistakes. Let us begin this discussion with a consideration of the types of mistakes that are made before the machine in question is actually brought into the world.

First we have the mistakes made in the planning stage of manufacturing equipment. This stage is based on the company's mid-term management plans, product development plans, and the mid-term plans of the production departments. Further, the specifications needed from equipment also will tend to vary according to the type of control system in use.

Next we have action taken against mistakes made at the design and fabrication stages. One problem here is the volume of data related to preventive maintenance available to the designers. If the designers have no such data, they will be forced to continue with their previous designs, and the same cries of agony as before soon will be heard from the shop floor. It is necessary to create a special taskforce from people directly involved in manufacturing and people directly involved in maintenance prior to entering the design stage, for this will ensure that the designers will have ample data to work with in their tasks.

Another indispensable element is the inspection of the equipment after it has been fabricated. If designers are not involved in this process, too, it is all too likely that the shop floor will end up with equipment which is not exactly what is needed.

To guard against this possibility, a quality assurance specialist should be called in to check the equipment as a regular part of the overall system for equipment design and fabrication. Most companies which have a high rate of equipment usage have already taken this step, and will not ship equipment to the floor until it has been okayed by the quality assurance team. This has proven quite effective.

The second of our two types of actions is those taken against mistakes made after the machine is brought into the world. For these problems, the proper implementation of conventional TPM activities is normally the best countermeasure. Of course it is necessary to practice the 5S's, and to use suggestions and small group activities, but *the* most important thing is standardization—"doing things in the way that it has been decided they should be done." Further, it is a lamentable trend these days that people are overlooking the importance of learning the basics of their machinery's capacity, and we would like to stress that operators be well-schooled in this area. Controls never will be fully possible without adequate knowledge of what it is you wish to control.

Taking Action against Loss due to Brief Stops

The Mistakes: *Equipment design and fabrication; setup maintenance; overloading*

The Resulting Losses: *Increased costs*

Brief stops are the parasites of the equipment world. They nibble away and are virtually unnoticeable under normal circumstances, but these days, when automation is the name of the game in so many shops, brief stops leap out at us in ways that they never did before.

One of the major problems is brief stops in automated assembly machines. This is probably only natural, given the fact that we are entrusting a process—assembly—that has always relied on the full set of human senses to an unfeeling mass of metal. Further, the parts to be assembled may include some defects, and may vary greatly, which compounds the problem. If the assembly machine could just be a bit more feeling, like a human being, and if parts quality could be stabilized, then we should be able to eliminate the parasitic "brief-stop bug" from our lives.

Brief stops are something like athlete's foot—they are not very serious in and of themselves, and often go unreported, but they still cause a certain amount of pain in the journey forward. They cannot be allowed to fester, especially in a plant that is striving toward unmanned production. The ideal equipment of the future will not be plagued by problems with brief stops.

■ The example

The example shown in Figure 2 is one of a fixture for an automatic assembly machine. Automated assembly is the most difficult of all design jobs for those who design production equipment, and at the same time, as the peak in manufacturing technology, it presents a challenge that most designers cannot resist.

Nearly all brief stops involving automated assembly equipment are related somehow to the parts feeder. Natural drop type chutes must be eliminated from the picture if these problems are to be solved, and should be replaced with a direct feed system that does not depend on dead weight. Parts should not be fed in random batches, but should be stored in a magazine, or marked with tape. Many designs these days eliminate the parts feeder altogether.

In the example shown in the figure, the fixture and finger are related directly to the workpiece. Before improvements were made, the workpiece sometimes would not be fully cleared out by the finger, or, on occasion, it would fail to fully enter the fixture, coming in at a slant. These mistakes occurred frequently, and they of course resulted in a brief stop, with the maintenance man being forced to poke at the workpieces with a needle to straighten them out. The improvements made to the design of this mechanism perfected the process. Now, the finger uses a vacuum, and when it

Figure 2 Action against Loss due to Brief Stops

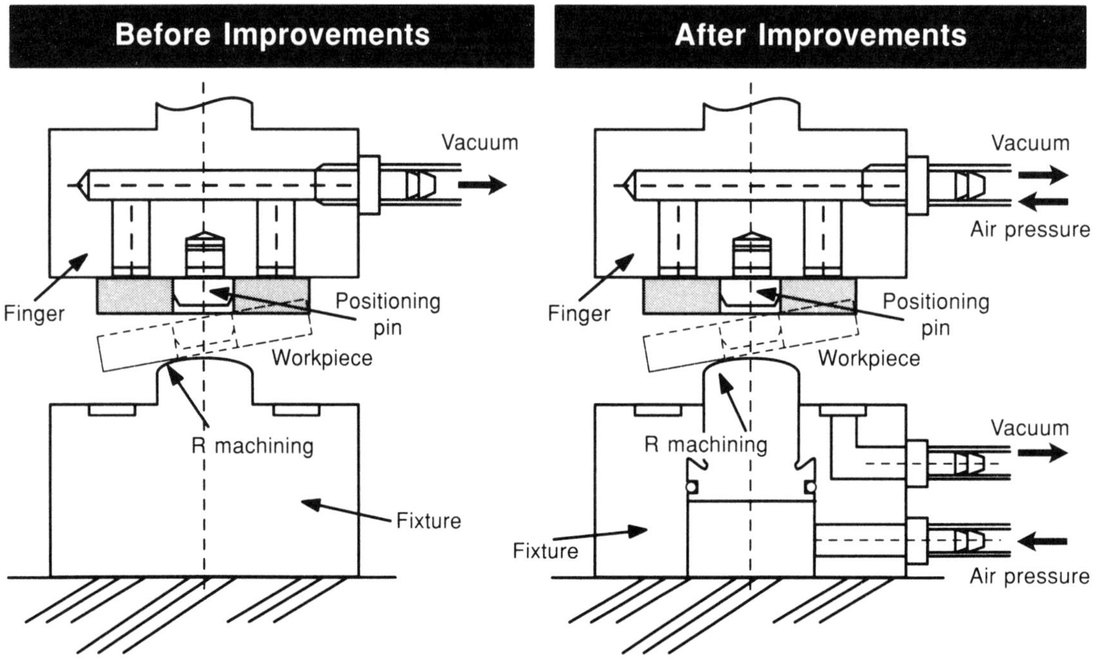

goes into motion this vacuum is converted to air pressure, so that the part is fully cleared out. The fixture was also improved and now functions perfectly.

Taking Action against Loss due to Spontaneous Machine Failure

The Mistakes: *From equipment planning on*

The Resulting Losses: *Late deliveries, increased costs*

Some people think of failures as being demons which possess equipment, but think for a moment of the common refrigerator, a consumer good necessary to our daily lives and one which almost never breaks down. Electric fans are the same. These are mirrors of the equipment used in a manufacturing plant. When there are failures in household electrical equipment, they inevitably come in the part of the equipment that contains the newest technology. In other words, equipment failures vary inversely with the length of the history of the item in question—the longer the history, the less frequent the breakdowns. The reason we see so few failures in refrigerators or electric fans, then, is due to the fact that their major component is their motor.

Motors have been well wrought over the course of history, so they have very little likelihood of failing.

Equipment failures could be controlled more efficiently by using market theories of quality assurance and reliability when the equipment is first introduced. Plants tend to over-rely on their maintenance staff, and are apt to be far too forgiving in their adaptation of countermeasures against failures. Designers, in particular, simply *must* take failures (especially spontaneous failures) into account in their first set of drawings. It's not enough to design a machine that simply "operates."

■ The example

As one precaution against spontaneous failures, the preventive maintenance staff would perform periodic inspections and compile data so that abnormal conditions could be predicted. Unfortunately, though, on occasions these conditions were not predicted, and resulted in spontaneous machine failure, throwing the workplace into commotion. On reflection, it was decided that there were several reasons for the failure of the prediction system:

✓ Data was not completely gathered
✓ The data collection cycle was wrong
✓ Data was being collected at the wrong places
✓ Sensors failed, leading to insufficient accuracy in data collected
✓ Data was not adequately analyzed

A good deal of thought was given to these problems, and it was decided that, despite the added cost, it would be worthwhile to introduce a computer control system. The computer was connected to all of the sensors in the system, data was constantly gathered and updated in real time, and the computer compared the data it collected with the data stored in its decision circuits. The computer also was able to alert human operators to any failures in the sensors, so they could be replaced immediately. The system of course cut down on the traveling inspections made by the maintenance staff, and enabled them to focus their energies on preparing for emergency situations. This system is depicted in Figure 3.

Figure 3 Action against Loss due to Spontaneous Failures

Taking Action against Loss due to Speed Drops

The Mistakes: *Equipment design, overload operations, setup adjustments*

The Resulting Losses: *Increased costs, late deliveries*

The appreciation of the yen and the unfavorable impact this had on their position in international trade caused most Japanese companies to begin looking long and hard at ways to lower costs. It was a particularly difficult task for companies which were exporting products made through mass production, for they had to bring their costs down by the same rate that the yen was appreciating to maintain sales, and they could not do this easily. Many managers suffered through this period. But, they had to do *something*, and so they started by speeding up their production lines. They were successful in producing at speeds that they would never have dreamed of when the original takt times were designed. No matter what types of safety indices were input to these processes, there was no way that they could hide the fact that the speeds were unreasonable, due to the congenital limitations of their equipment. It was shop floor technology that enabled these firms to exceed the speeds for which their equipment was designed. Many wished that these possibilities had been foreseen when the equipment was first planned, and that the base sections of the equipment had been made from cast iron, but at least the situation taught them something.

The first step was to reinforce the bases with channel material to damp vibration. Pneumatic cylinders in the motive portions of the equipment were then changed to cams. First one step, then another was taken.

■ The example

We do not need to say that high speed and high precision are two of the major goals of engineers. The problem is that high speeds generally result in a drop in accuracy, and working for high precision usually means that speeds must be cut. It is the engineer who must reconcile these two mutually exclusive goals.

Conventionally, the plant shown in Figure 4 used a P&P unit, with workpieces being loaded from a feed conveyor

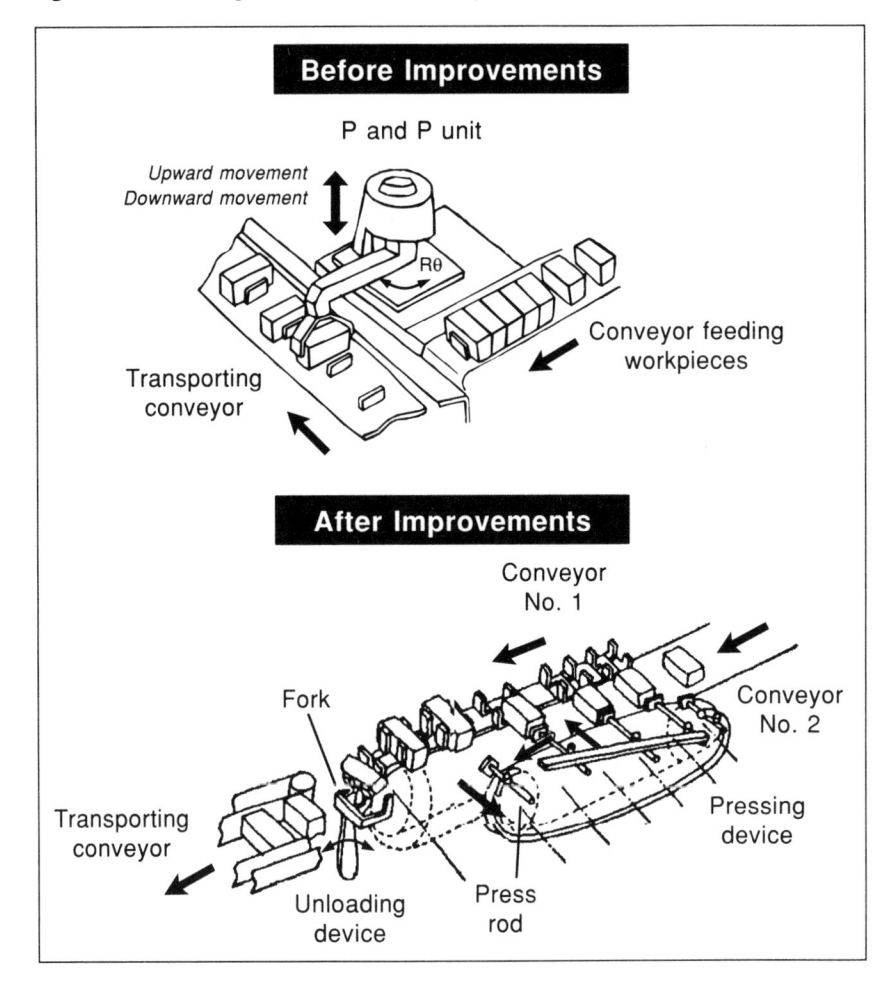

Figure 4 Action against Loss due to Speed Drops

to the main transporting conveyor. The workpieces came at three-second intervals. The workpieces were about the size of a VCR cassette, and this three-second interval was thought sufficient at the design stage.

But the plant manager ordered that this time be cut to 1.5 seconds, or half the time that had been allowed, an order which gave the designers fits. There was only one solution—they would have to change from a takt time type feed system to a continuous feed system. They went back to the drawing board to consider what types of mechanisms could be used to load workpieces on a moving conveyor. The mechanism they came up with, shown in Figure 4, was judged to be the most economic and reliable method available. It enabled workpieces to be loaded at intervals of one second each.

Taking Action against Loss due to Setup Adjustments

The Mistakes: *Equipment design, setup maintenance*

The Resulting Losses: *Late deliveries, defects, increased costs*

It has long been said that it takes seven minutes to do the setup and three to do the job. The first jobs done in the morning would have many defects, and this would make it difficult to meet deliveries. Conversely, some famous operators could go right into the production of acceptable parts from the setup—so it also was said, "he who is good at setups is good at the job." Jobs on days that the setup adjustments went well from the beginning would be smooth, with no defects. So let's trace the reason for this back to the design stage. First, the design of a machine will differ depending on whether it is a general use machine or a dedicated machine. One design factor for dedicated machines is to minimize setup adjustments, and to increase the accuracy of all fixtures so that they will need only to be slid into place.

This is a difficult approach to take with general purpose machines, though. General purpose machines and dedicated machines that approach general purpose machines in their designs will need the skills of a setup professional. Even so, it is best if these skills are dependent, to as great a degree as possible, on the fixtures and tools used. Of course, it is necessary to organize and dedicate tools according to the 5S principles. The video camera is a great asset here, as well—shooting the setup sequence will enable supervisors to spot many types of waste.

■ The example

A numerically controlled machine is a general use dedicated machine. Machining centers have a greater amount of general applicability. These two types of machines are currently the principal weapons used in the campaign to move to the multiple model, small-lot production system needed in today's world. But it takes time to mount the fixtures and attachments used even for these machines. This is a problem that has been met successfully on machining

Figure 5 Action against Loss due to Setup Adjustments

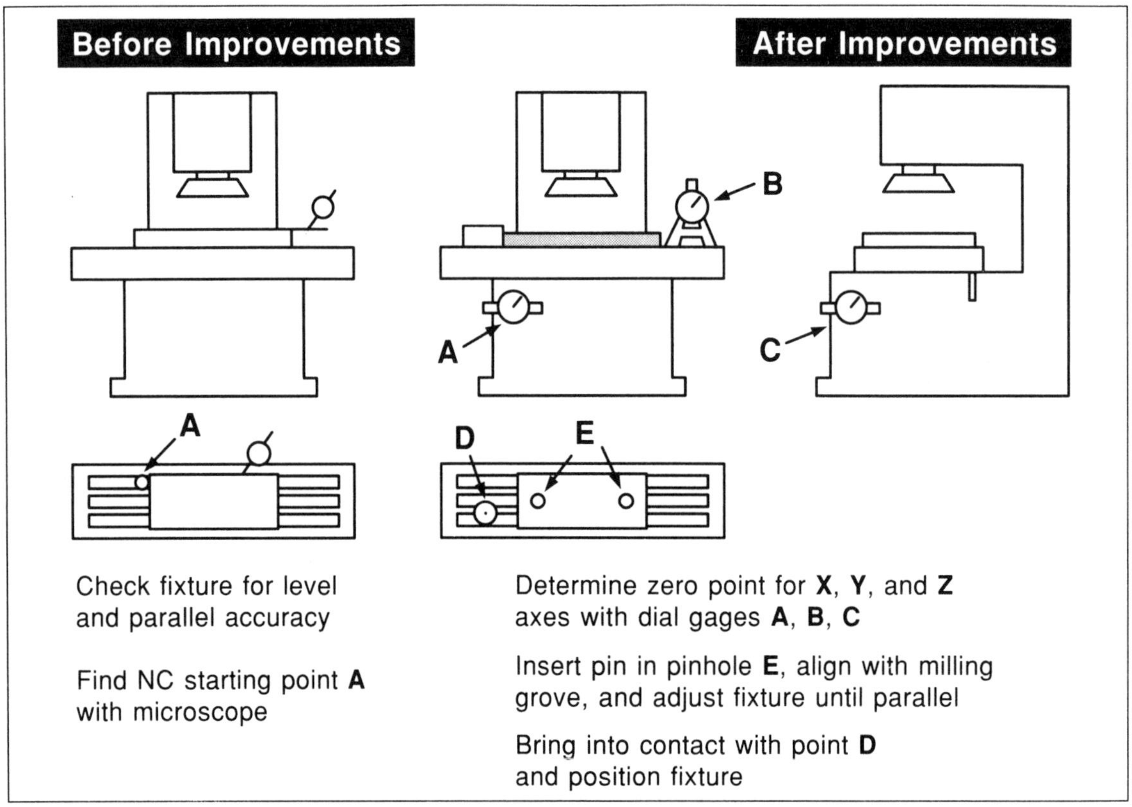

Before Improvements

Check fixture for level and parallel accuracy

Find NC starting point **A** with microscope

After Improvements

Determine zero point for **X**, **Y**, and **Z** axes with dial gages **A**, **B**, **C**

Insert pin in pinhole **E**, align with milling grove, and adjust fixture until parallel

Bring into contact with point **D** and position fixture

centers recently through the skillful use of the pallet system, but it remains a sore spot on NC machines.

As shown in Figure 5, the first step was to load the fixture on a table, then make it level and parallel. The NC zero point (A) was then discovered with a microscope. This takes some time—it was about an hour until the elimination of cutting chips. So careful consideration was given to the table. Holes were drilled in the table, and positioning pins inserted. Zero positioning for the X, Y, and Z axes was done with dial gages, the fixture was slid into place and attached with pins, and that was the end of the job. Quick turning screws or pneumatic clamps can be used to secure the fixture in place, and the whole operation can now be accomplished within five minutes. The breakthrough here was the idea of drilling holes in the NC machine table itself.

Taking Action against the Loss due to Changing Consumable Parts

The Mistakes: *Equipment design, overloaded operation*

The Resulting Losses: *Increased costs, late deliveries*

Value-added design is all the rage for products these days, and failures now occur here and there. The automobile is a good example of this. Periodic inspections are performed after a vehicle has run a specific distance or after a specific amount of time has passed, and at this time anything loose is tightened, the oil is changed, and parts with design flaws can be changed before they become a problem. Sometimes, though, problems such as a screwdriver being left under the hood after adjustments can occur as well. After three years, the battery goes dead, the rubber on the windshield wipers starts to peel off, or the tires go flat. But with skillful design, when the vehicle is driven to a certain fixed number of miles, the whole chassis will start to squeak. And, of course, the car will start to look old and out of style.

Is production equipment, too, calculated to die at a certain point? Some parts of a machine could last as long as 100 years, while others need maintenance after three months. It is an especially bothersome task to have to change what we call the "consumable" parts of a machine.

■ The example

What role does oil, say, occupy within a piece of equipment? Is it like the oil or tires of the car that we were discussing above? If you simply say that it should be changed when it goes bad, there is no way to measure the process.

Oil is used in vacuum pumps, too, but failures that can be traced to the oil in these pumps make up about 90 percent of all problems that occur with vacuum pumps.

These problems include the deterioration of the oil, oil temperature increases, insufficient oil, oil leaks, and defective oil lubrication. The first job is to find an oil with high performance and to use it. Then, to guard against deterioration, devise ways to keep the oil temperature from rising, such as the use of an oil cooler in current machinery, which

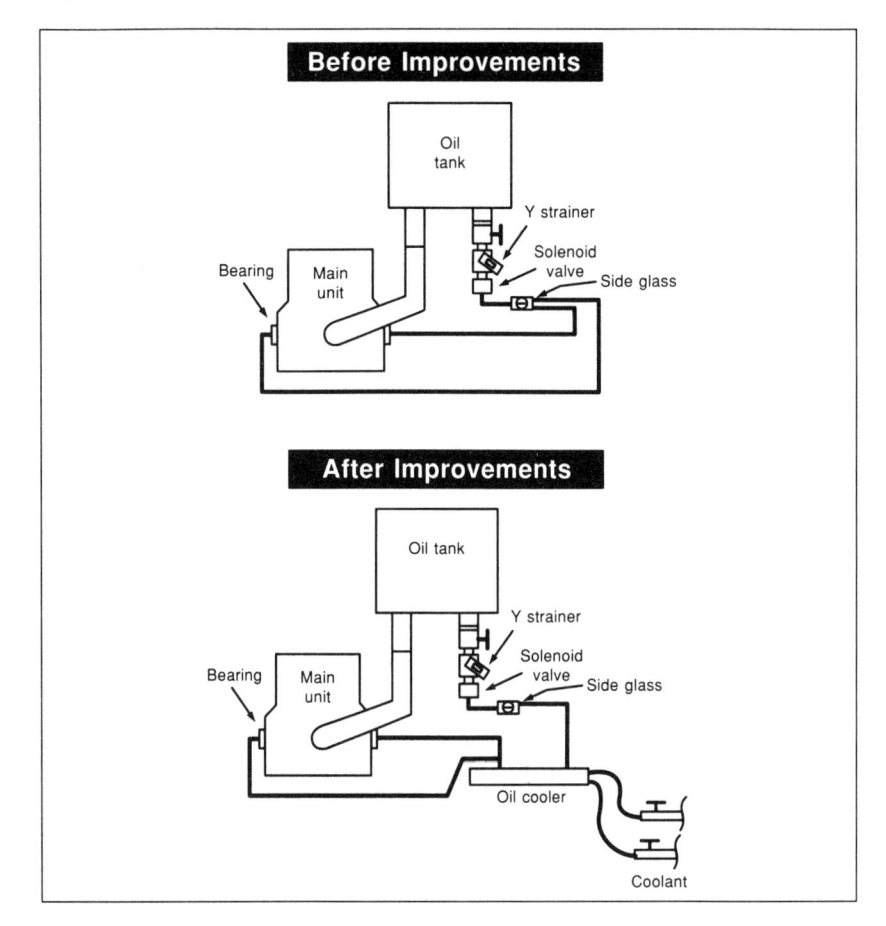

Figure 6 Action against Loss due to Changing Consumable Parts

will lengthen the interval between oil changes. This is what was done in the situation shown in Figure 6, where a large number of vacuum pumps were in operation, and changing the oil for them was unnecessarily difficult. The system also brought about a significant decrease in cost for new oil. The strainer also was improved, and this and other small group activities by the maintenance staff were instrumental in combatting a significant source of loss.

Taking Action against Loss due to Instable Precision

The Mistakes: *Equipment design stages, setup maintenance, overload operations*

The Resulting Losses: *Quality defects, late deliveries, increased costs*

One of the most significant problems caused by equipment, and one which has the most significant impact on the plant, is instable accuracy. Operation overloads or the need for greater accuracy than is possible with the equipment involved are problems that of course can be understood, but the real difficulty is when there is excessive deviation in accuracy within the framework set out by the machine's specifications. There frequently will be differences in accuracy from work performed first thing in the morning to work performed late in the day; seasonal shifts in accuracy; or differences that are dependent on the workpiece itself. There is a real question in these cases as to whether the problems can be adequately dealt with by existing workplace technology or the abilities of the setup staff. But problems with deviations in accuracy must be dealt with in some way.

The first and most important issue is to determine whether the problem must be tackled at the design level, or whether it can be handled with adjustments in the plant during production. Design-related problems cannot be solved no matter how much shop floor expertise is applied. But if they are allowed to go unchecked, without anything being said, they will soon turn into chronic problems.

■ The example

Defects due to eccentricity in an NC lathe were costing up to $25,000 a year, and the time needed for the 100 percent inspections necessitated by these problems amounted to up to some 3,000 hours a year.

This was more than just a problem with quality defects—it also spilled over into delivery problems. Workplace supervisors studied their products carefully to determine its cause.

This product had strict constrictions regarding balance and eccentricity. Eccentricity, in particular, had to be held within a variation of 0.01, but the finished product was falling within a variation of 0.015. A study of the reasons for

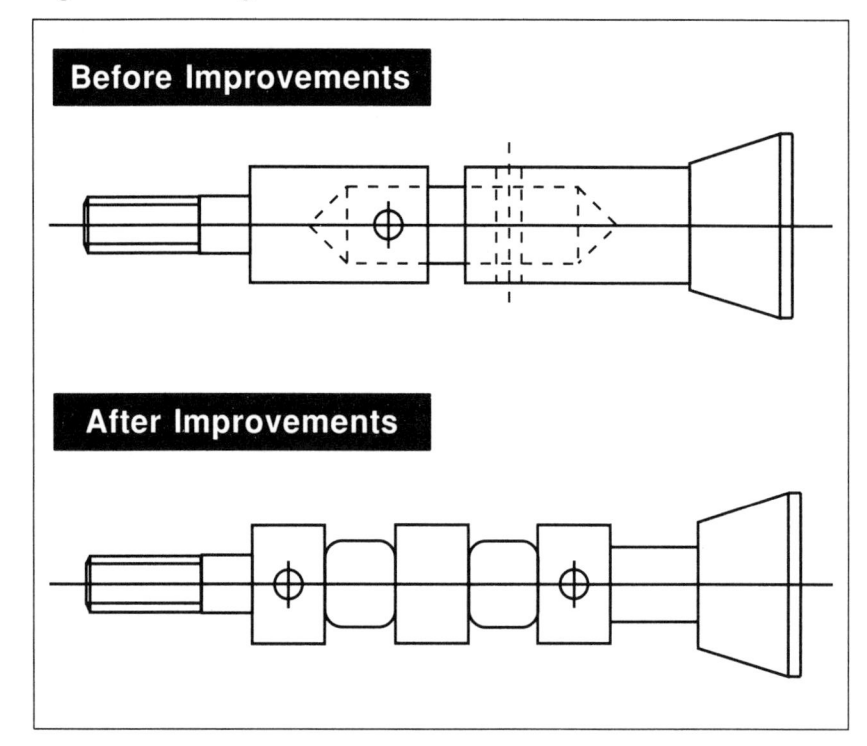

Figure 7 Action against Loss due to Instable Precision

[Before Improvements / After Improvements diagrams of chuck draw bar]

this revealed a bias in the chuck draw bar in the secondary machining process.

This draw bar was manufactured by the chuck manufacturer at the request of the lathe manufacturer, and was done in two parts, as shown in Figure 7. This made it impossible for the chuck taper to fully engage. It was determined that this was the main problem, so a decision was made to use commercially available ball joints to make the draw bar more flexible. Strength was of course taken into account, and the goal was to increase performance. Highly flexible ball joints were used, and the problem was solved by using products available on the commercial market.

Developing "TPM Eyes"

Increasing Human, Equipment, and Material Efficiency to Lower Failures

By Masayori Katoh
Togo Seisakusyo

The Togo Seisakusyo TPM Program

Togo Seisakusyo Corporation was founded in 1881 for the fabrication of forged agricultural implements. In 1947 the current version of the company was formed, and it recently celebrated its 40th anniversary as an integrated manufacturer of small springs.

The company's principal products are wire springs and thin plate springs made mainly from steel, resin springs, and subassemblies for these springs. The major applications for these products are in the automotive industry.

Background to the TPM Movement

The first fuel crisis exposed many of the weaknesses in the company's corporate structure, prompting a series of structural improvements that resulted in the creation of a structure sound enough to be awarded the Toyota Quality Control Prize. Following this, corporate performance continued to improve, but the voluntary restrictions on automo-

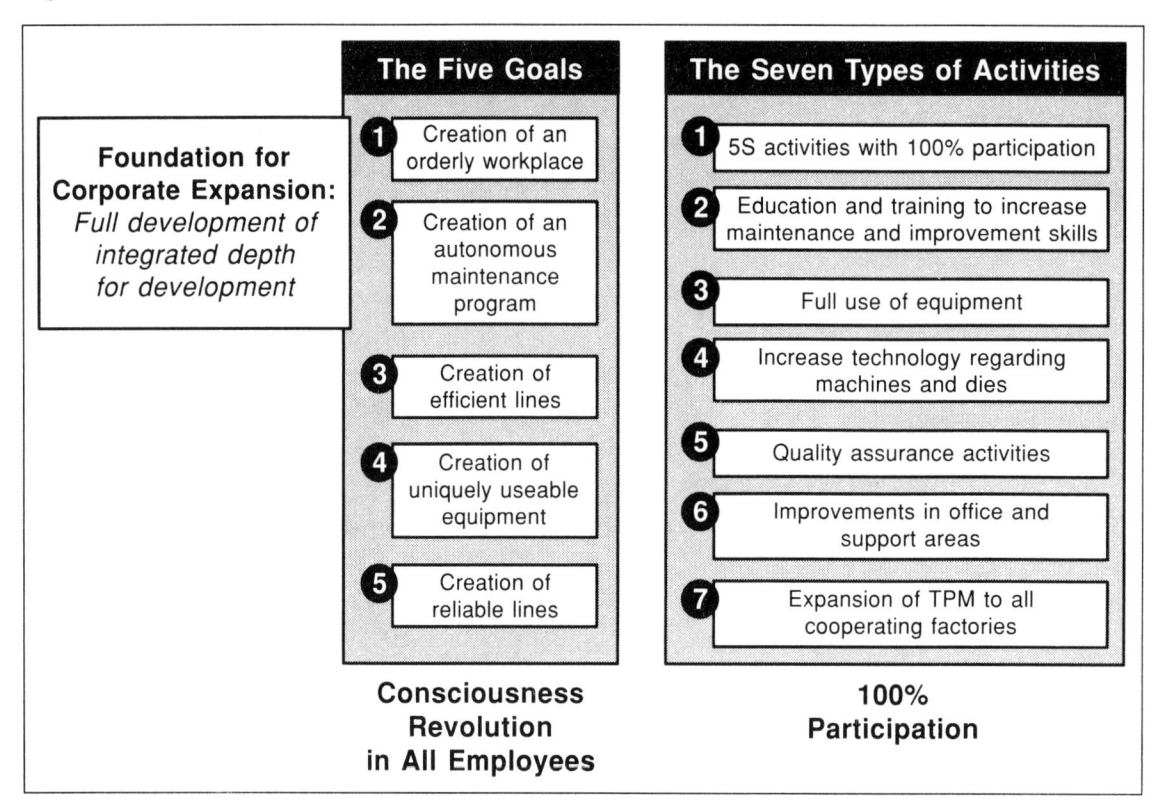

Figure 1 The Five Goals and the Seven Activities

Foundation for Corporate Expansion: *Full development of integrated depth for development*	**The Five Goals**	**The Seven Types of Activities**
	① Creation of an orderly workplace	① 5S activities with 100% participation
	② Creation of an autonomous maintenance program	② Education and training to increase maintenance and improvement skills
	③ Creation of efficient lines	③ Full use of equipment
	④ Creation of uniquely useable equipment	④ Increase technology regarding machines and dies
	⑤ Creation of reliable lines	⑤ Quality assurance activities
		⑥ Improvements in office and support areas
		⑦ Expansion of TPM to all cooperating factories
	Consciousness Revolution in All Employees	**100% Participation**

tive exports eventually blunted sales and caused a worsening of the company's position. At the same time, competition was stiffening on the general market.

The company thus was faced with a pressing need to increase its competitive power. A survey conducted in 1983 revealed TPM as a desirable program for needed improvements, and a TPM program was launched in 1984.

At the time of introduction, then, there was no particular thought in the company concerning the PM Prize competition, but a reflection on corporate performance in 1985 made clear the necessity to somehow vitalize the TPM activities being undertaken. In early 1986, the company set its sights on winning this prize, and promoted all activities on this basis. As a result, the company was fortunate enough to win the prize in 1987.

An Overview of TPM Activities

The basic goal of the TPM program was to utilize the participation of all company employees in PM activities that would increase the efficiency of all personnel and equipment in the company, expand the corporate base, and nurture an ever-broader foundation of overall capability. In order to reach this goal, attention was focused on activities that would result in 100 percent participation throughout the company (see Figure 1).

All of the company's production is based on orders received. In order to strengthen its competitive position in the industry, the company adopted the slogan, "The workplace itself is a product for sale for a parts manufacturing company," and strove to use TPM as a tool with which to create highly efficient, reliable lines.

The company also implemented a 5S program for the workplace, in an effort to create a fitting backdrop to the TPM activities it was implementing. In addition to the main thrust of the program—which was aimed at organizational activities centered around production technology—activities included improvements in the company's craftsmanship program, the strengthening of quality control circle activities, and the utilization of improvement teams on an individual workplace level.

The result of these activities was a systemization of improvement activities, and the creation of a plant environment with considerable vitality.

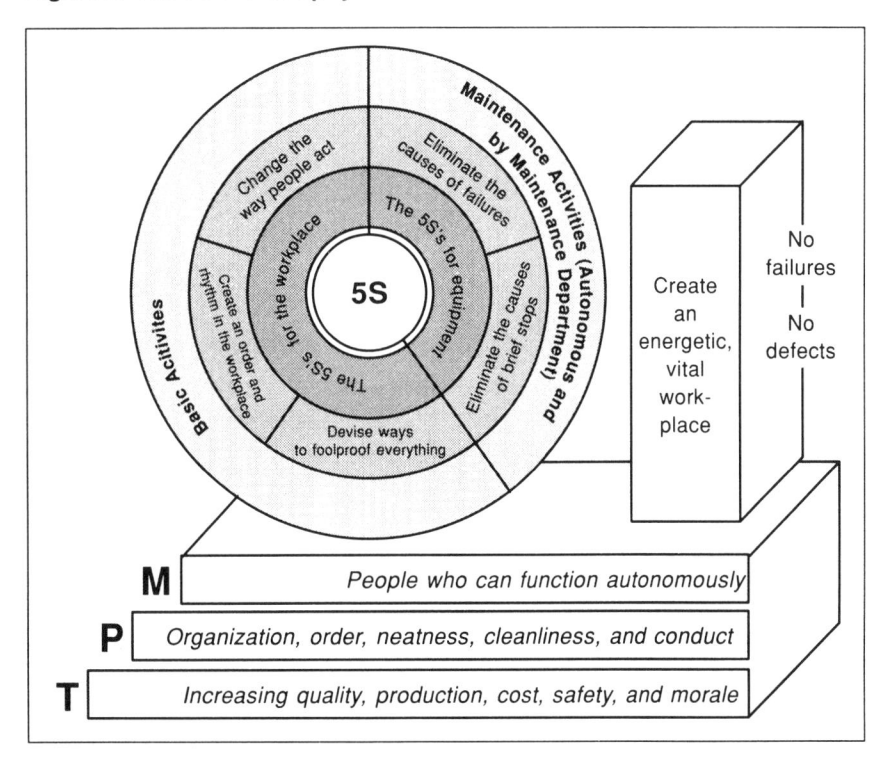

Figure 2 The 5S Philosophy

Figure 3 The Three Guidelines for 5S Activities

The Three Guidelines	I	II	III
	Creation of an orderly workplace	Creation of a clean workplace	Creation of a workplace conducive to visual controls
Goals	All employees carry out the decisions that have been made	Clean every corner of the work area and all the equipment so that it sparkles to the eye	Create an environment in which visual checks will lead to action by revealing problems
	Change the way people act	*Organize the workplace environment*	*Devise ways to foolproof everything*

The 5S's for the Workplace

In order to be effective, TPM activities must have 100 percent participation, and each individual must have his own role in the workplace. Training is thus very important. The company reworked its Toyota Prize-winning 5S program, making it into a "Workplace 5S" program. The major energy of the TPM program for its first year and a half was directed toward these 5S activities, as is shown in Figures 2 and 3.

A thorough implementation of the 5S's in the workplace is the foundation for autonomous maintenance activities. The two main pillars on which the structure is built are equipment and die technology (including maintenance) as organizational activities on the one hand, and production maintenance (the creation of more efficient lines) on the other.

Tools needed to maintain and continually build on the workplace 5S activities include the 5S calendar, the division of labor chart, the various types of maps, and individual TPM pronouncements. The use of activities crafted from these tools enables the continuous building of a workplace in which each person can perform his or her own individual role, as well as a role in the expansion of TPM.

Production Maintenance

By "production maintenance," we mean the creation of more efficient lines. The TPM activities instituted by Togo Seisakusyo to increase production line efficiency were improvement activities centered mainly around production technology. By systematizing conventional approaches, it was possible to achieve a more efficient level of improvement results.

In short, in order to respond to the demands posed by an order-based production system involving a large number of different parts in lot sizes ranging from small to large, it was necessary to view human efficiency, machine efficiency, and materials flow from the perspective of efficiency, uncovering the problems inherent in each major product and process. The method used was to study possible actions against each of these problems, and to solve them in stages (see Figure 4).

■ Human efficiency

As is the case with most other products, manual labor is generally not efficient in the manufacture of springs. Even so, many of the companies manufacturing springs are very small businesses, relying primarily on manual labor as they always have. For this reason, Togo Seisakusyo decided that the development of a machine-oriented production system would be the key to domination in the industry. From a comparatively early stage, the company was involved in using its own unique strengths to mechanize jobs once done by human workers, and to establish an unmanned production system.

Despite the fact that processes selected for manpower reduction or unmanned operation were those which were busy in the short term, certain long-term benefits also became apparent after the implementation of the TPM program. Not only were the problems in products and processes clarified, but so were the implementation period and implementation steps. This created an organization that enabled the maintenance of an overall, company-wide balance.

Although this now might seem painfully obvious, the four stages described below were used in the construction of a matrix in the study of problems and the implementation steps, so that the whole program (company-wide and process-wide) could proceed with improvements in the most efficient manner possible:

Figure 4 The Basic Concepts of Production Activities

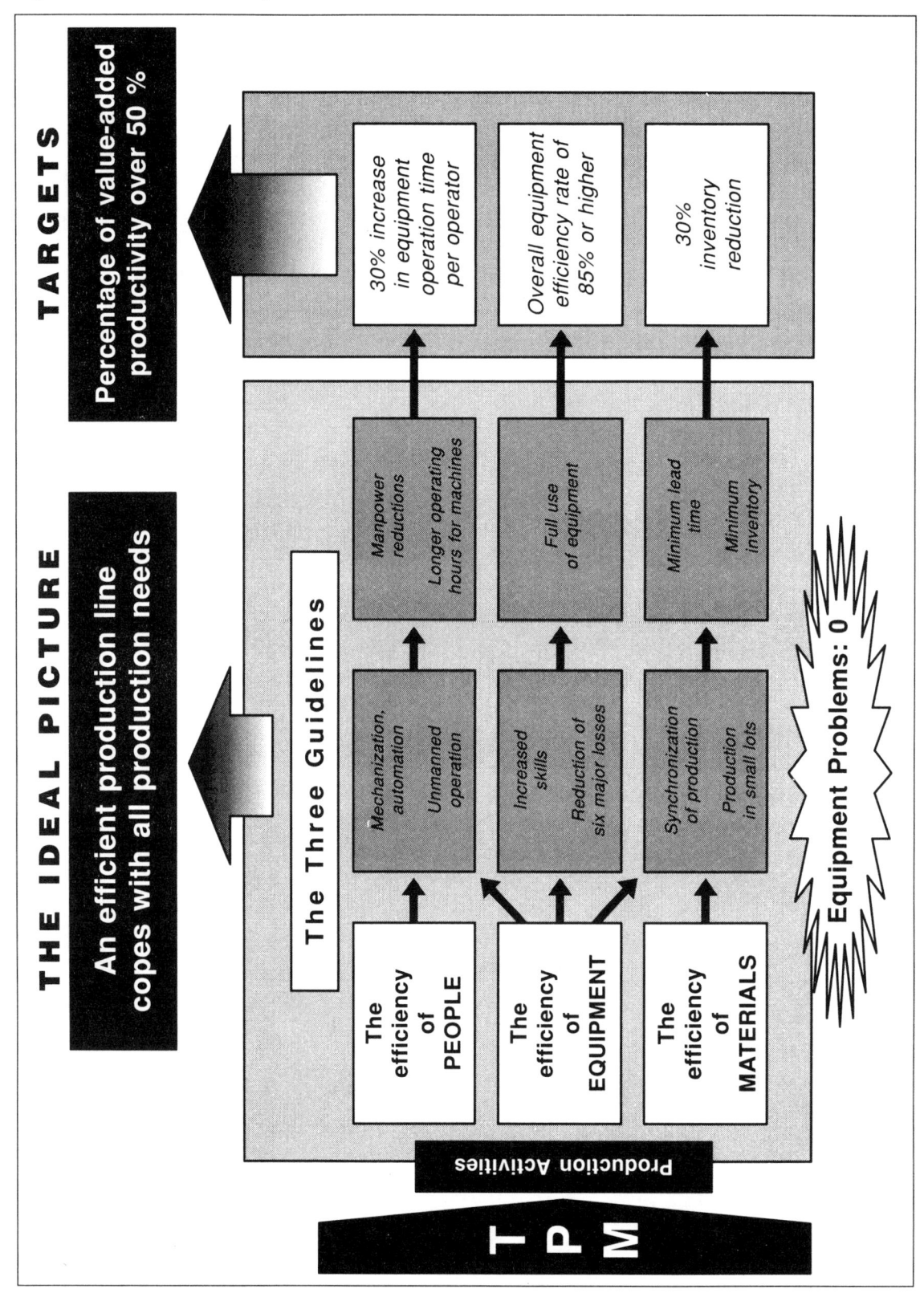

✓ Stage 1: The mechanization of manual jobs
✓ Stage 2: The automation of machinery and other equipment
✓ Stage 3: Unmanned operation of machines and other equipment
✓ Stage 4: The synchronization of processes (creation of one unified line)

These activities, which are shown in the Example 1 box at the end of this chapter, were developed in a systematic manner, along with the sensors needed for autonomation and unmanned production, and the product transporting devices needed to synchronize processes.

■ Equipment efficiency

Conventionally, equipment efficiency has been judged by its rate of hours in operation, so improvements have been aimed at setups and setup adjustments, which have always accounted for most of the hours equipment was not in operation. Although failures were noticed, they were nearly always left up to the maintenance staff, and people simply gave up on brief stops. They seldom even noticed problems such as air cuts or speed drops.

Consideration of overall equipment efficiency, however, makes it necessary to think of all of these problems, and to devise actions to make improvements in these areas. Once this is done, impressive results will follow.

■ Material flow efficiency

If production is to remain efficient for a large number of different products, made in lot sizes ranging from small to large, then problems in material flow and inventory handling must be overcome. This poses a large number of problems in layout plans for lines, workplaces, and, by extension, the entire company; many factors must be taken into account in order to synchronize processes, to coordinate incoming orders from outside vendors, and the like. The company worked to expose hidden loss in the current processes and make improvements on all fronts, including transporting, the warehousing of work in process and completed work, packing, work space used, auxiliary materials, error processing, and the like. These improvements have only just begun, and have not yet resulted in conspicuous results.

Reducing Failures

Perhaps the most effective sorts of activities undertaken against loss in the TPM program are those aimed at the reduction of failures in equipment and dies. These activities were implemented at each workplace, overseen by teams composed for that purpose and with full operator participation.

The Togo Seisakusyo autonomous maintenance program starts with team activities designed to reduce equipment failures, and is made up of four distinct stages. These are Failure Reduction 1 (lubrication and tightening), Failure Reduction 2 (component inspection), Defect Reduction (quality control), and Autonomous Control. Each is described below.

■ Stage 1

The member of the maintenance staff assigned to each workplace came to the workplace to conduct classes in both theory and practice concerning lubrication, tightening, and the cleaning of air blowers. A number of improvements were made at this stage, including changing areas where lubrication was difficult to perform and the like; the results were that the number of failures was cut in half.

■ Stage 2

Teams were formed, composed of representatives from manufacturing, maintenance, and production engineering. These teams performed thorough studies of areas where failures had been the most conspicuous during the previous year, established what the ideal situation should be at such areas, and implemented a number of improvements to recover that ideal. Among the improvements implemented were the installation of limit switches and bearings.

These thorough inspections clarified the overall level of deterioration. Limit switches uncovered 80 percent of the defects, and bearings about 60 percent, thus making it comparatively easy for operators to take the steps needed to recover from problems. Further, activities based on the varied experiences of people in the three areas noted above ensured that improvements were smoothly incorporated in all of the workplaces. These improvements were such that operators themselves could maintain after implementation.

These thorough inspections were expanded to eight different components on the basis of the failure records for 1985, a structure for maintenance skills training was introduced, and training was expanded to reach more people. Each team prepared an "eight component inspection table" for each machine in its jurisdiction, and training was offered in inspection procedures and recovery methods. These activities marked a surge forward in preventive maintenance that cut the number of failures to 1/40th their former rate. This resulted in a far-reaching reduction in loss due to failure, and several workplaces actually totally eliminated spontaneous failures from their lives. An "All Green Campaign" is currently underway to this zero failure rate.

■ Stage 3

All reasons for quality defects in the past were inventories in order to eliminate the generation of defects attributable to equipment problems. Equipment components (or states) that clearly needed to be controlled as causes of defects were labeled as "Quality Components," and chronic defects for which no cause had yet been determined were subjected to "MQ analysis" to determine what components required controls. After being discovered, these factors were controlled by means of daily inspection tables and PM calendars.

These measures have been taken only recently, and firm results have yet to be obtained. There has already been a 25 percent drop in the number of problems reported, and problems caused by defects in equipment and dies have dropped from 38 percent to 29 percent of the total. There is still ample room for improvement.

■ Stage 4

Stage four is the final step toward the complete elimination of failures from the workplace through the stepping up of autonomous maintenance activities. In this stage, steps are taken to ensure that the activities of the first three stages can be implemented and maintained in the individual workplaces. Inspection cycles are lengthened in accordance with the expansion of preventive maintenance activities in the workplace, inspections are simplified, and predictive maintenance is introduced to maintain a trouble-free environment and cut costs.

Because the materials used for dies are hard and the die structure is complicated by the need for one-shot forming, it always had been considered that a certain level of failure would be unavoidable. But after being stimulated by their high rate of success in reducing equipment failures, operators turned their attention to die failures, beginning activities designed to eliminate totally this type of failure, as well. Teams were formed from operators (and setup personnel), designers, and die fabricators to assist the maintenance staff in their PM activities directed at dies.

Looking Back

We have attempted in this article to introduce some of the TPM activities and general improvement examples that were a part of our efforts to create more efficient lines (lines with minimal waste and loss).

Togo Seisakusyo's experiments with TPM were not "smart" developments based on some type of overall program, but they were an attempt to develop "TPM Eyes" throughout the workplace, to lead to the discovery of problems that had been overlooked formerly, and to ways of dealing with these problems. These activities were conducted on an individual basis and a small group activity basis, marked by the formation of projects teams that were known mainly as "improvement teams." By dividing the labor through a number of different layers of organization, it was possible to match the problems discovered with their solutions in such a way that a generally high level of results was obtained.

But this is by no means a full picture of what TPM can do. We have merely laid the foundation for further activities. It is now time to become involved in activities aimed at an overall efficiency increase, to place new emphasis on production controls, and to work harder for individual improvements that will increase efficiency further.

Looking Forward

As has been noted, many of the activities undertaken in this campaign to increase line efficiency were borne by the company's strength in production technology. This will be an important tool of the firm in the future, as well, and increasing this strength must be the first priority in any program.

But daily controls and efforts to shave seconds from times must be stressed, for if they are not, overall production efficiency will not increase despite the fact that innumerable individual improvements have been implemented.

Further, the activities taken to date have come from the many leading firms that have developed their programs to the point of being able to write textbooks and handbooks for improvements. In the future, we will gradually find ourselves in ground that is unique to our own experience, and we will be forced to rely on our own knowledge and expertise.

The company must use its reception of the PM Prize as a springboard from which to develop the types of improvements that are needed to improve line efficiency even further. We must make efforts to improve in the other six types of TPM activities (see Figure 1) as we have in the first (5S workplace activities). This is the first step in the next stage of our TPM program, where, we believe, true TPM activities will really begin.

Examples of Loss Reduction

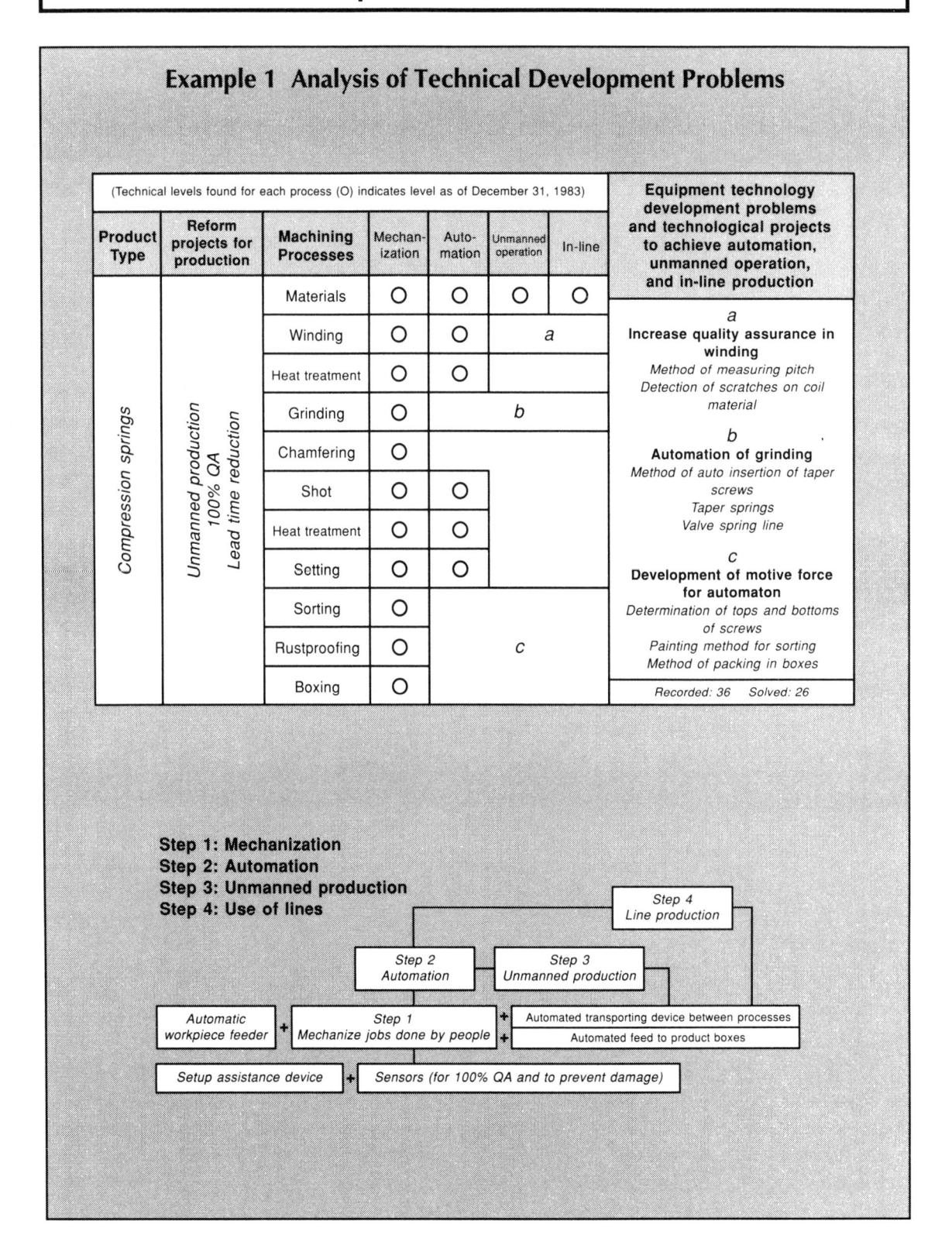

Example 1 Analysis of Technical Development Problems

(Technical levels found for each process (O) indicates level as of December 31, 1983)

Product Type	Reform projects for production	Machining Processes	Mechan-ization	Auto-mation	Unmanned operation	In-line
Compression springs	Unmanned production 100% QA Lead time reduction	Materials	O	O	O	O
		Winding	O	O	a	
		Heat treatment	O	O		
		Grinding	O		b	
		Chamfering	O			
		Shot	O	O		
		Heat treatment	O	O		
		Setting	O	O		
		Sorting	O			
		Rustproofing	O		c	
		Boxing	O			

Equipment technology development problems and technological projects to achieve automation, unmanned operation, and in-line production

a
Increase quality assurance in winding
Method of measuring pitch
Detection of scratches on coil material

b
Automation of grinding
Method of auto insertion of taper screws
Taper springs
Valve spring line

c
Development of motive force for automaton
Determination of tops and bottoms of screws
Painting method for sorting
Method of packing in boxes

Recorded: 36   Solved: 26

Step 1: Mechanization
Step 2: Automation
Step 3: Unmanned production
Step 4: Use of lines

```
                                                          ┌─────────────────┐
                                                          │ Step 4          │
                                                          │ Line production │
                                                          └─────────────────┘
                         ┌──────────────┐  ┌────────────────────┐
                         │ Step 2       │  │ Step 3             │
                         │ Automation   │  │ Unmanned production│
                         └──────────────┘  └────────────────────┘
┌─────────────────┐  ┌────────────────────────────┐  ┌──────────────────────────────────────┐
│ Automatic       │+ │ Step 1                     │+ │ Automated transporting device        │
│ workpiece feeder│+ │ Mechanize jobs done by     │+ │ between processes                    │
│                 │  │ people                     │  │ Automated feed to product boxes      │
└─────────────────┘  └────────────────────────────┘  └──────────────────────────────────────┘
┌─────────────────────────┐  ┌──────────────────────────────────────────────┐
│ Setup assistance device │+ │ Sensors (for 100% QA and to prevent damage) │
└─────────────────────────┘  └──────────────────────────────────────────────┘
```

Example 2 Unmanned Operation of the Small Press

The unmanned operation of machining equipment proceeded according to the four steps outlined below. At each step in the implementation, care was taken to meet all necessary operating conditions, and improvement activities were implemented to raise the overall level of operation.

Step 1: One box, one coil
Step 2: Operation during breaks and shift changes (one hour)
Step 3: Over three hours operation (after work hours)
Step 4: Operation on vacation days (half-day to full day)

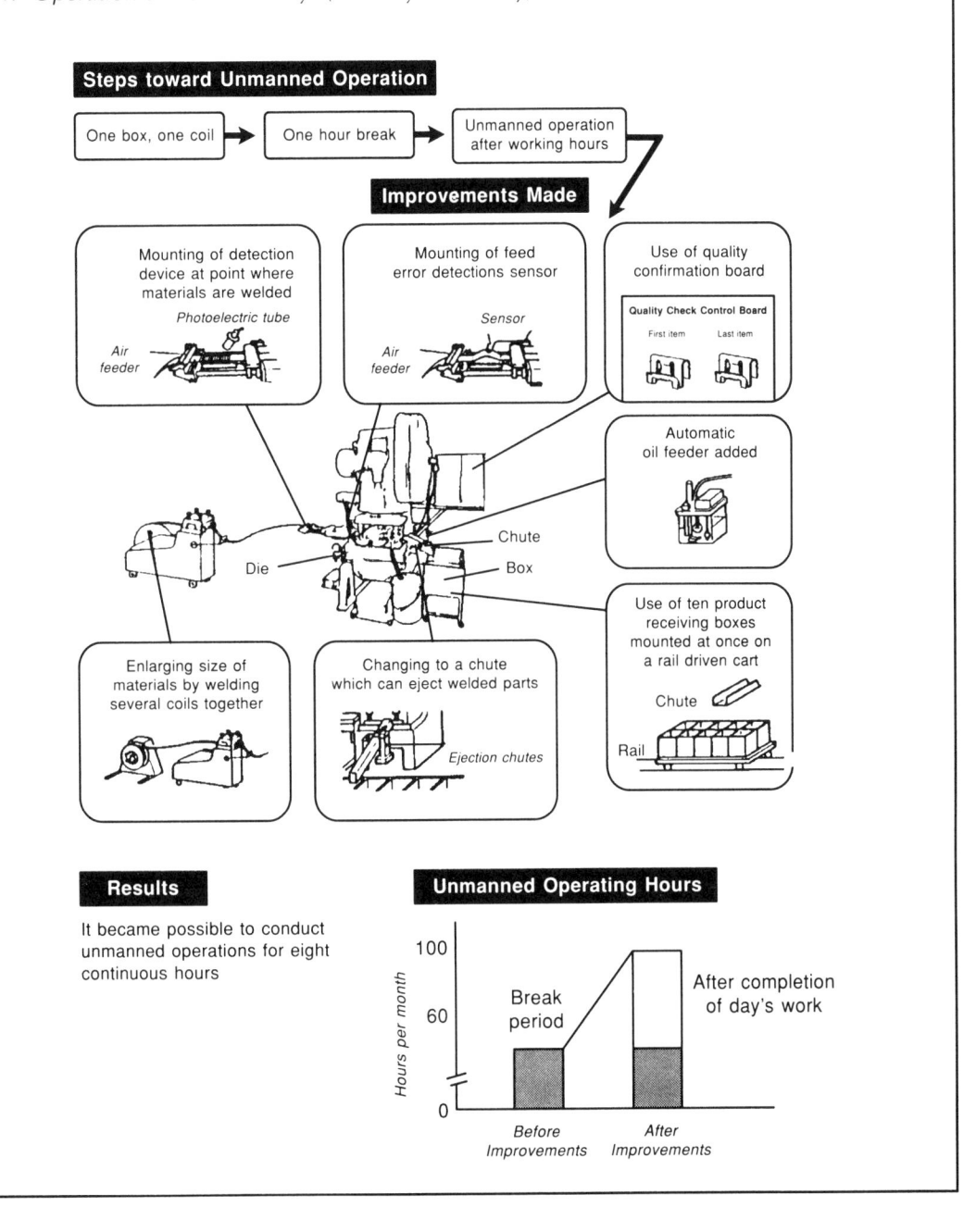

Steps toward Unmanned Operation

One box, one coil → One hour break → Unmanned operation after working hours

Improvements Made

- Mounting of detection device at point where materials are welded (Photoelectric tube, Air feeder)
- Mounting of feed error detections sensor (Sensor, Air feeder)
- Use of quality confirmation board (Quality Check Control Board — First item, Last item)
- Automatic oil feeder added
- Use of ten product receiving boxes mounted at once on a rail driven cart (Chute, Rail)
- Enlarging size of materials by welding several coils together
- Changing to a chute which can eject welded parts (Ejection chutes)

Die, Chute, Box

Results

It became possible to conduct unmanned operations for eight continuous hours

Unmanned Operating Hours

Hours per month: 0, 60, 100
Break period / After completion of day's work
Before Improvements / After Improvements

Example 3 Synchronization of Damper Spring Production Line

Providing autonomated machining equipment, with features such as a materials feeding device and devices for transporting workpieces to the next process, were development and improvement actions. These enabled the further development of lines through the synchronization of all processes performed on the line.

Parts feeders were used in these cases, according to the size, shape, quantity, and equipment technology level of the products involved. These parts feeders inserted the workpieces into the machines involved, and were used for both small-lot partial batch flow production and full one-piece flow production from the first process on.

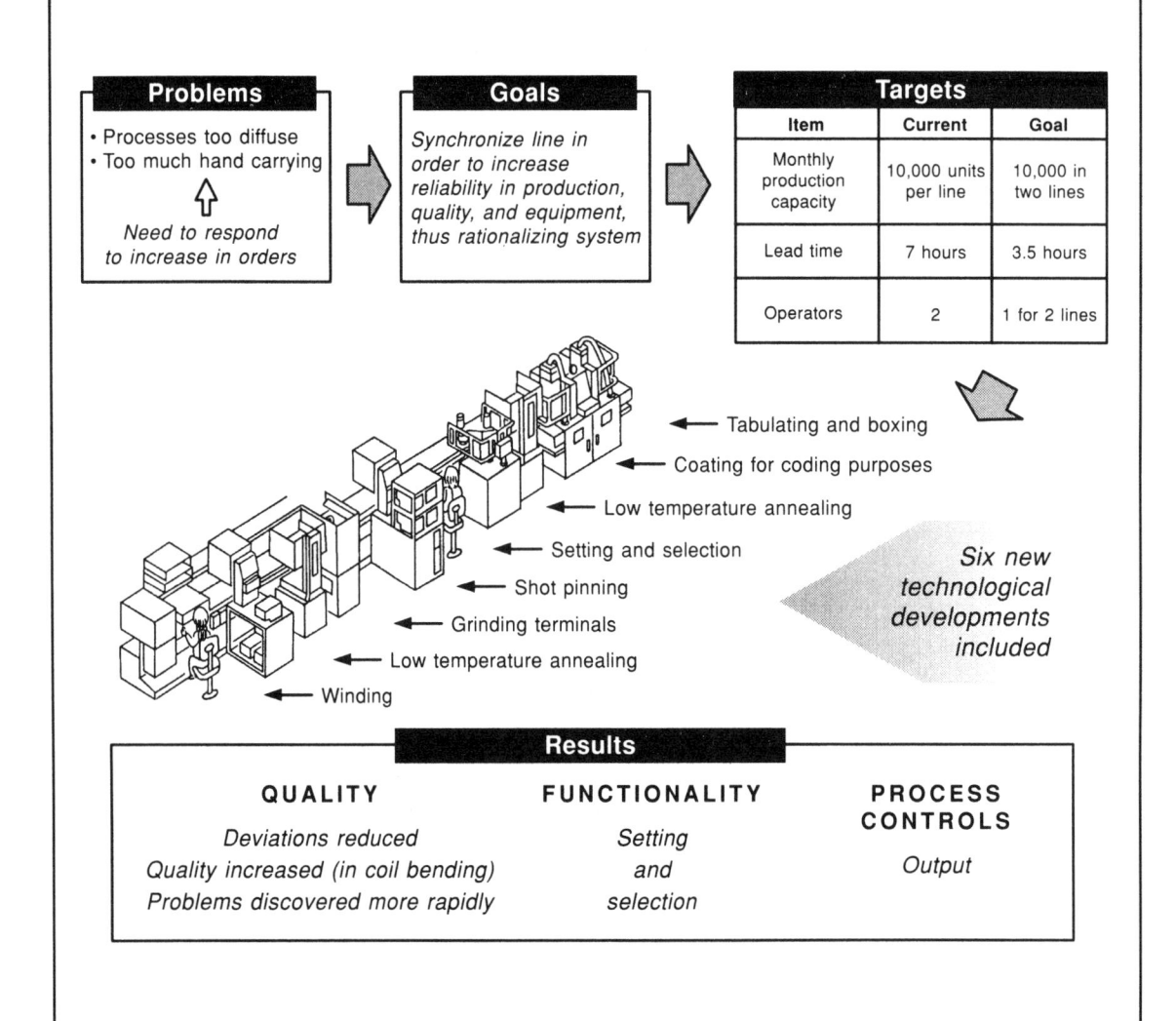

Problems
- Processes too diffuse
- Too much hand carrying

⇧

Need to respond to increase in orders

Goals

Synchronize line in order to increase reliability in production, quality, and equipment, thus rationalizing system

Targets

Item	Current	Goal
Monthly production capacity	10,000 units per line	10,000 in two lines
Lead time	7 hours	3.5 hours
Operators	2	1 for 2 lines

Process flow (from end to start):
- Tabulating and boxing
- Coating for coding purposes
- Low temperature annealing
- Setting and selection
- Shot pinning
- Grinding terminals
- Low temperature annealing
- Winding

Six new technological developments included

Results

QUALITY	FUNCTIONALITY	PROCESS CONTROLS
Deviations reduced	Setting	Output
Quality increased (in coil bending)	and	
Problems discovered more rapidly	selection	

Increasing Human, Equipment, and Material Efficiency to Lower Failures

Example 4 Die Design and Fabrication

The majority of the products made by Togo Seisakusyo require the use of dies, and these dies determine the quality, quantity, and cost of the product. From the efficiency standpoint, in particular, it is necessary to use one-shot forming dies that require no work in subsequent processes. This, in turn, required the development of new technologies, and new machining methods and mechanisms that are not to be found in the conventional approaches.

A system thus was devised to study the development of new mechanisms. The expansion of the CAD system, in particular, provided greater efficiency in the design of dies.

Major Products	New Technology and Processes	Ease of maintenance	Setup ease	Starting and stopping	Speed	Quality	Information Activities MP	Information Activities CD	Effects
	Tool to synchronize extraction and bending			√		√	30	5	Selection operation eliminated due to dimensional stability
	Multi-stroke forming method	√	√				40	4	Die length cut to 1/7, thus enabling press size reduction
	Slanted tool design for press				√		55	7	Processes compressed (from three processes to immediate forming)
	3-D movement of bending tool				√		23	4	Tool stroke distance reduced from 150 to 25 mm
	Synchronization of attaching two parts and bending				√	√	20	5	Processes compressed (from five processes to two processes)

Example 5 Setup Loss

Some time before, the company had gone to the use of diesets and other devices to develop the so-called "single-minute exchange of die" (SMED) system, in which setups are performed in under ten minutes. In this case, however, the changes were being made in the multi-forming and winding machines, which have a large number of built-in tools and cams, and improvements proved more difficult to implement than had been anticipated. It was decided that, lacking a main road to the destination, side roads would have to be utilized. A switch to off-line setups proved remarkably effective.

Problems

Approximately two hours required for forming setups

No trial operations could be made during time tool was being dressed

⬇

Development of Equipment for Setup Reduction

⬇

Two parallel trial operations possible

Effect: forming changeover went from 120 min. to 1 min.

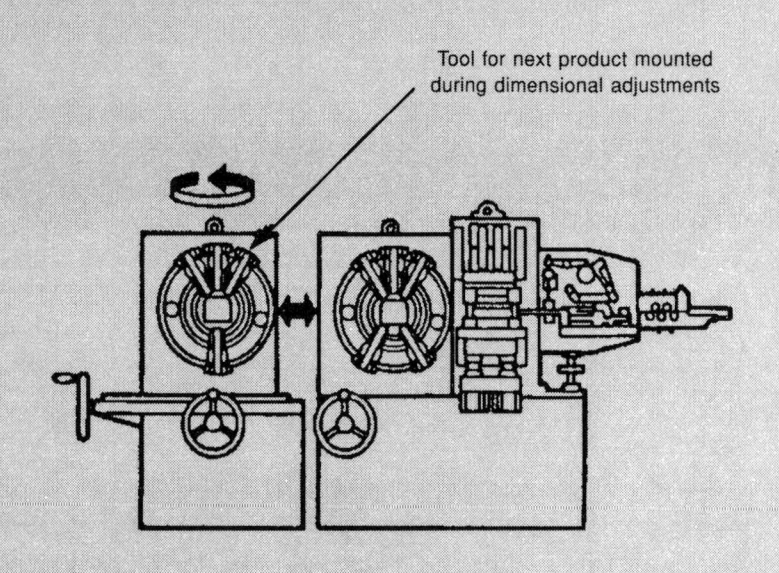

Tool for next product mounted during dimensional adjustments

Example 6 Shortening Setups

A study of setups shows that there are two major types: some involve the use of diesets, and some involve the need to change a number of tools or cams. These latter types are primarily for the multi-forming machines and compression spring winding machines, which are the major types of machines used at Togo Seisakusyo. The length of time needed for setups, then, has a major impact on production time.

The Philosophy and Implementation of Setup Improvements

Setup

Setup Methods
- Complex due to the large number of tools and cams which must be changed
- Changing diesets

Equipment
- Multi-Forming Machine
  - 11 press-type bending tools
  - 13 slide cams
- Winding Machine
- Extrusion-Forming Machine
- Small Press

Multi-Forming Machine Winding Machine	Reasons for Problems	Extrusion Forming Machine Small Press
●	Full change of tools	
	Die dimensions not uniform	●
●	Dimensional adjustments too complex	
●	Requires long experience	
	Needs preparations	●

Points of Improvements

- Distinction between on- and off-line setups
- Quantify and gage
- Simplify attachments
- Standardize
- Operation training

- Distinction between on- and off-line setups
- Unify dimensions of dies
- One-shot positioning

Target Time
- Less than 1/3
- Under ten minutes for setup change

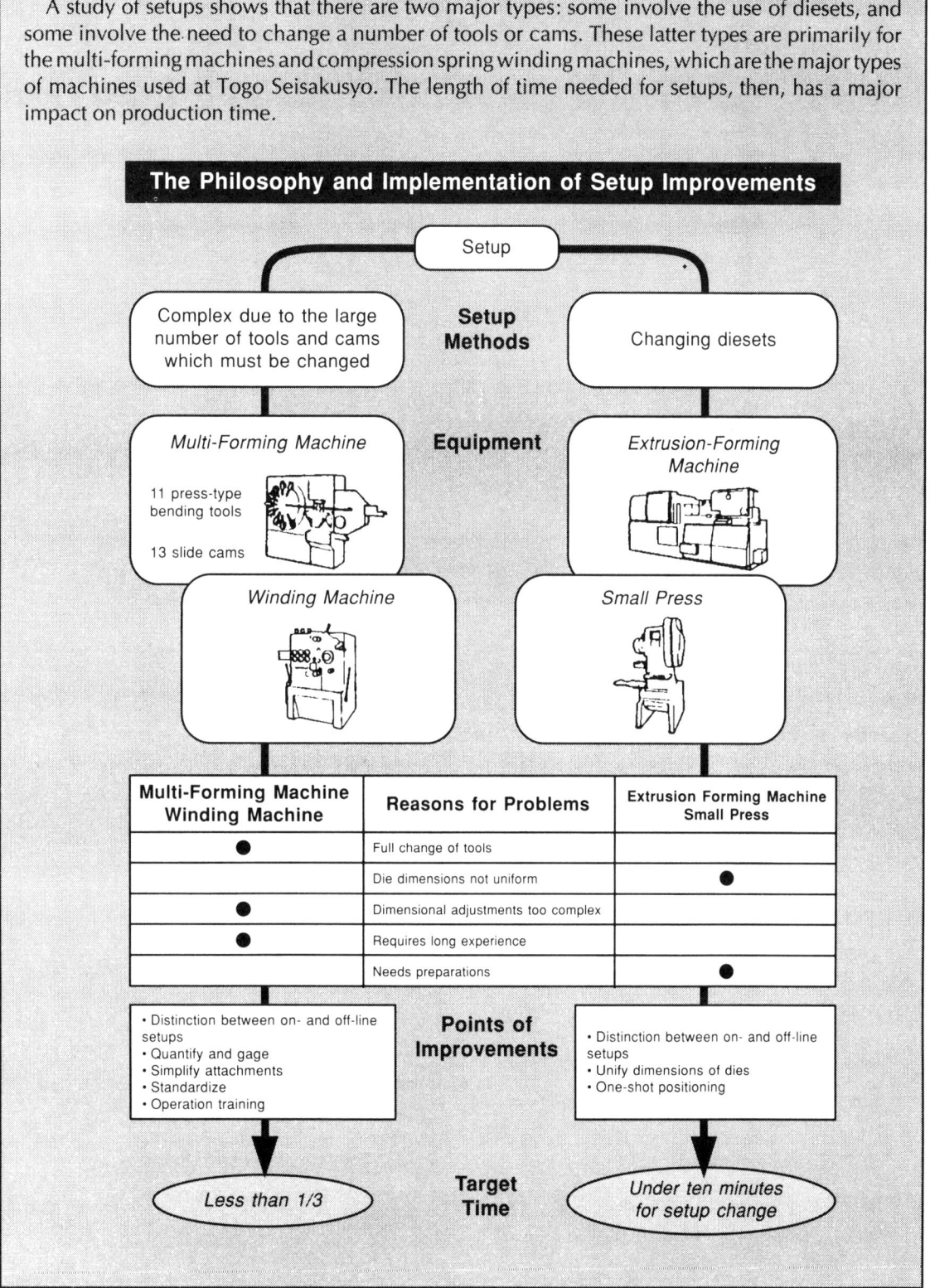

Example 7 Loss due to Brief Stops

As mechanization and automation proceeded, a large number of parts feeders and transporting devices came into use. This intensified problems with brief stops, and in some workplaces, recovery from these stops became the major tasks faced by the operators.

Due to the difficulty in taking up the problem of brief stops systematically, most of these individual problems were assigned to the quality control circles as on-going improvement activities. Considerable success was achieved in this area.

Reasons for Taking Up Project

(1) Too many brief stops, requiring the response of female operators

(2) Need to increase production with current operator level

Way Assembly Performed

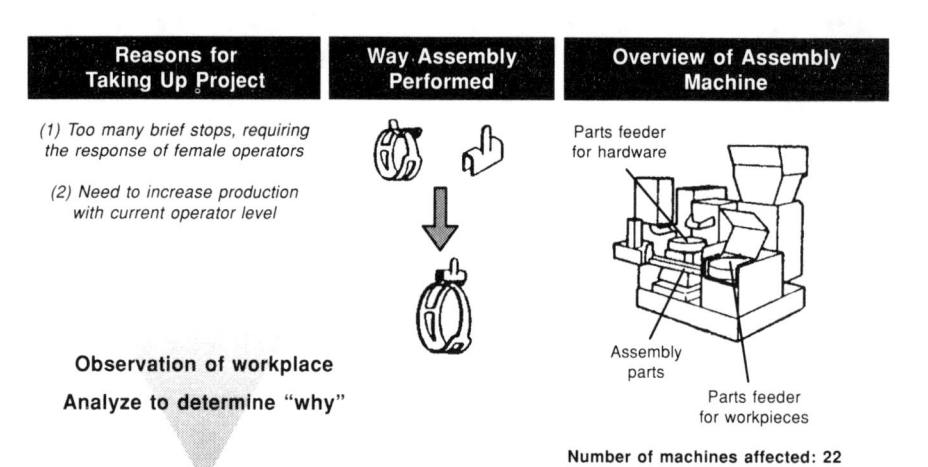

Observation of workplace

Analyze to determine "why"

Overview of Assembly Machine

Parts feeder for hardware

Assembly parts

Parts feeder for workpieces

Number of machines affected: 22

AREAS WHERE PROBLEMS OCCUR	CAUSES	ACTIONS TAKEN	EFFECTS
❶  Caught in hole for sensor	There is a sensor hole in curved section of hardware chute	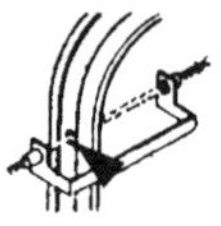 Hole position changed from curved to perpendicular area	From 40 times daily to once
❷ 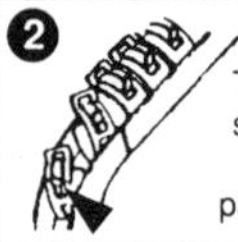 Turned on side when leaving parts feeder	Workpieces vibrate and catch in the corners of the chute entrance	 Stabilizing guide added (will not change direction even if they hit the corner)	From four times daily to once
❸ 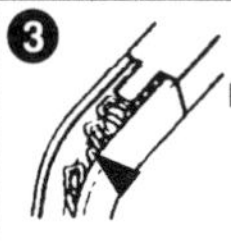 Reversed inside chute	 Get turned around in areas with large gaps	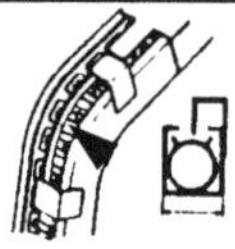 Guide mounted to be aligned with work (aligns gaps)	From five times daily to never
❹ 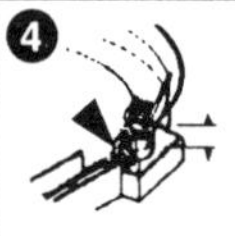 Caught in parts feeder chute	Get caught in gaps between the workpiece dividing rods	 Workpiece dividing rod lengthened (for three horizontal units)	From 48 times daily to seven

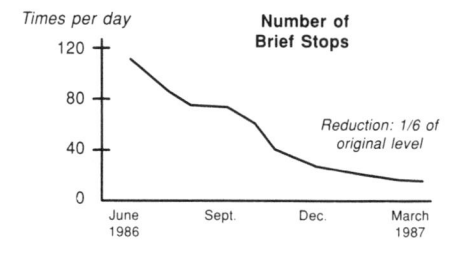

Number of Brief Stops

Reduction: 1/6 of original level

(Times per day: June 1986 ~120, Sept., Dec., March 1987)

Example 8 Loss due to Air Cuts

The widespread use of parts feeders and transporting devices led to a considerable increase in loss due to air cuts. In these cases, springs might get caught or hung up in the parts feeder when they were being fed to the end surface polishing or setting processes, for example, which would result in some or all of the springs not being fed to the process. In these cases, the machines would go on cutting anyway, leading to air cut loss.

Further, when injection molding dies, which form multiple pieces at one time, are not prepared because of quality problems, from one to several pieces will be eliminated from the forming process and the process will be carried out with a smaller number of pieces than normal. This, too, is a form of air cutting and a source of loss.

These sorts of losses are among the major reasons for drops in process speed efficiency. Once this is understood fully by everyone, they can be dealt with by QC circles, and major improvements can be achieved.

Example 9 The "Clean the Dies" Campaign

Before this campaign was begun, there were numerous failures due to mistakes in die maintenance and mistakes in die handling and setups. The reason for these mistakes was that overall concern regarding dies was low, making it difficult to determine the cause of failures. In order to raise the consciousness of those directly concerned with the problem, a number of company-wide activities were begun:

✓ The elimination of broken diesets

✓ The cleaning of all dies

✓ The improvement of die storage methods

This campaign was aimed at increasing workplace morale, and as a result, the number of defects related to resin dies was greatly reduced, which was an unexpected but fortunate by-product of the campaign.

Example 10 Disaster Die Countermeasures

Prior to beginning this campaign, there had been a number of failures regarding dies, so dies which had experienced two or more failures in any given month were designated as "disaster dies," and given the special attention of the improvement teams. These activities revealed the fact that the spare parts system was poor, and also that failures often recurred. As a result of positive actions taken to reduce machining mistakes by departments involved in the machining of dies (the machine tool department and outside contractors), and to improve the wirecut machining system, failures caused by problems with spare parts were reduced to ten percent of their former level.

> **Example 11 Increasing Die Maintenance Skills**
>
> Conventional technical training was inadequate, resulting in a low reliability rate for die preparation, so technical skills maps were made for each operator and concerned person to evaluate the overall level of technical expertise. Academic and technical training programs were also instituted, with mottoes such as "everyone a teacher, everyone a student," or "everyone an instructor, everyone a trainee." Lesson sheets were prepared for these and training was undertaken so that the general level of die maintenance skills was increased for the entire maintenance staff.
>
> In conjunction with this, a planning maintenance base was constructed to increase the reliability of die preparation. The maintenance cycle was clarified, and die preparation was conducted in a planned manner, in three stages. As a result, the number of die failures was reduced to ten percent of its former level.
>
> These activities greatly reduced the loss due to die failures, and increased production rates; it also reduced problems with some processes lagging behind others. Particularly large increases in performance and productivity were achieved with the resin dies, in particular.

100 Percent Participation

Improving Corporate Structure with TPM Activities

By Katsumi Takeichi
NBC Corporation Electric Wire Company

The NBC Corporation TPM Program

NBC Corporation was founded in 1931 as a manufacturer of electrical wire, and since 1955 has functioned as a specialist in the manufacture of wire harnesses for automotive use. Its growth has kept pace with that of the automotive industry in general. In 1969, it anticipated the demands of the new age and moved into the production of printed circuit boards, and today it is at the forefront of the automotive electronics field.

The company functions in what is essentially a harsh environment, however, and considerable reflection on the future convinced management that problems such as low productivity and chronic quality defects caused by equipment are common to all of its operations. Declaring the need to maintain a level of quality and reliability that would satisfy the company's customers, the president of the company recently launched a TPM program with one set of unified goals for all corporate divisions. The TPM program was aimed primarily at securing 100 percent participation from all employees in order to improve corporate structure and efficiency.

The Basic Policies of the TPM Program

The main goals of the program are to secure 100 percent employee involvement to create TPM activities that will increase the levels of control, technology, and skills within the company, thus strengthening corporate structure. There are three main components to this:

✓ Reduce quality defects caused by equipment problems in order to maintain a high standard of quality

✓ Increase productivity rates for equipment and use it more effectively, in order to increase overall productivity

✓ Create a clean and pleasant atmosphere in the workplace in order to make it more vital

These three basic goals of the program are to be implemented through 100 percent employee participation in activities designed around five major concerns:

✓ Quality and preventive maintenance (PM)

✓ Increased productivity

✓ Maintenance programs

✓ A revitalized workplace

✓ Safety, health, and environmental controls

Figure 1 The TPM Promotional Organization

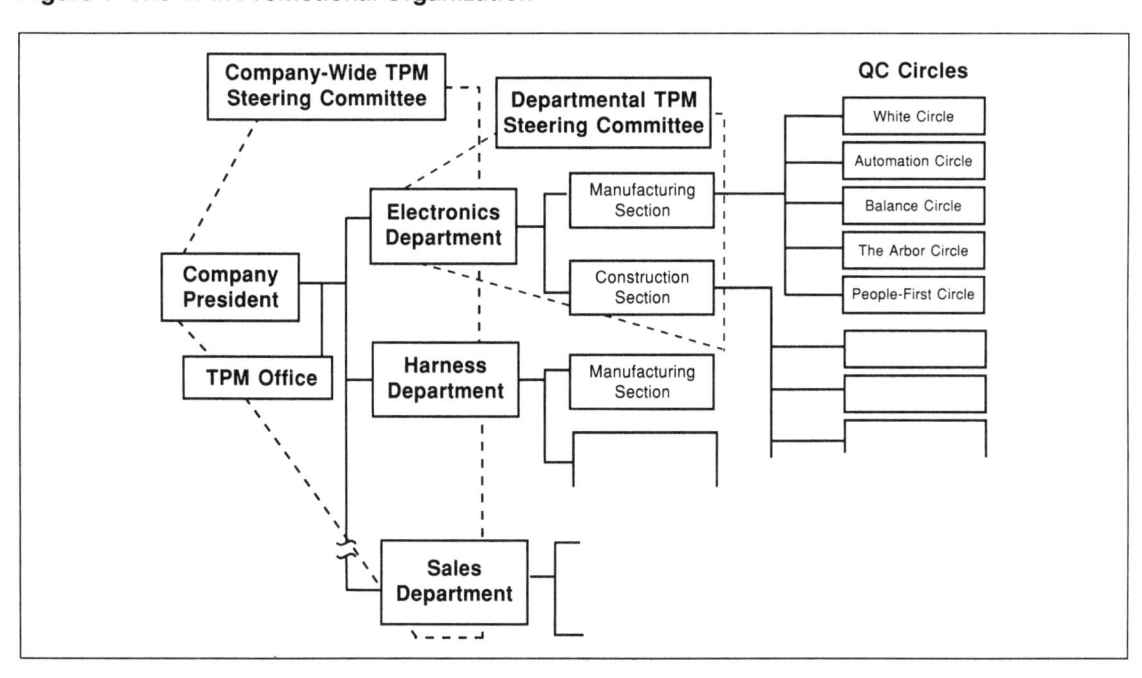

guard against problems with dirt and foreign matter. Also, TPM activities and concurrent improvements were launched on a plant-wide basis to counter defect-related problems.

The Wire Harness Division is made up of the cutting and application processes primarily—which use automated cutting and application machines—and manual installation, often jobbed out to outside contractors. This division had implemented TPM activities to guard against cutting and application defects made by the machines, and installation errors made by the human workers. The quality situation at the time the TPM program was first introduced to the company is shown in Figure 4.

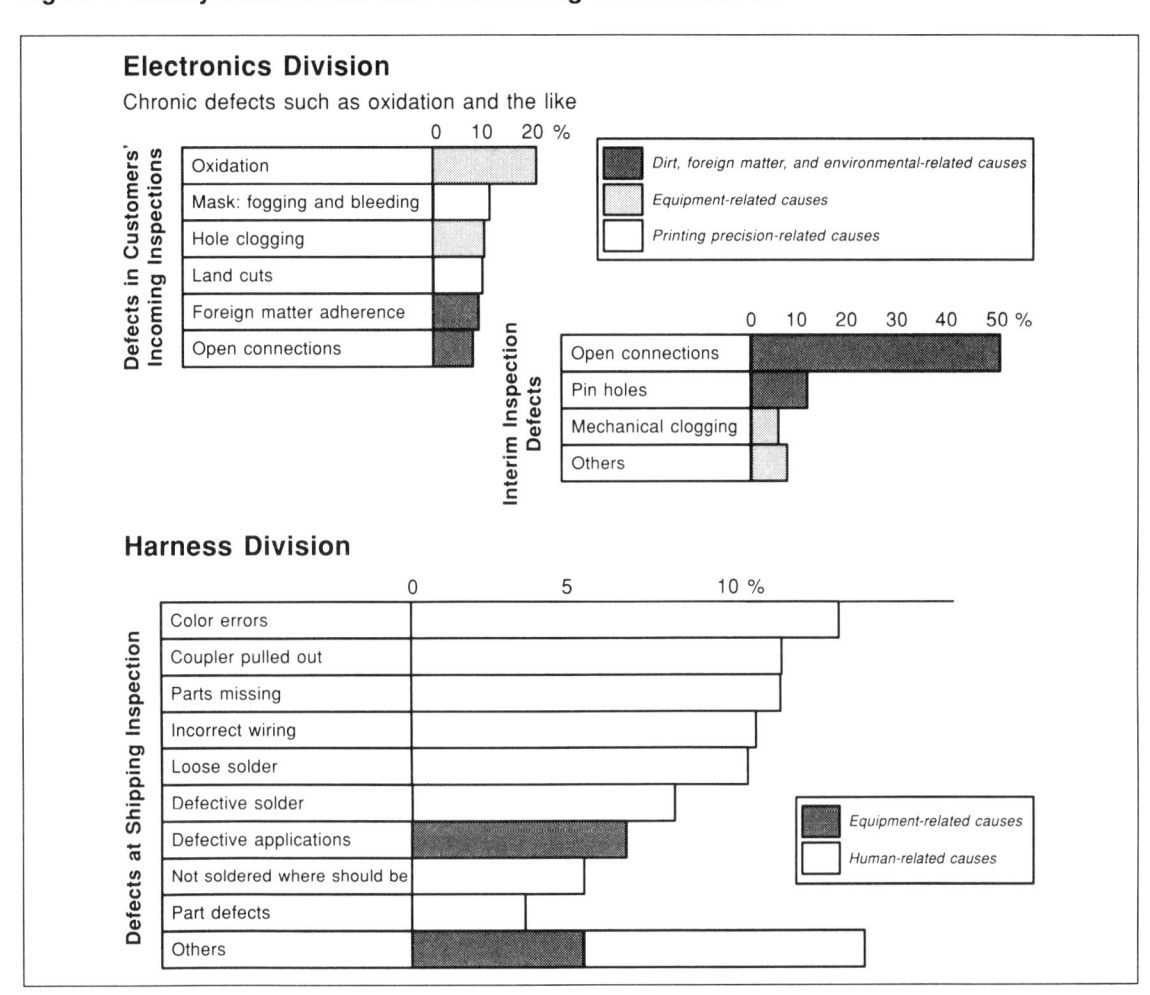

Figure 4 Quality Status at the Time of TPM Program Introduction

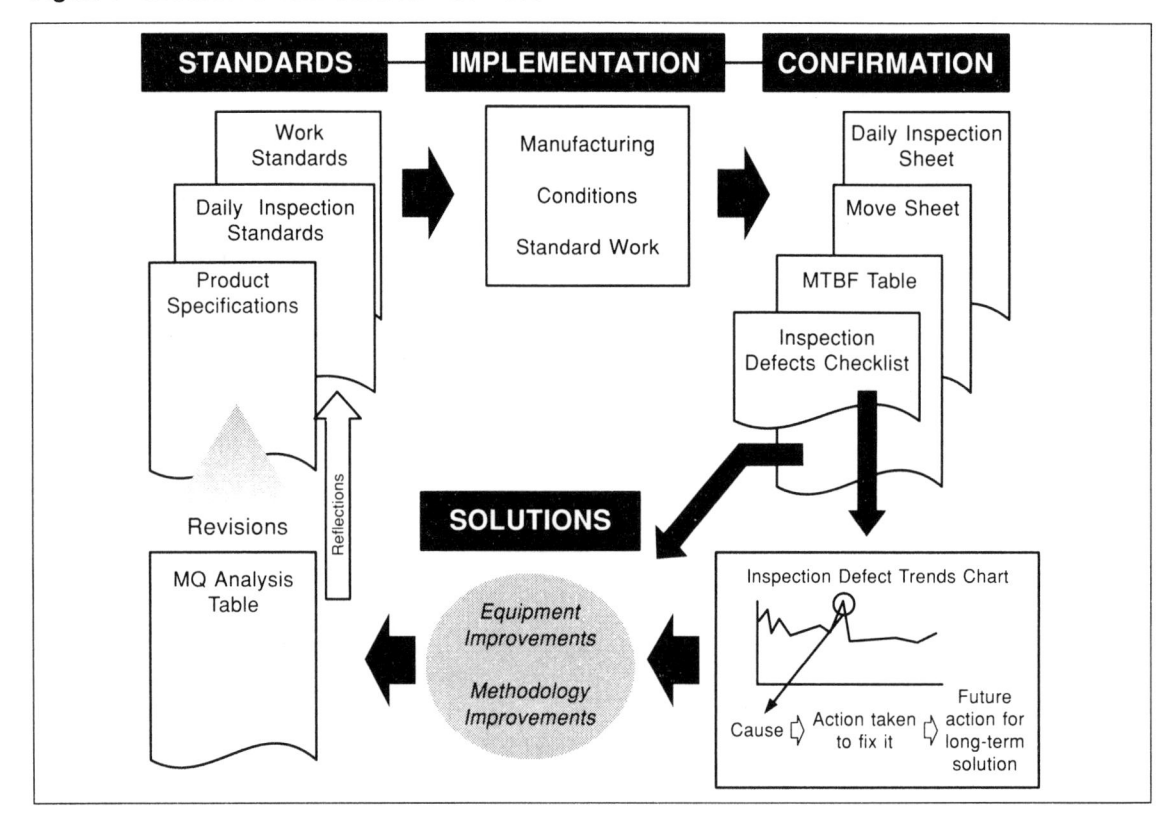

Figure 5 The Mechanism Used for Activities

■ The "Build in Quality" campaign of the Electronics Division

Prior to the introduction of TPM, quality problems were dealt with in a very superficial manner, and with improvements which seldom had any true impact on the situation. With the introduction of TPM, though, more effort was made to get to the root of quality problems and to take steps to prevent their recurrence. The mechanism used for this is shown in Figure 5.

■ Elimination of dirt and foreign matter, and environmental preparation

Open connections, pinholes, and other quality defects are caused by dirt and foreign matter. Flaws under one-third the pattern width are permissible under JPCA standards, and 83 percent of the dirt generated during the cutting process—the major dirt generator—is a cause of defects. The measures taken by NBC Corporation against dust particles of 83μ or larger from the pattern printing processing to the

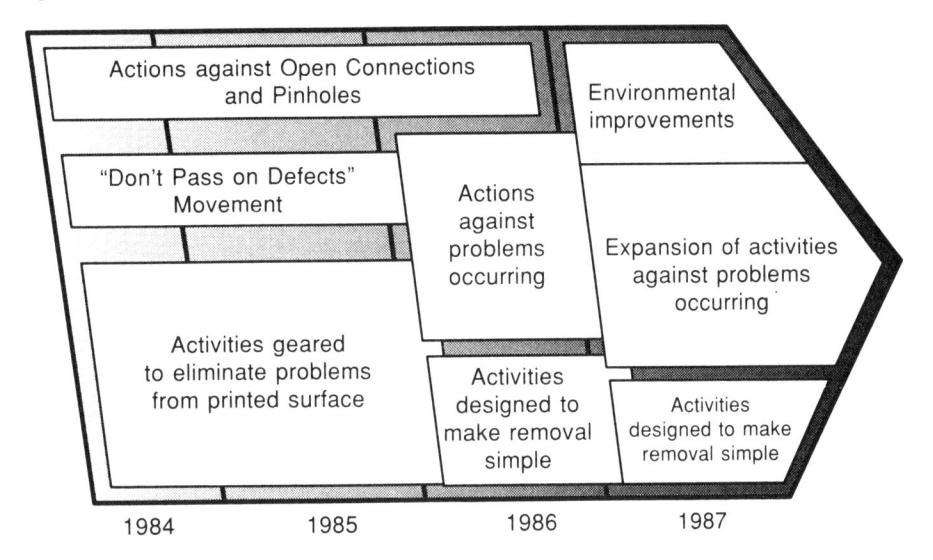

Figure 6 Historical Development of Activities

Actions against Open Connections and Pinholes		Environmental improvements
"Don't Pass on Defects" Movement	Actions against problems occurring	Expansion of activities against problems occurring
Activities geared to eliminate problems from printed surface	Activities designed to make removal simple	Activities designed to make removal simple
1984	1985	1986	1987

cutting process are shown in Figure 6 in historical perspective.

■ The reduction of equipment-related defects

Nearly all defects in printed circuit boards are due to equipment problems. A program of daily and periodic inspections thus was implemented for the equipment, along with mean time between failures (MTBF) analysis. These tools were used for equipment improvements and maintenance activities. Then MQ analysis was performed to settle on the maintenance method which would have the

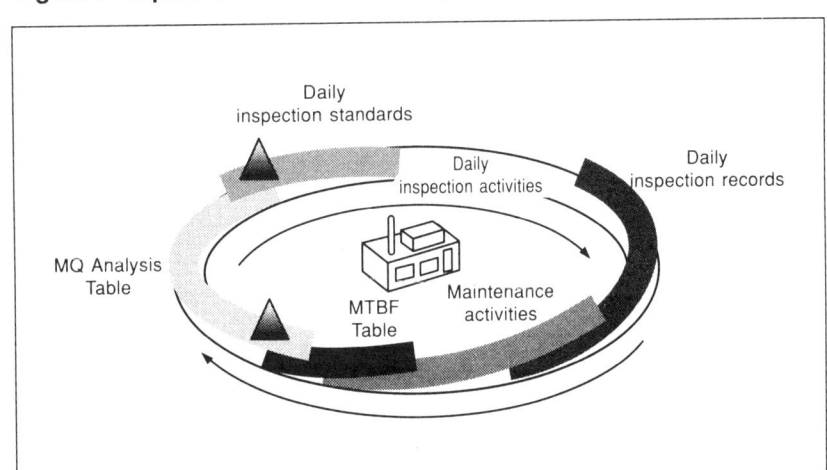

Figure 7 Implementation of MQ Analysis

greatest impact on quality. The implementation of this program is shown in Figure 7.

■ The "Build in Quality" campaign of the Wire Harness Division

The major goal in this division was the reduction of equipment-related defects in the cutting and application process.

The primary causes of equipment-related defects in the application of wire harnesses are the automated application machine cords and terminal shift positions.

These relationships between quality and equipment are shown in Figure 8. In addition to dealing with these areas individually to implement improvements, daily and periodic inspections also were used to maintain quality as a part of a preventive maintenance program.

To lower these defects even further, MQ analysis was performed to determine the relationship between quality and the specific parts of the machines. This enabled the determination of a preventive maintenance program that was able to keep quality levels high.

Figure 8 The Relationships between Quality and Equipment

Process	Item	Sags	Missing parts	Extrusion	Neck balance	Cover peeling	Meat peeling	Other
Terminal Shifting	Reel	○	○		●			
	Terminal feed	○	○					
	Terminal application	○	●	●				
Cord Shifting	Cord feed							●
	Cord clamping					●	○	
	Cut skin peeling					○	●	
	Clamp shifting		●	●				
	Application position	○	○	●	●			
	Terminal application	○	○					

● *Process and Factor with Impact on Problem*   ○ *Process and Factor with Particular Impact on Problem*

Increasing Productivity

Expanding business requires adding more devices to the existing equipment, which greatly increases setup time when operators are insufficiently skilled and products must be made in small lots. This is a major obstacle to improving productivity.

For this reason, the introduction of the TPM program in 1984 was used as the opportunity to increase overall equipment efficiency. To do this, work improvements were undertaken with 100 percent employee participation to increase production rates of critical equipment, to use equipment more effectively, and to automate equipment. The main goal of all of this activity was to increase productivity (see Figure 9).

Regarding the efforts to increase the production rates of critical equipment in particular, the numbers in Figure 10

Figure 9 Critical Activities

Maximize Equipment Efficiency

- *Increase production rate of critical equipment*
    - Reducing time equipment not in operation
        - Reducing time for setups
            - Motion improvement based on video recordings
            - Reduce number of times setup needed
            - Encourage the use of off-line setups
        - Reduce number of brief stops
            - Stop electrical cords from becoming entangled
            - Stop terminals from catching
            - Stop plate clogging
        - Reduce amount of loss due to speed drops
            - Lower speed loss on automated applicator
            - Reduce speed loss on etching line
- *More efficient use of equipment and automation*
    - Automate equipment to increase cycle speed
    - Achieve compatibility among automated applicators
- *Work improvements with 100% participation*
    - Detection and improvement of problem based on work improvement questionnaires

102 REDUCING THE SIX MAJOR LOSSES

Figure 10 Types of Non-Productive Machine Hours

EQUIPMENT ITEM	Automated cutter and applicator	Pattern printing machine	Percentage of time stopped
Setup change	○	○	~45%
Plate correction		●	~15%
Measurement	●		~5%
Brief stop	●	●	~5%
Other	●	●	~10%

Automated cutter and applicator
- Setup changes 91%
- Measurements 31%
- Brief stops 6%
- Other 3%

Pattern printing machine
- Setup changes 76%
- Plate correction 33%
- Brief stops 3%
- Other 21%

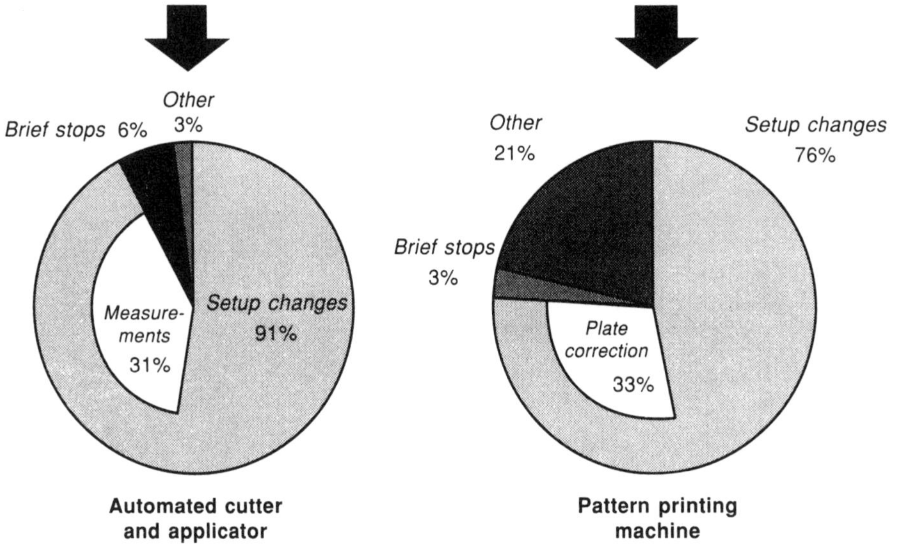

make it clear that the major reason for equipment being out of production was setups. In order to reduce setup time, video tapes of the setup operations were shot and studied in order to formulate work improvements. One-lesson texts and tape recordings also were used for operational training. The reduction of time required for changing materials, cutting tools, and the like was accomplished by equipment improvements to eliminate the need for repeated adjustments. One of these improvements will be discussed below.

■ Reducing setup time through equipment improvements

As can be seen in Figure 11, setups and measurements for the cutting and application of electric wires are done in

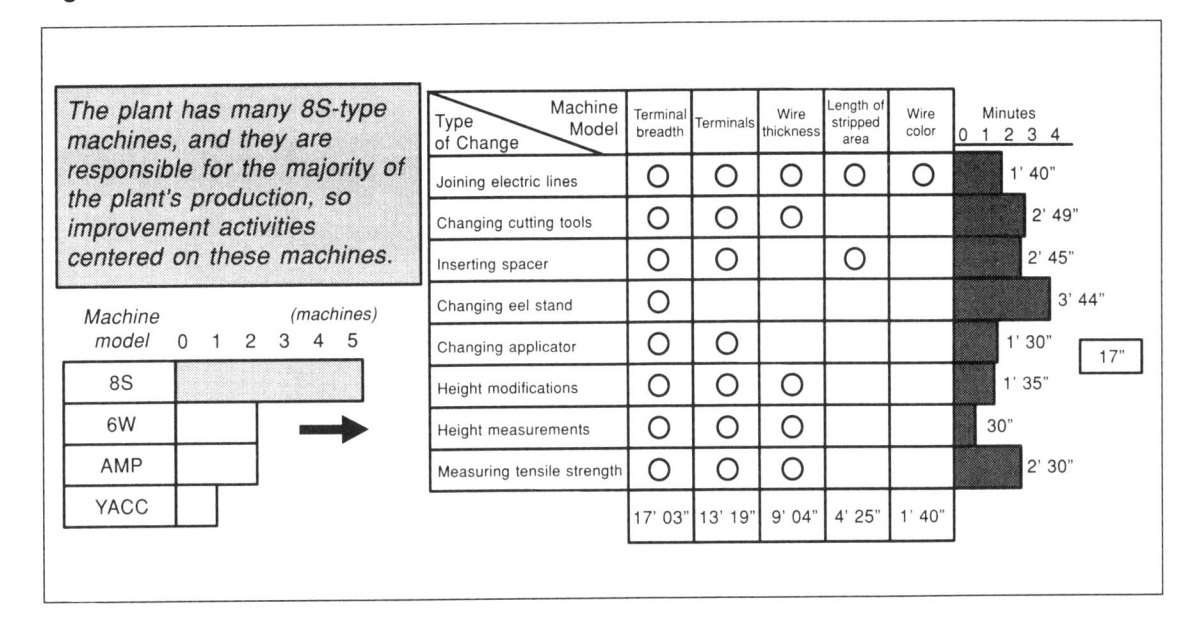

Improving Corporate Structure with TPM Activities 103

Figure 11 The Status of Critical Machines and Time Requirements of 8S Machine Setups

Type of Change \ Machine Model	Terminal breadth	Terminals	Wire thickness	Length of stripped area	Wire color	Minutes
Joining electric lines	O	O	O	O	O	1' 40"
Changing cutting tools	O	O	O			2' 49"
Inserting spacer	O	O		O		2' 45"
Changing eel stand	O					3' 44"
Changing applicator	O	O				1' 30"
Height modifications	O	O	O			1' 35"
Height measurements	O	O	O			30"
Measuring tensile strength	O	O	O			2' 30"
	17' 03"	13' 19"	9' 04"	4' 25"	1' 40"	

The plant has many 8S-type machines, and they are responsible for the majority of the plant's production, so improvement activities centered on these machines.

Machine model (machines): 8S, 6W, AMP, YACC

small setup increments, so equipment improvements were conducted for each item separately.

Maintenance Activities

The mechanism for maintenance activities shown in Figure 12 was established as a part of the creation of a system that would allow full scope for preventive maintenance. Short texts were created for autonomous maintenance, so that operators could get to the point of being able to perform minor repairs and improvements on their machines to maintain machine performance and become acquainted with basic inspection techniques. In the Electronics Division, in particular, a good deal of highly corrosive solvent was used, and a campaign was begun to eliminate the rust that this solvent caused.

The maintenance staff, meanwhile, began a program of corrective maintenance that involved the use of MTBF analysis and PM analysis, as a part of the activities designed to lower the number of failures.

Revitalization of the Workplace

Four approaches were taken to the creation of a clean, safe, and comfortable workplace. These were:

✓ 5S activities with 100 percent employee involvement
✓ The creation of QC circles
✓ A creative suggestion system
✓ Personnel training

104   REDUCING THE SIX MAJOR LOSSES

Figure 12 Mechanisms for Maintenance Activities

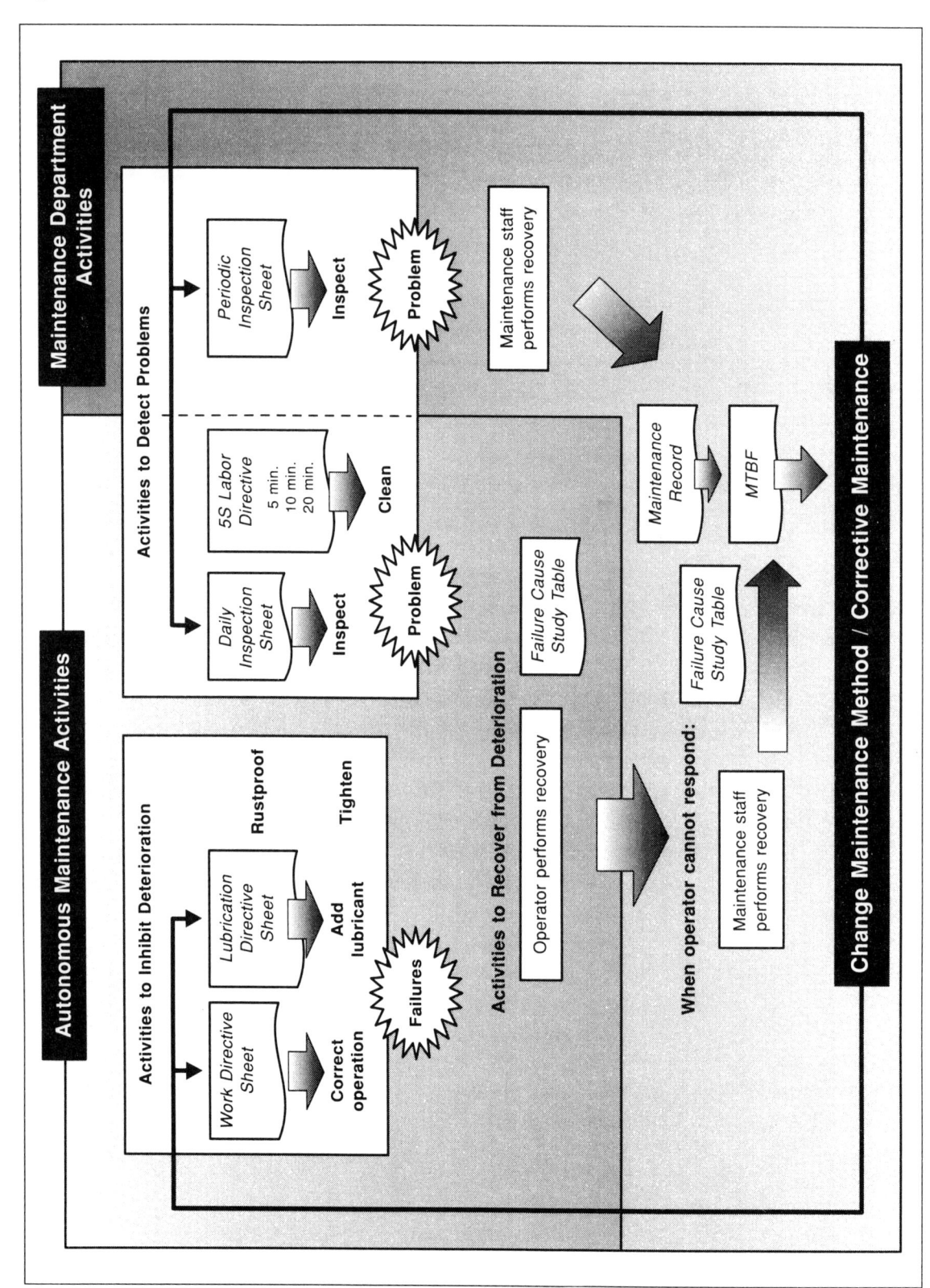

Activities were particularly intense in the Electronics Division, where a number of fluids and other liquids are used. Here policies were enacted to counter oil spills, water spills, the scattering of chips, dust buildup, and the like. This was launched by the use of a red tag campaign.

In the Wire Harness Division, where nearly all of the operators are female part-timers, setups and daily inspections always had been performed by women. Failures, however, were treated by the male members of the maintenance staff.

As a part of the TPM program, the female operators were trained to handle all failures that could be repaired in ten minutes or less.

Safety, Health, and Environmental Controls

Steps also were taken to ensure that the control system would be effective against disasters and pollution problems. In order to maintain an accident-free, non-polluting work environment, safety patrols were inaugurated to discover potentially unsafe areas and improve them. Other efforts to ensure the preservation of a safe and healthy work environment involved training people for the proper certifications. Figure 13 shows the safety, health, and environmental controls implemented.

Overall Effects of the Program

The most tangible effect of the TPM activities was the fact that major progress was made in each of the four areas discussed above. This progress is shown in Figure 14.

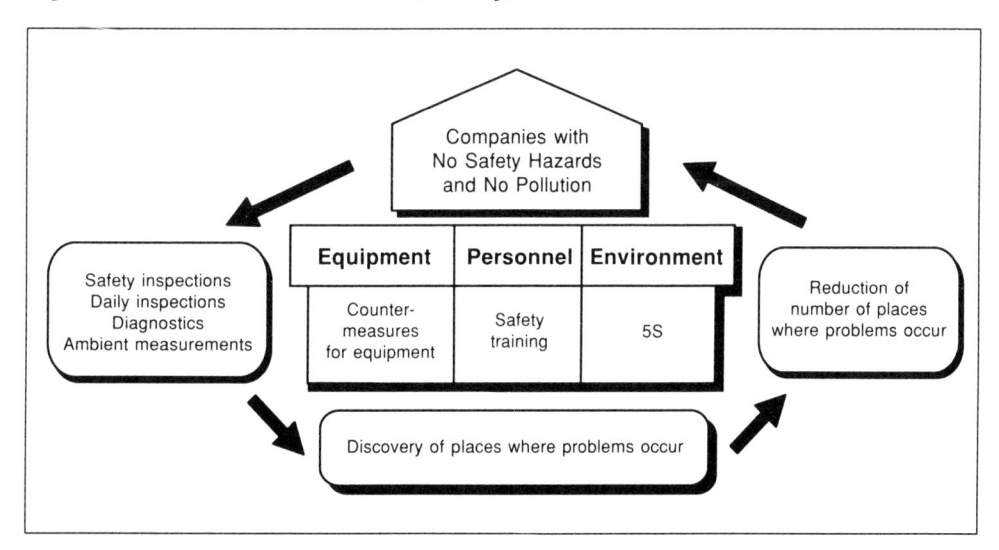

Figure 13 Mechanisms for Health, Safety, and Environmental Controls

Ultimately, we believe that even in the cutthroat price competition of today's world, the program returned satisfactory management results.

One of the main intangible benefits that the program brought about was an increased feeling of self confidence on the part of the work force, which realized that 100 percent employee participation could enable the solving of even the most difficult problems. This benefit will be reaped by the company for many years to come.

Figure 14 Overall Progress toward Goals

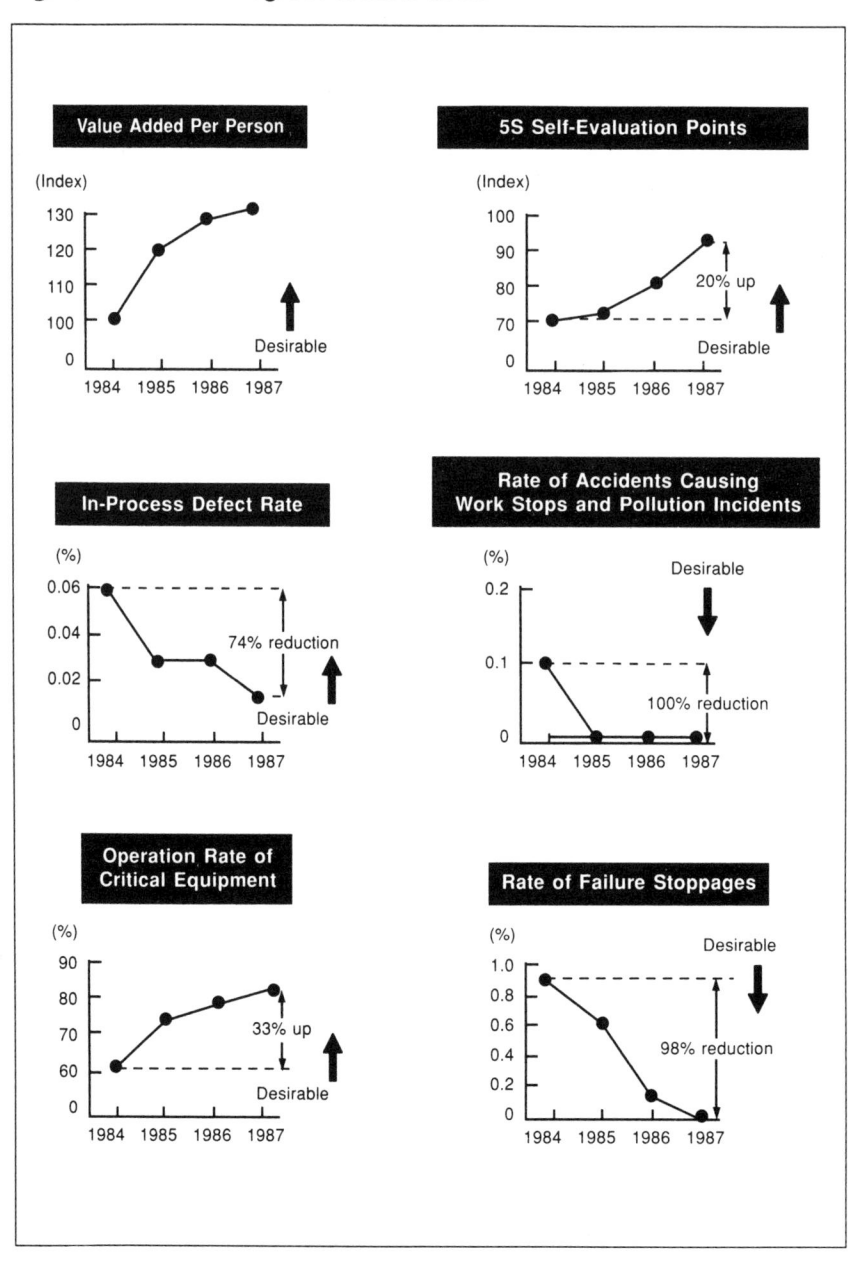

**Plans for
the Future**

Three major steps now must be taken to lay the foundation for an ongoing successful management program. These are:

- ✓ The interrelationship between quality and equipment must be clarified, improvement activities intensified, and higher quality secured
- ✓ Improvements on equipment must be pursued even further, and equipment production rates increased
- ✓ Efforts must be continued to train personnel in the proper understanding and use of the equipment, harmony established between human operators and their equipment, and workplace morale kept at a high level

In order to accomplish this, the company will intensify the TPM activities discussed in this article, continue with its efforts to improve corporate structure through 100 percent employee involvement, and work to promote managerial efficiency.

Examples of Loss Reduction

Example 1 Defect Reduction with MQ Analysis

Oxidation on the copper plating surface gives rise to complaints from customers that they cannot make proper solder connections in those areas. To combat this problem, five specific items were selected for improvement on the flux equipment. Parts replacement and other measures also were taken to lengthen service life. Finally an MQ analysis was undertaken in conjunction with a study of the causes of the problems, which is what enabled the focusing on these five specific items. The result of this work is that oxidation defects generated by the flux equipment were cut to one-eighth of their former levels.

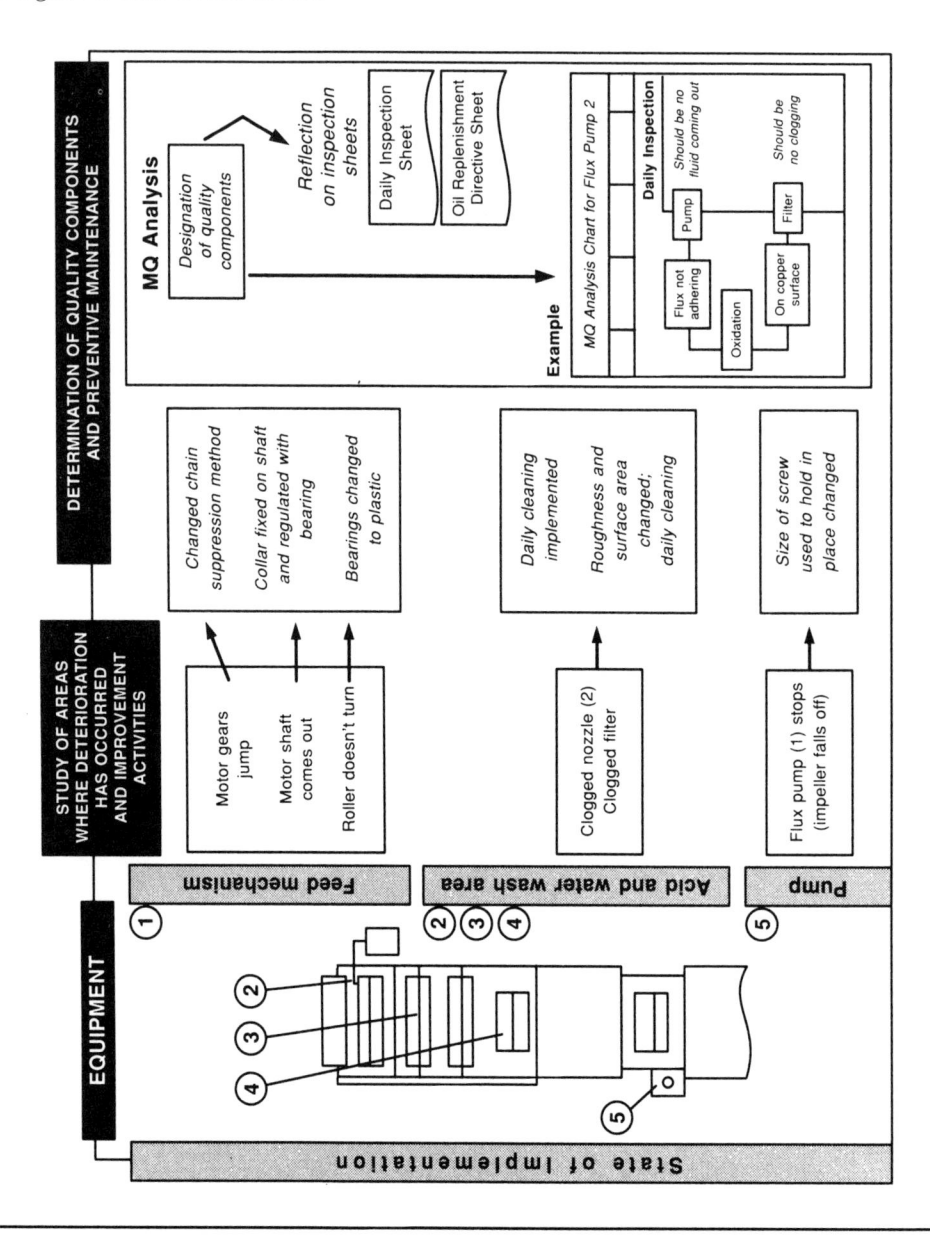

Example 2
Reduction of Sagging Defects

Sagging defects often were generated in the cutting and application process, particularly at Machine No. 12, an 8S type of machine. This machine thus was singled out as a sort of test case, and anti-sagging measures were implemented.

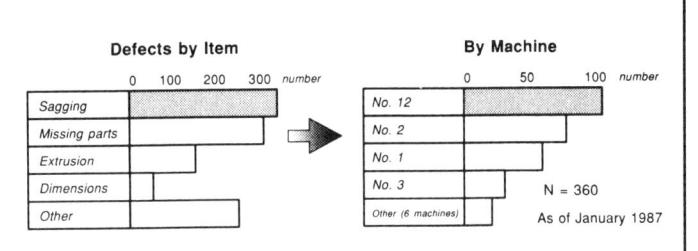

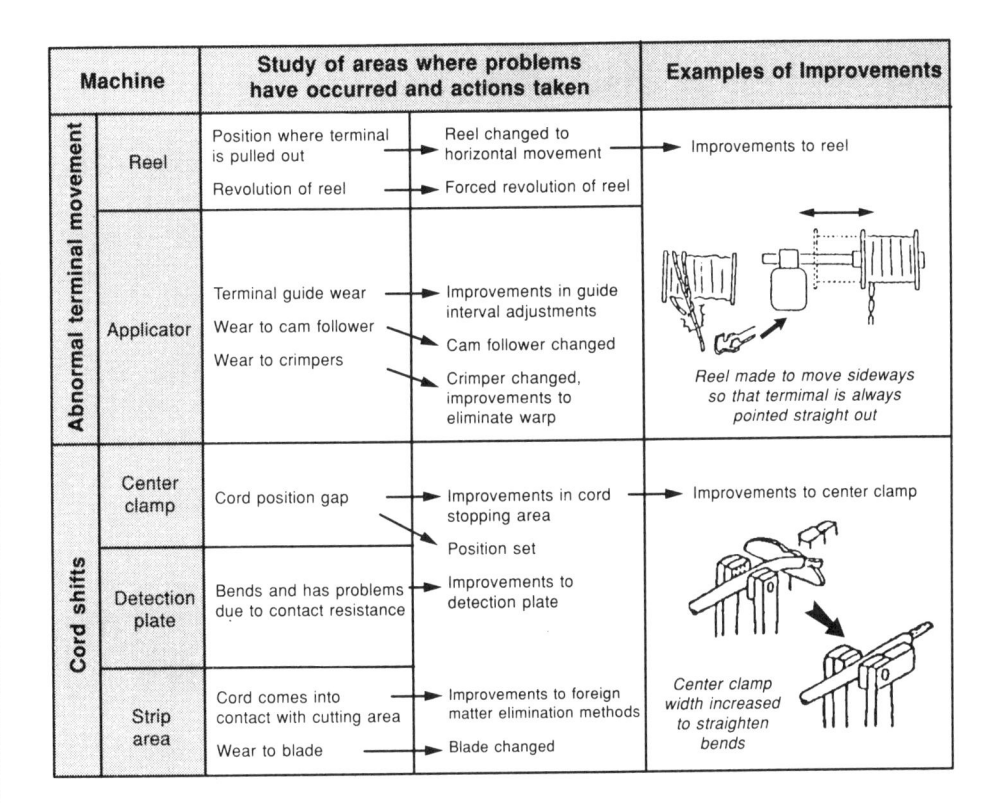

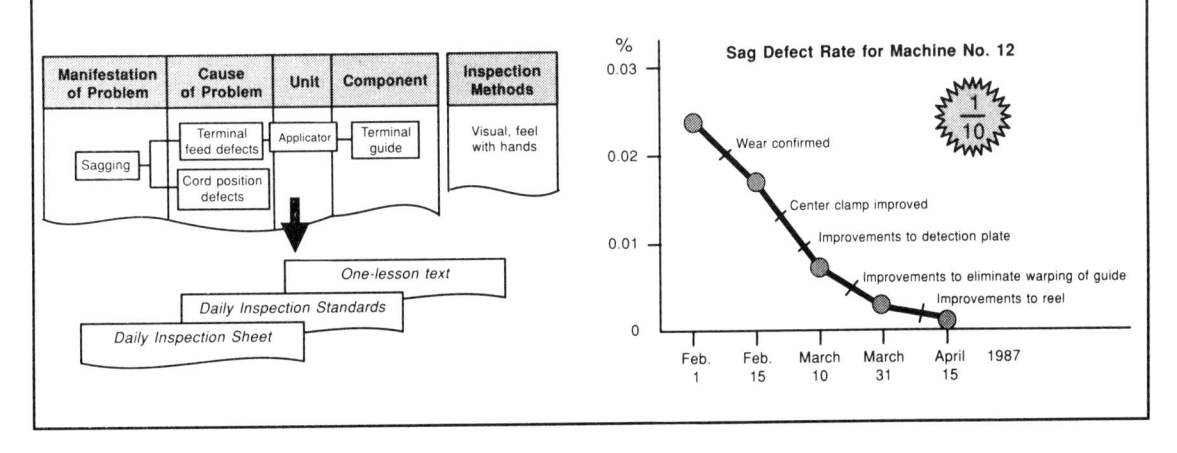

Defects by Item

Sagging	(≈300)
Missing parts	
Extrusion	
Dimensions	
Other	

By Machine

Machine	
No. 12	(≈100)
No. 2	
No. 1	
No. 3	
Other (6 machines)	

N = 360
As of January 1987

Machine		Study of areas where problems have occurred and actions taken		Examples of Improvements
Abnormal terminal movement	Reel	Position where terminal is pulled out	Reel changed to horizontal movement	Improvements to reel
		Revolution of reel	Forced revolution of reel	Reel made to move sideways so that terminal is always pointed straight out
	Applicator	Terminal guide wear	Improvements in guide interval adjustments	
		Wear to cam follower	Cam follower changed	
		Wear to crimpers	Crimper changed, improvements to eliminate warp	
Cord shifts	Center clamp	Cord position gap	Improvements in cord stopping area	Improvements to center clamp
			Position set	
	Detection plate	Bends and has problems due to contact resistance	Improvements to detection plate	Center clamp width increased to straighten bends
	Strip area	Cord comes into contact with cutting area	Improvements to foreign matter elimination methods	
		Wear to blade	Blade changed	

Sag Defect Rate for Machine No. 12

1/10

- Feb. 1 — 0.024 — Wear confirmed
- Feb. 15 — Center clamp improved
- March 10 — Improvements to detection plate
- March 31 — Improvements to eliminate warping of guide
- April 15, 1987 — Improvements to reel

Manifestation of Problem	Cause of Problem	Unit	Component	Inspection Methods
Sagging	Terminal feed defects	Applicator	Terminal guide	Visual, feel with hands
	Cord position defects			

↓
One-lesson text
Daily Inspection Standards
Daily Inspection Sheet

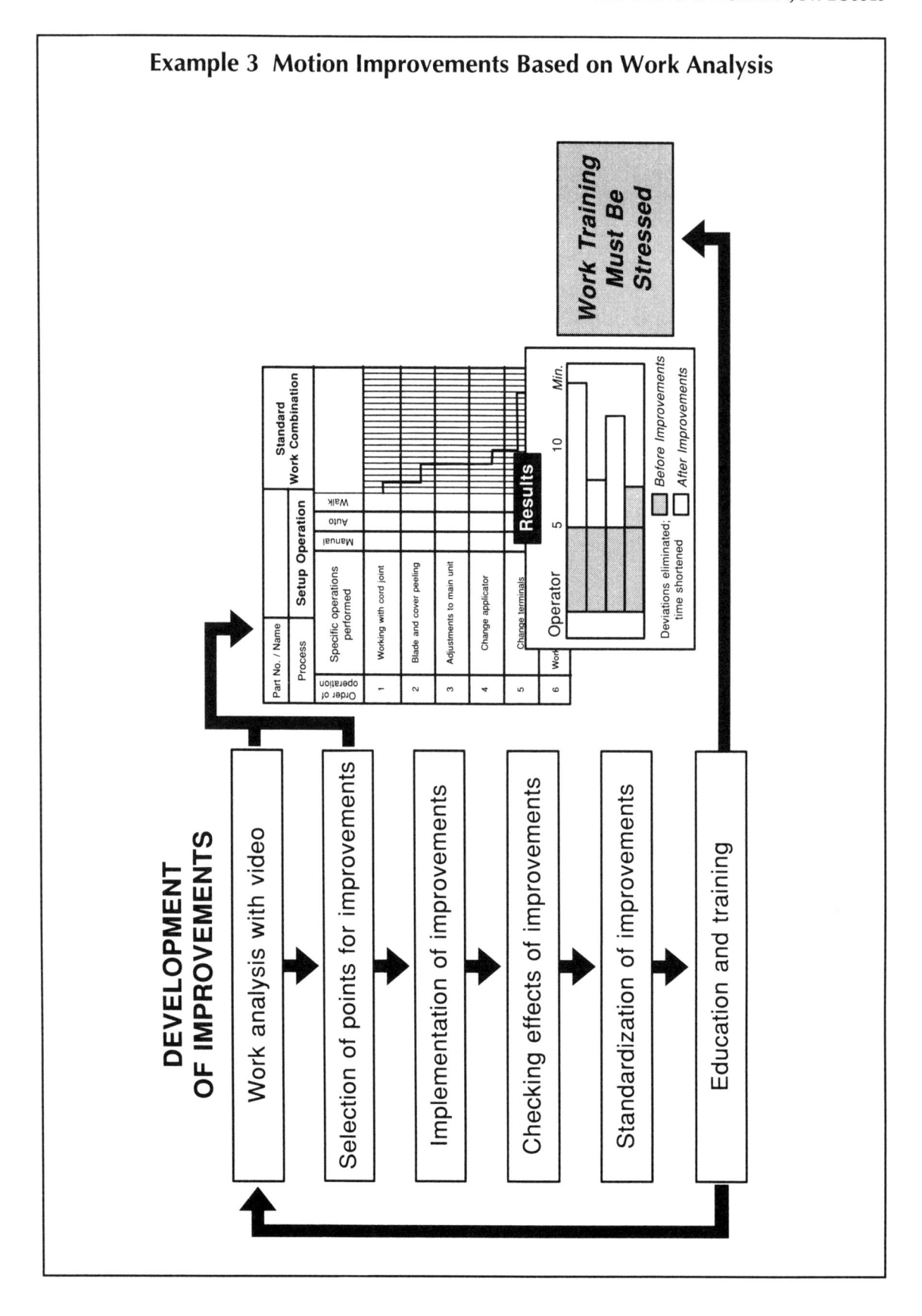

Example 3 Motion Improvements Based on Work Analysis

DEVELOPMENT OF IMPROVEMENTS

Work analysis with video → Selection of points for improvements → Implementation of improvements → Checking effects of improvements → Standardization of improvements → Education and training

Work Training Must Be Stressed

Standard Work Combination table with Setup Operation (Manual, Auto, Walk) listing:
1. Working with cord joint
2. Blade and cover peeling
3. Adjustments to main unit
4. Change applicator
5. Change terminals
6. Work

Results: Operator chart showing Before Improvements and After Improvements (Min., 5, 10). Deviations eliminated; time shortened.

Improving Corporate Structure with TPM Activities 111

Example 4 Shortening Setups and Times for the 8S Machines

	Before Improvements	Problems	Improvements Made	Effects
Changing Reel Stand		When terminal feed direction is wrong, time is required to take off bolts to change the position of the reel stand	Overlapping reel stand positions	3' 44" → 30" Before / After Improvements
Inserting Spacers		A number of different types of spacers are mixed together, and must be confirmed with calipers	Imprinted with plate thickness to enable visual controls	Shifted to off-line setup for one-touch setup 2' 45" → 0" Before / After Improvements
Inserting Spacers and Changing Cutting Tool		Time required to put together (it is necessary to take off four bolts and change them)	Fabricated one-touch fixture to change cutting tool	2' 49" → 25" Before / After Improvements

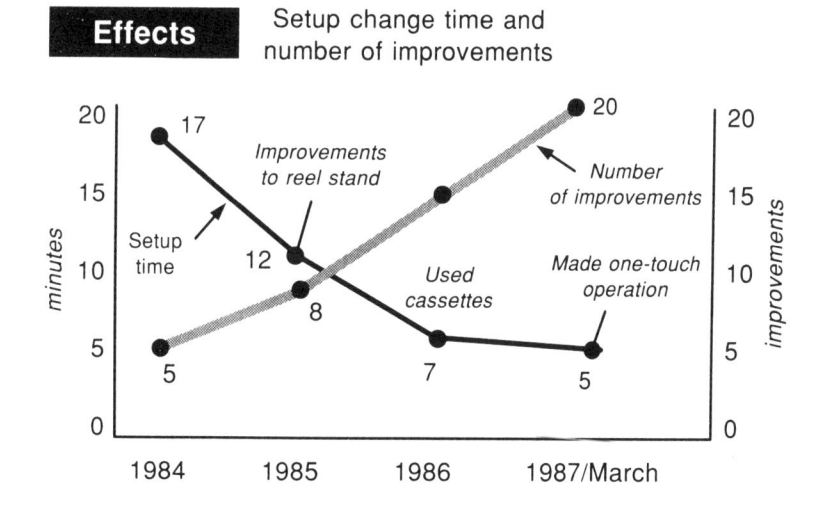

Effects — Setup change time and number of improvements

- Setup time (minutes): 17 (1984), 12 (1985), 8, 7 (1986), 5 (1987/March)
  - Improvements to reel stand
  - Used cassettes
  - Made one-touch operation
- Number of improvements: 5 (1984), →, →, 20 (1987/March)

Example 5 The Anti-Rust Campaign

Because Plant No. 3 uses ferric chloride and hydrochloric acid as an etching solution, special attention must be paid to ventilation in the plant. Even with this extra attention, though, the amount of rust being generated in all areas was conspicuous.

Areas Where Rust Is Generated

Machine Name	Area	Areas to be Treated
Takeup machine	Shaft area	10
"	Motor	2
"	Transmission	
"	Switch area	
	Handle	

Rust Generation by Type of Material Used

Material	Surface Treatment	Rust Generation	Red rust	Location
Fe	Ni	X	Red rust	Shaft area
"	NiCr	X	"	Pushbutton areas
"	Zn	▲	White rust	Transmission
"	Bluing	X	Red rust	Springs
"	Hardened	O	None	Body
"	Ni shell	X	Red rust	Screws
Stainless Steel	←	O	None	"

Changing Materials

- Use materials that survey has shown are slow to rust
- Use materials that can be acquired on commercial market (for economic reasons)

Coating

Because so many hours are required for rust removal, coating has impact on quality as well as becoming a factor in economy

Status of Implementation

Category	Degree of Criticality		Steps Implemented	Number of Locations
Changes in Materials	Impacts Quality		Stainless Steel used for screws and bolts	450
Coating Used	Quality	Critical	Polyurethane coating	223
		Near critical	Epoxy coating	202
	Operability	Critical	Rustproof oils and wax	105
		Near critical	Epoxy coating	88
	No Critical Impact		Epoxy coating	382
Total				1,450

Implementing the Rust-Away Campaign

Rust-Away Campaign
- Environmental preparation — Lower rust generation by studying in-plant environment and making needed improvements
- Improvements in areas where rust is generated — Inventory each area where rust is generated, and apply rustproofing actions individually

Example 6 Scheduled Inspections and Corrective Maintenance

Set Periodic Inspection Method

Annual Plan

Set Items

Select from company written procedures, manuals, and records of failures

Set Inspection Cycles

AMP equipment should be overhauled once each year from part service life

Monthly Plans

Items and Inspection Cycle

Set from MTBF Chart

Maintenance Plans

Periodic Inspection Plans for 1987

Periodic Inspection Checklist

Periodic Inspection Sheet for March

Trends in Machine Failure

Effects

Problems Detected and PM Performed

| Gear wear |
| Abnormal noise in main clutch |
| Brake lining wear |
| Decelerator lube problems |
| Drive switch contact burnout |

Trends in Machine Failure

Broken springs N=11

Clutch operation N=25

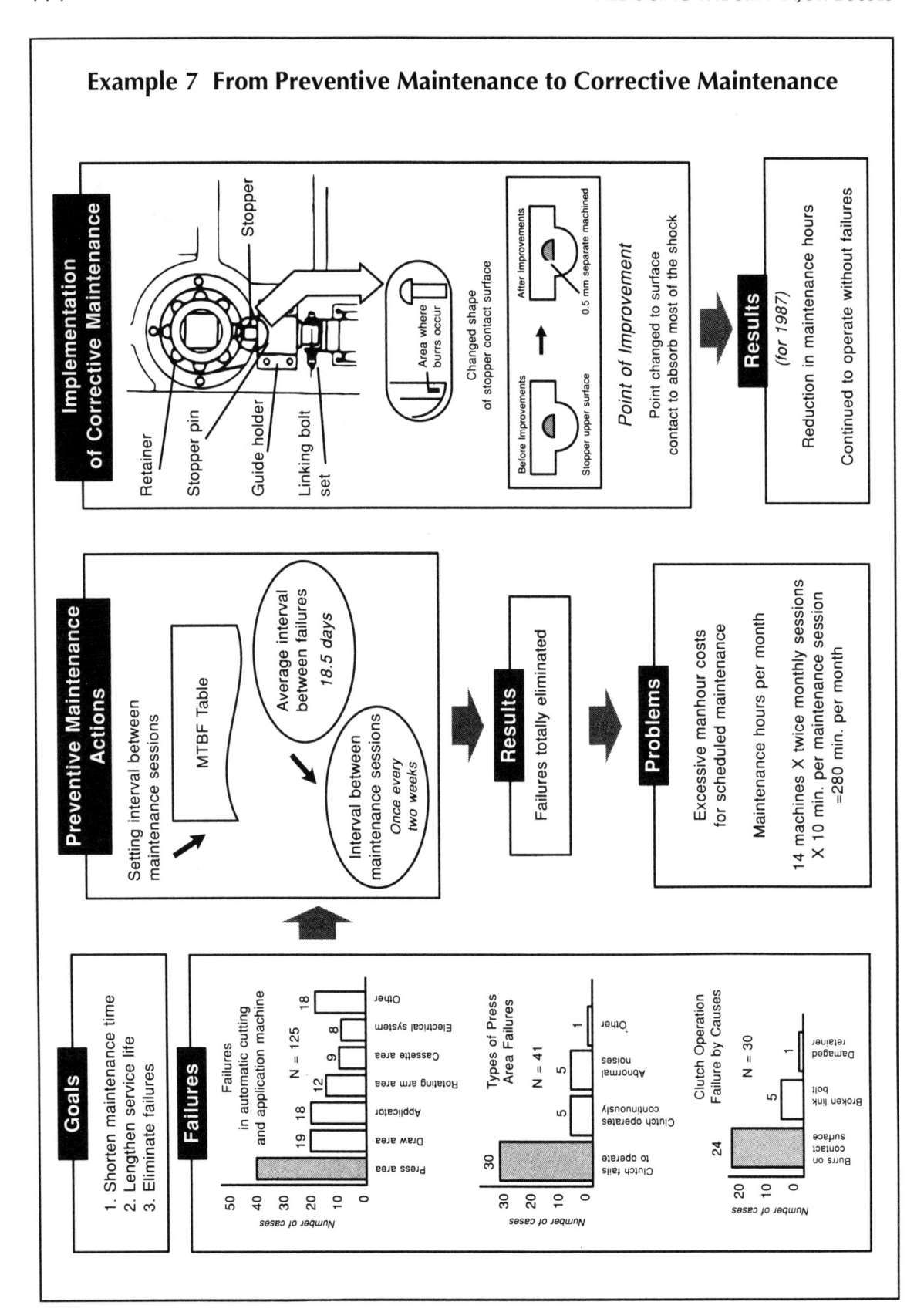

Example 7 From Preventive Maintenance to Corrective Maintenance

Goals
1. Shorten maintenance time
2. Lengthen service life
3. Eliminate failures

Failures

Failures in automatic cutting and application machine (N = 125):
- Press area: 40
- Draw area: 19
- Applicator: 18
- Rotating arm area: 12
- Cassette area: 9
- Electrical system: 8
- Other: 18

Types of Press Area Failures (N = 41):
- Clutch fails to operate: 30
- Clutch operates continuously: 5
- Abnormal noises: 5
- Other: 1

Clutch Operation Failure by Causes (N = 30):
- Burrs on contact surface: 24
- Broken link bolt: 5
- Damaged retainer: 1

Preventive Maintenance Actions

Setting interval between maintenance sessions → MTBF Table
- Average interval between failures: *18.5 days*
- Interval between maintenance sessions: *Once every two weeks*

Results: Failures totally eliminated

Problems:
Excessive manhour costs for scheduled maintenance

Maintenance hours per month:
14 machines × twice monthly sessions × 10 min. per maintenance session = 280 min. per month

Implementation of Corrective Maintenance

Retainer, Stopper pin, Stopper, Guide holder, Linking bolt set

Area where burrs occur

Changed shape of stopper contact surface

Before Improvements — Stopper upper surface
After Improvements — 0.5 mm separate machined

Point of Improvement
Point changed to surface contact to absorb most of the shock

Results *(for 1987)*
Reduction in maintenance hours
Continued to operate without failures

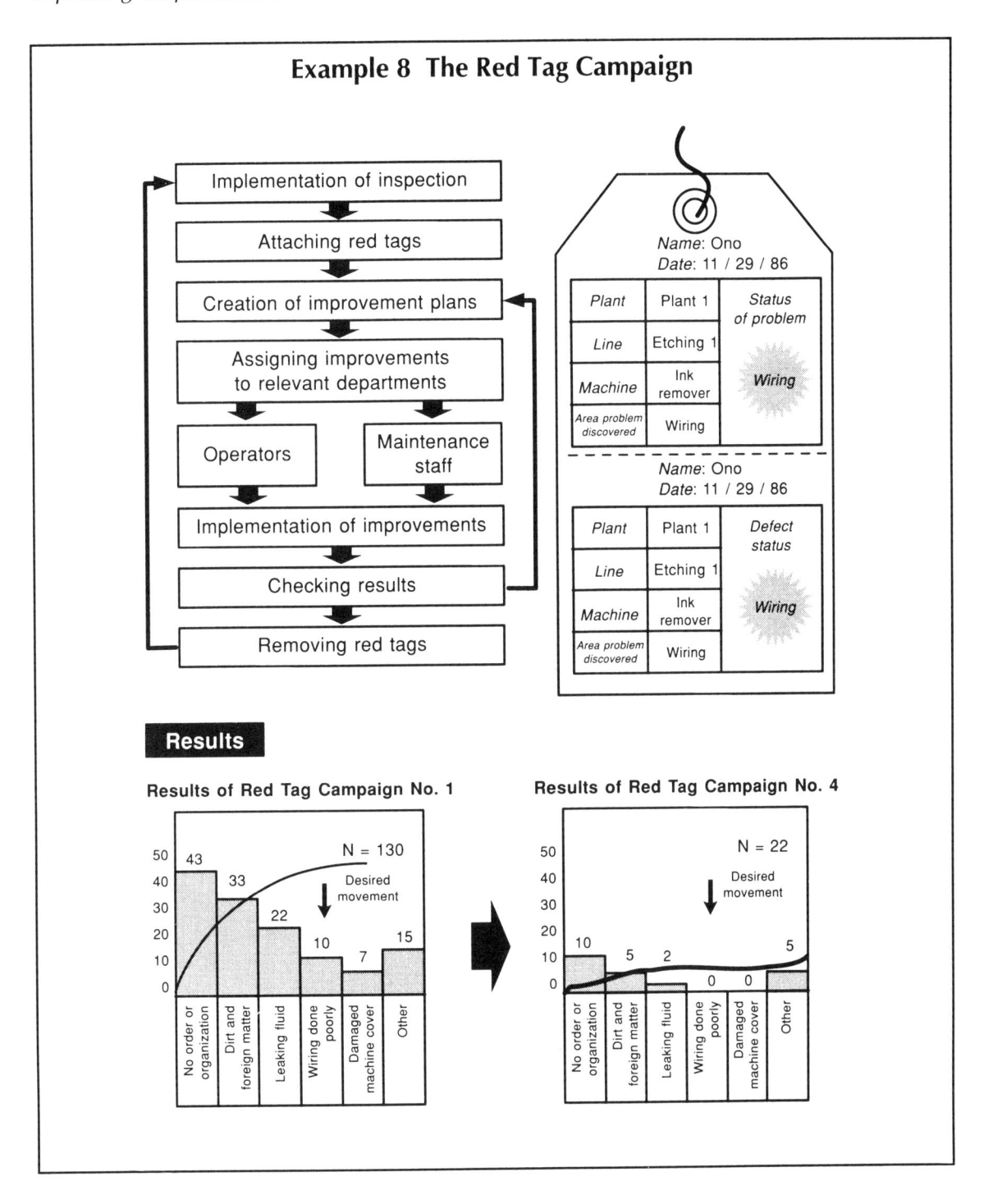

Improving Corporate Structure with TPM Activities 115

Example 8 The Red Tag Campaign

Flow chart:
- Implementation of inspection
- Attaching red tags
- Creation of improvement plans
- Assigning improvements to relevant departments
  - Operators
  - Maintenance staff
- Implementation of improvements
- Checking results
- Removing red tags

(Loop: Checking results → Creation of improvement plans; Removing red tags → Implementation of inspection)

Red tag sample:

Name: Ono		
Date: 11 / 29 / 86		
Plant	Plant 1	Status of problem
Line	Etching 1	
Machine	Ink remover	*Wiring*
Area problem discovered	Wiring	

Name: Ono		
Date: 11 / 29 / 86		
Plant	Plant 1	Defect status
Line	Etching 1	
Machine	Ink remover	*Wiring*
Area problem discovered	Wiring	

Results

Results of Red Tag Campaign No. 1 (N = 130)

No order or organization	43
Dirt and foreign matter	33
Leaking fluid	22
Wiring done poorly	10
Damaged machine cover	7
Other	15

Desired movement ↓

Results of Red Tag Campaign No. 4 (N = 22)

No order or organization	10
Dirt and foreign matter	5
Leaking fluid	2
Wiring done poorly	0
Damaged machine cover	0
Other	5

Desired movement ↓

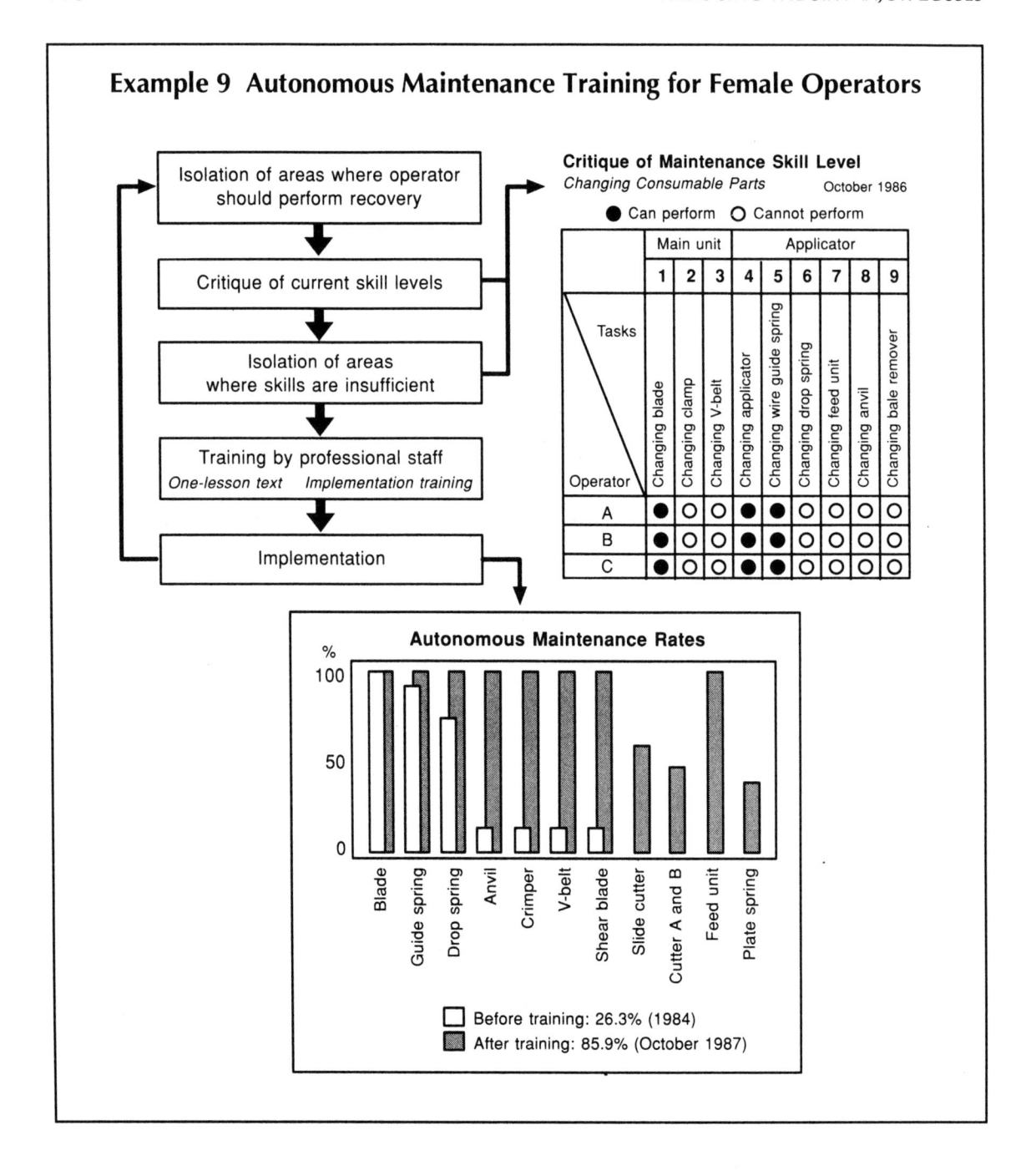

Example 9 Autonomous Maintenance Training for Female Operators

```
┌─ Isolation of areas where operator
│   should perform recovery
│          ↓
│   Critique of current skill levels
│          ↓
│   Isolation of areas
│   where skills are insufficient
│          ↓
│   Training by professional staff
│   One-lesson text   Implementation training
│          ↓
└── Implementation
```

Critique of Maintenance Skill Level
Changing Consumable Parts   October 1986

● Can perform   ○ Cannot perform

		Main unit			Applicator					
	Tasks	1	2	3	4	5	6	7	8	9
		Changing blade	Changing clamp	Changing V-belt	Changing applicator	Changing wire guide spring	Changing drop spring	Changing feed unit	Changing anvil	Changing bale remover
Operator	A	●	○	○	●	●	○	○	○	○
	B	●	○	○	●	●	○	○	○	○
	C	●	○	○	●	●	○	○	○	○

Autonomous Maintenance Rates

(Bar chart showing % for: Blade, Guide spring, Drop spring, Anvil, Crimper, V-belt, Shear blade, Slide cutter, Cutter A and B, Feed unit, Plate spring)

□ Before training: 26.3% (1984)
▨ After training: 85.9% (October 1987)

Sparking a Consciousness Revolution

Specialized Maintenance and Autonomous Maintenance in the Process Industries

By Kyoichi Nakazato
Nishi Nihon Sugar Manufacturing Co., Ltd.

TPM in the Process Industries

Nishi Nihon Sugar Manufacturing Co., Ltd. was founded in 1982 as a joint production company for Dainippon Sugar and Meiji Sugar. It is located in Fukuoka Prefecture, the key entryway prefecture on the island of Kyushu.

The plant itself has a long history. It was started in 1901 as the Ozato Sugar Manufacturing Plant, and despite having gone through several name and capitalization changes, has continued to produce sugar since opening its doors. It occupies more than 676,000 sq. ft. of land, and owns a private pond of nearly 500,000 sq. ft. (water capacity is 140,000 tons when filled) in the foothills of the nearby mountain range. Its daily sugar production capacity is 450 tons.

> ## Basic Guidelines
>
> 1. Minimize equipment failures to establish a stable work environment and commission-based production system.
> 2. Create an equipment control system that combines specialized and autonomous maintenance procedures, and achieve a high degree of planning and economy in maintenance.
> 3. Minimize the need for manual work and operator supervision by taking all actions possible against leaks, spills, and potential maintenance problems.
> 4. Tear down the walls between the equipment and production components of the company, and create an improvement structure that consists of these two departments plus production control.
> 5. Create a company-wide management structure that combines office and production staffs, and promote the streamlining of the support staff.

The main products of this facility include refined sugar products such as granulated, powdered, and the like, plus liquid sugar and sugar cubes. Through the efforts of Dainippon Sugar and Meiji Sugar, the two founding partners, it supplies sugar to nearly all parts of Japan west of Hiroshima.

Events Leading to the TPM Program

The industry has long been in a period of structural instability, and despite the increase in plant productivity ratios—brought about as the result of the centralized production from an early stage by the Mitsubishi Sugar Group—competition within the industry remains fierce. Nishi Nihon Sugar Manufacturing Co., Ltd., working from

Figure 1 The FE Campaign

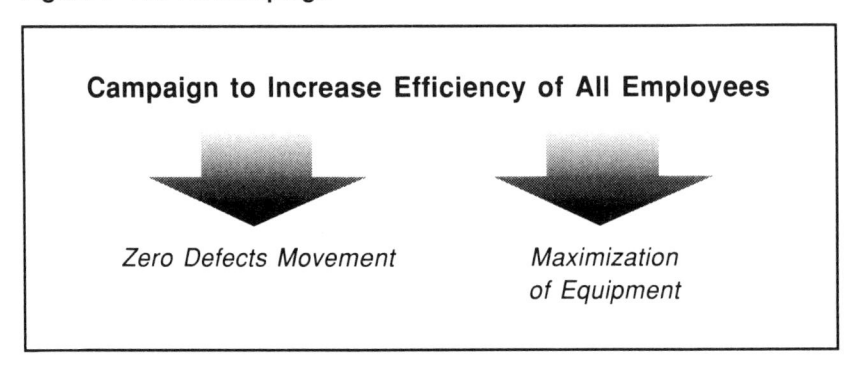

Campaign to Increase Efficiency of All Employees

Zero Defects Movement   *Maximization of Equipment*

Table 1 The Six Major Guidelines for TPM Activities

Activities	Goal of Activities	Overview of Activities
1. Autonomous Maintenance Activities	Creation of an autonomous control system by operators for equipment, creation of active program of small group activities, and establishment of innovative and action-oriented structure for maintenance	1. Test-case development: Stages 1–3 2. Block development: Stages 1–3 3. Area development: Stages 1–4 4. Area development: Stages 5–6 5. Thorough development of visual maintenance
2. Specialized Maintenance Activities	Creation of a systematic maintenance program that incorporates planned and predictive maintenance, stabilize plant operations by reducing the number of failures—thus increasing productivity—and make equipment installation more economical	1. Ranking and evaluating equipment and failures 2. Support activities for autonomous maintenance 3. After-the-fact maintenance and activities to prevent recurrence of problems 4. Planned maintenance and strengthening equipment installation controls 5. Introduction of predictive maintenance and diagnostic technology 6. Controls for spare parts, blueprints, and documents 7. Structure for equipment controls 8. Equipment investment plans and MP activities
3. Education and Training Activities	Implementation of thorough-going program for technical training and on-the-job training to vitalize both operators and the overall system, and the expansion of creativity and skill levels through skill training	1. Sequence training based on skill expansion format 2. TPM introduction training 3. On-the-job operation training for autonomous maintenance 4. Stage 4 skills training for autonomous maintenance 5. Introduction of general business improvement proposal system
4. 5S Activities	Working to eliminate loss totally through a thorough implementation of the 5S activities, and working more on personal conduct in order to create a work atmosphere proper for a plant that manufactures foodstuffs	1. Creation of a model room 2. Environmental 5S activities: safety aisles, parking lots, evaluations, etc. 3. Workplace 5S activities: cleaning tools, bulletin boards, room names posted
5. Individual Improvement Activities	Unifying equipment, operation, and production control staffs in order to make significant improvements on equipment experiencing frequent breakdowns, quality problems, or energy loss, and thus cut overall costs	1. Corrective maintenance activities for equipment 2. Product quality improvement activities 3. Activities to conserve energy and labor
6. Office Streamlining Activities	Streamline office activities through the use of mechanization and up-to-date technology, and instill cost-consciousness in workforce to encourage widescale elimination of waste	1. Introduction of automation to office and development of office system 2. Promote efficient use of filing 3. Rationalize in-office flow of work

the need for the strength to survive, and to acquire this strength as quickly as possible, introduced a basic program for corporate structural improvement. This program was based on the twin pillars of zero defects and maximization of equipment. The decision was made to pursue what was named the "FE Campaign" (full efficiency campaign, a campaign to increase the efficiency of all employees, as shown in Figure 1), and to make TPM activities the main support of this campaign.

The primary goal of firms introducing TPM programs is to win the PM Prize. Working toward this prize proved to be a way to unite the hearts and minds of employees who had come originally from two competing companies, and to make them into a single, coherent team.

The Goals and Guidelines of the TPM Program

There were three major goals in the development of the TPM program. These were to eliminate the following factors, which could have been obstacles to the development of the FE Campaign:

✓ Human weaknesses
✓ Organizational weaknesses
✓ Equipment weaknesses

Six major guidelines were established to bring this about, as shown in Table 1.

The general outline of the FE Campaign and the TPM program is shown in Figure 2.

Figure 2 The FE Campaign and TPM

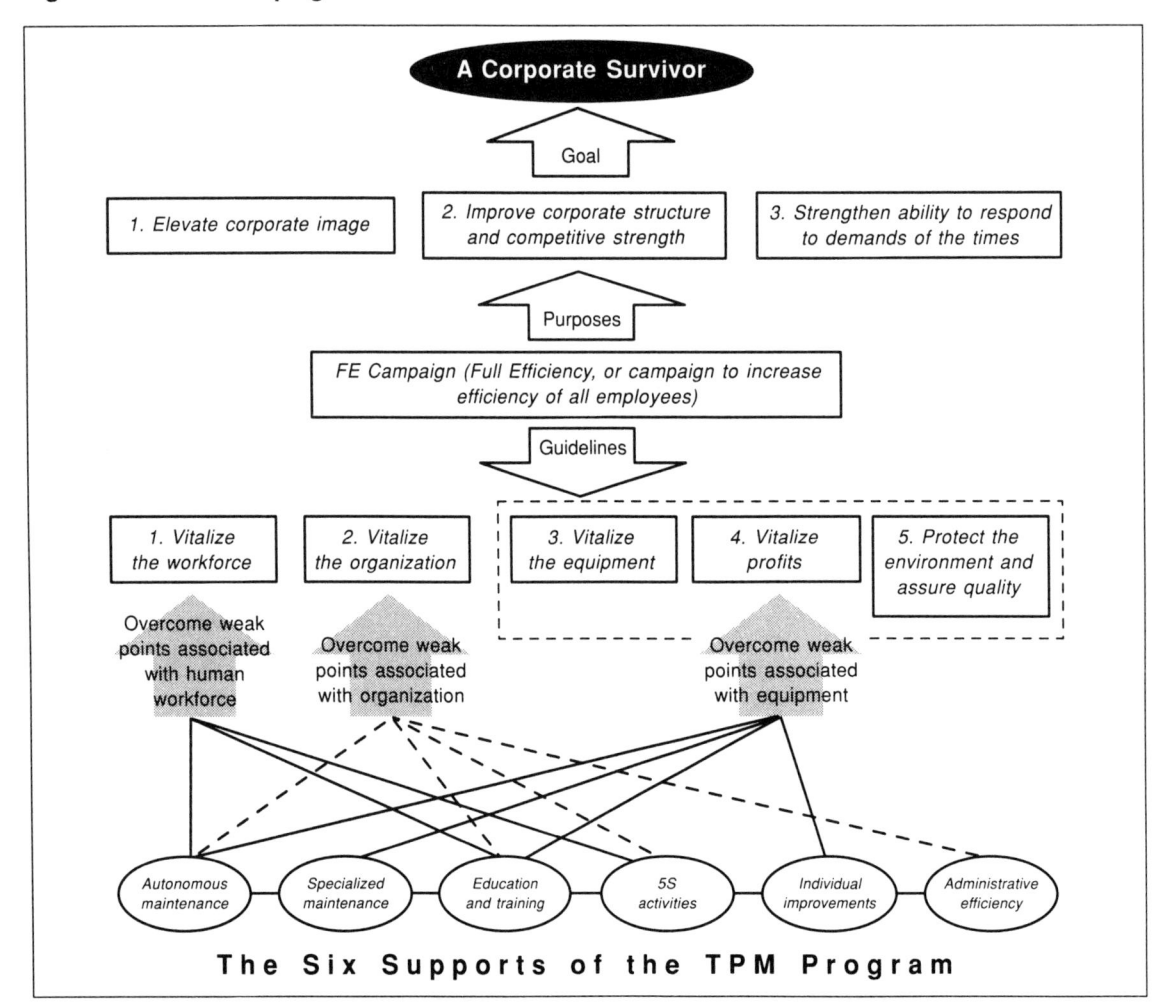

A Corporate Survivor (Goal)

1. Elevate corporate image
2. Improve corporate structure and competitive strength
3. Strengthen ability to respond to demands of the times

Purposes

FE Campaign (Full Efficiency, or campaign to increase efficiency of all employees)

Guidelines

1. Vitalize the workforce
2. Vitalize the organization
3. Vitalize the equipment
4. Vitalize profits
5. Protect the environment and assure quality

Overcome weak points associated with human workforce
Overcome weak points associated with organization
Overcome weak points associated with equipment

Autonomous maintenance · Specialized maintenance · Education and training · 5S activities · Individual improvements · Administrative efficiency

The Six Supports of the TPM Program

Specialized Maintenance and Autonomous Maintenance in the Process Industries 121

Figure 3 The Promotional Organization for the FE Campaign

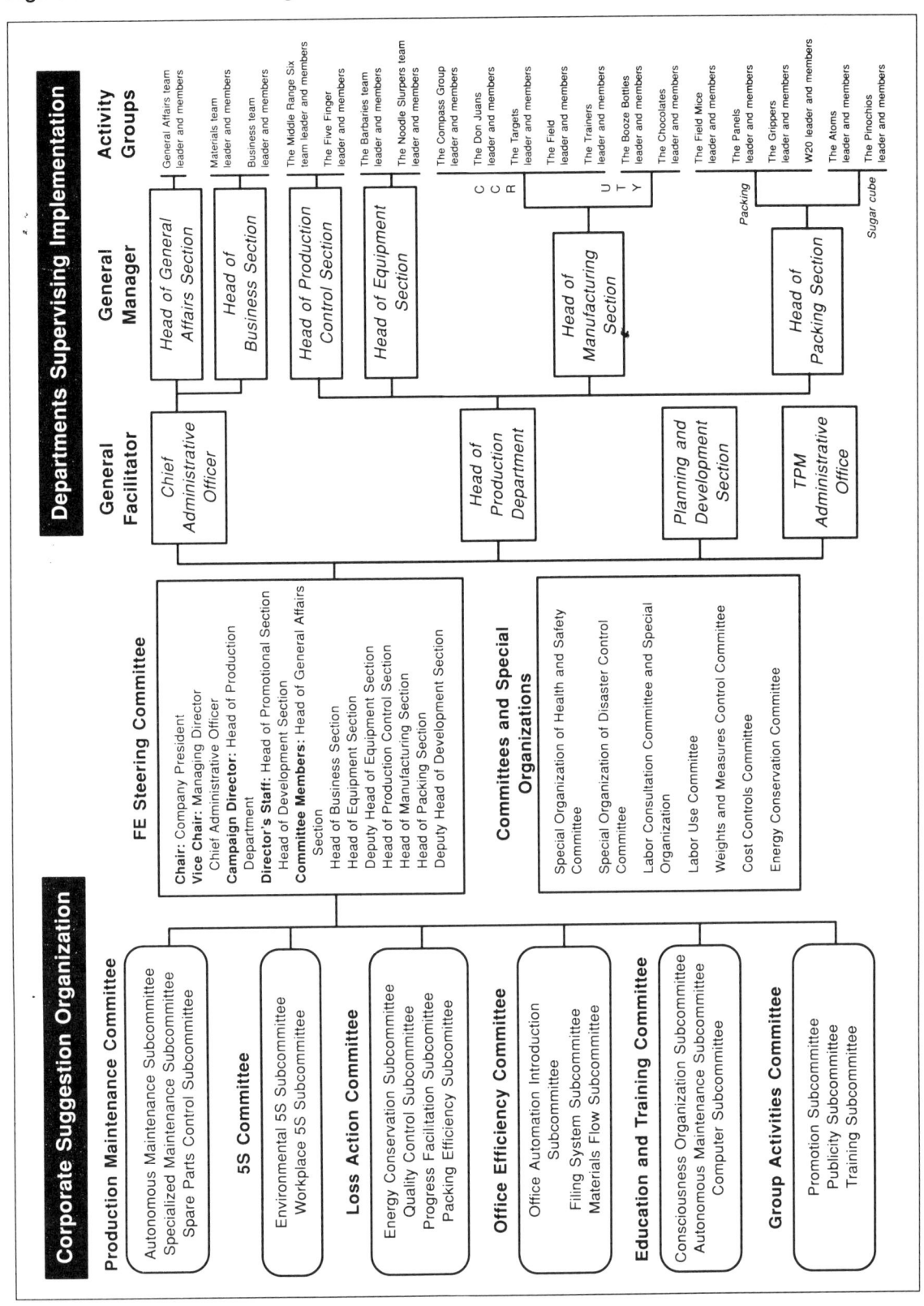

Promotional Organization and Activity History

The FE Campaign Steering Committee was at the peak of the TPM promotional activities, as shown in Figure 3. This steering committee was set up to supervise all corporate management activities, which it accomplished through a number of committees and other special organizations, including the Energy Conservation Committee and the like. The section at the left of Figure 3 shows the six main committees and 18 subcommittees involved in the overall process. This was a "corporate proposal structure" designed to perform TPM promotion and related activities.

On the right in Figure 3, we have the system of overlapping small groups which constituted the "execution brigade" for the program. The company president, as overall facilitator, brought the conventional corporate structure into the picture. Autonomous maintenance activities, which are at the core of all TPM activities, were at the head of the execution brigade, and provided the motivational force for most of the results secured by the program.

After a preparatory period of nearly six months, the Nishi Nihon Sugar Manufacturing Co., Ltd. TPM program was launched in May 1984. It was awarded the PM prize for excellence in 1987. These activities are outlined in Figure 4.

Characteristics of the Process Industries

A refined sugar manufacturing plant is typical of the process industries. The plant in question performs all operations from the dissolution of the raw sugar to the packing of the final products, an overall process that requires approximately 30 hours to complete. Failures in the processes where liquid sugar is refined are particularly serious, and can result in an overall shutdown, so equipment controls are of primary concern to management.

It cannot be said that the equipment control system used by Nishi Nihon Sugar Manufacturing Co., Ltd. was particularly strong. The goal was the establishment of a two-pronged systematic maintenance program featuring specialized and autonomous maintenance as defined by TPM. At the outset of the program, however, an understanding of the special characteristics of the process industries were used to determine the criticality of maintenance.

Specialized Maintenance and Autonomous Maintenance in the Process Industries 123

Figure 4 An Activity History of the Six TPM Guidelines

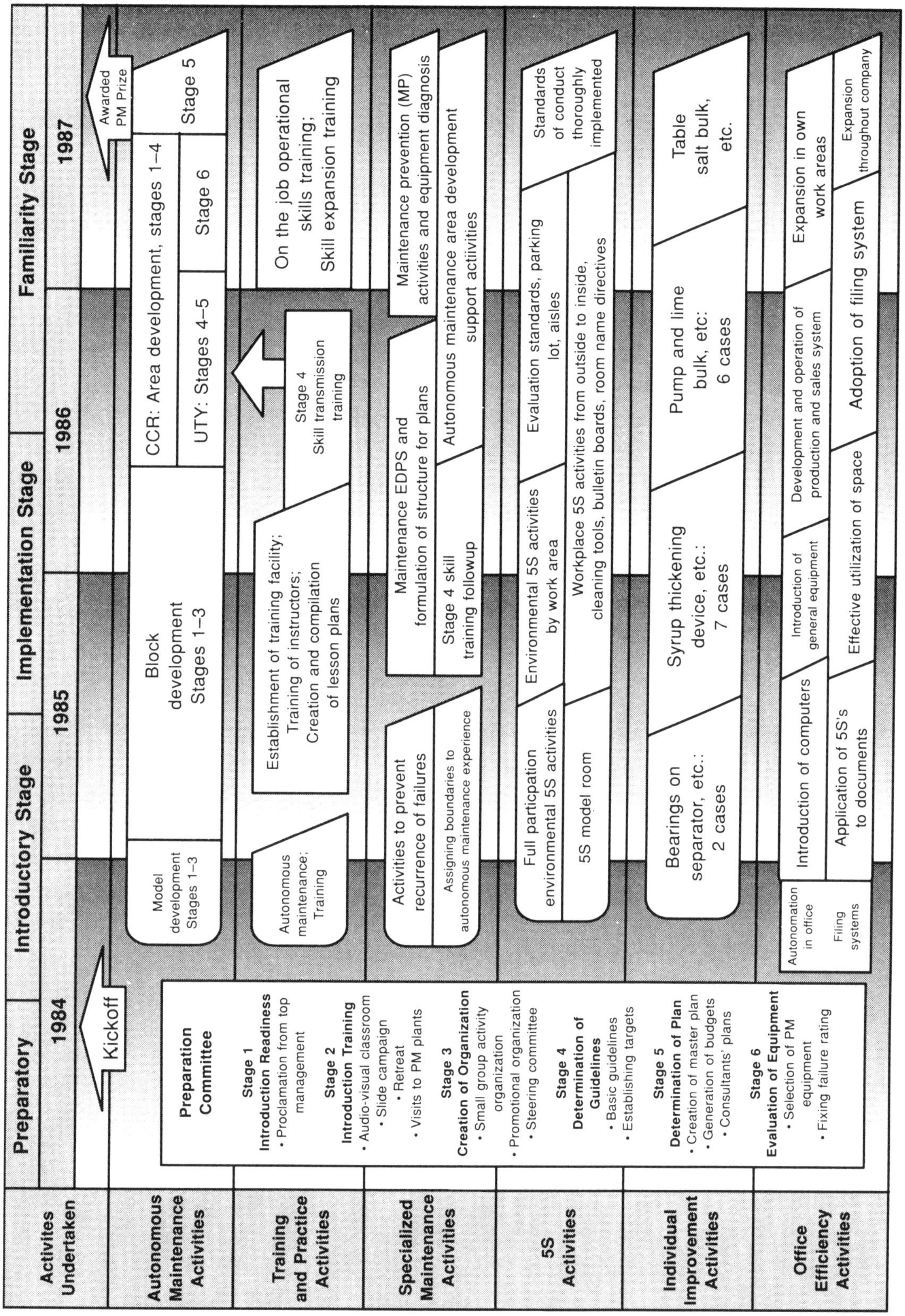

Table 2 Equipment Evaluation Standards

Category	Factors Evaluated	Standards of Evaluation		
		Rank A	Rank B	Rank C
S	Safety and pollution	Failures have impact in region in terms of safety and public health	Failures cause problems in region in terms of safety and public health	No problems
Q	Quality and progress	Failures cause quality defects or have major impact on machining progress	Failures cause deviations in quality or have impact on overall machining progress	No impact on either quality or machining progress
W	Availability status	In full production 24 hours a day	7 to 14 hours operation a day	Only operated infrequently
D	Opportunity loss	Failure would cause overall plant shutdown	Failure would cause shutdown in immediate area of machine	A backup machine available, or it is more economical to fix after failure
P	Frequency of failure	Frequent stops due to failures (frequency rate less than six months between stops)	Stops due to failure happen occasionally (frequency rate between six and 12 months between stops)	Almost never stops due to failure (fewer than one stop per year)
M	Maintainability	Repair time over four hours; repair cost over $1550	Time stopped between 1 and 4 hours; cost between $400 and $1550	Repair time under 1 hour; cost less than $400

■ Equipment evaluation and determining PM equipment

There are some 2,540 pieces of equipment at Nishi Nihon Sugar Manufacturing Co., Ltd., when all machines, devices, motors, and measuring devices are taken into account. This means that one operator must operate as many as 38 separate pieces of equipment. The development of specialized and autonomous maintenance programs for each of these pieces of equipment would be impossible given the capacity of the plant, and also would result in such a cumbersome organizational structure that no results could be realistically anticipated from the venture.

For this reason, a system of ranking equipment on the basis of equipment evaluation criteria was established, and equipment was categorized as being in rank A, B, or C, depending on its importance. The ranking system is shown in Table 2. Equipment in ranks A and B were then selected as "PM Equipment," enabling the concentration on safety and efficiency depending on importance.

Specialized Maintenance and Autonomous Maintenance in the Process Industries

Table 3 A PM Equipment Chart

	Machines and Devices	All Equipment Number	% of total	PM Equipment Number	% of category PM classified
1	Columns and vats	375	31.0	38	10.1
2	Rotating equipment	299	24.7	194	64.9
3	Transporting equipment	280	23.1	121	43.2
4	Eccentric separators	17	1.4	17	100.0
5	Filtering machines	40	3.3	29	72.5
6	Crystallizers and kilns	11	0.9	11	100.0
7	Heaters and coolers	59	4.9	23	39.0
8	Scales and metal detectors	44	3.6	39	88.6
9	Packing equipment and sewing machines	40	3.3	35	87.5
10	Boilers	3	0.3	3	100.0
11	Others	42	3.5	26	61.9
		1210 machines		536	44.3

Table 3 shows the evaluation results for 1,210 machines and devices. The percentage of PM equipment in this selection is 44.3. Among these, the PM rate for rotating machines and transporting machines was over 60, which adequately reflects the characteristics of the process industries.

■ An overview of maintenance intended to reduce failures

Maintenance activities were implemented with the idea of stabilizing operations through the reduction of failures. As shown in Figure 5, the first thing done on the implementation of these activities was to clarify what types of activities could be used to reduce what types of failures; after getting this overview, the system was put together.

For example, activities by the specialized maintenance staff to prevent the occurrence of spontaneous failures were approached through the reduction of serious and medium-serious failures on PM equipment. Planned maintenance and predictive maintenance also was expanded through the prioritization of rank A PM equipment on down.

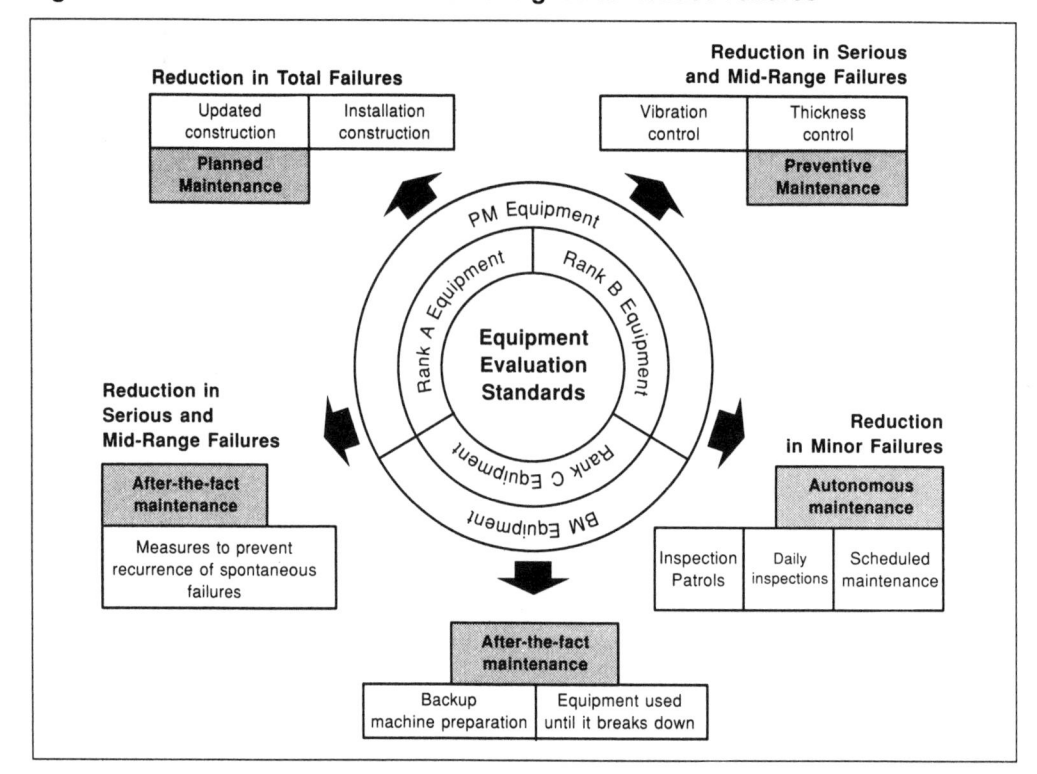

Figure 5 An Overview of Maintenance Designed to Reduce Failures

[Figure 5: Diagram showing Equipment Evaluation Standards at center, surrounded by ring of Rank A Equipment, Rank B Equipment, Rank C Equipment, BM Equipment, PM Equipment. Four quadrants: Reduction in Total Failures (Planned Maintenance: Updated construction, Installation construction); Reduction in Serious and Mid-Range Failures (Preventive Maintenance: Vibration control, Thickness control); Reduction in Minor Failures (Autonomous maintenance: Inspection Patrols, Daily inspections, Scheduled maintenance); Reduction in Serious and Mid-Range Failures (After-the-fact maintenance: Measures to prevent recurrence of spontaneous failures); After-the-fact maintenance (Backup machine preparation, Equipment used until it breaks down).]

The autonomous maintenance activities, which will be discussed below, also were focused on PM equipment and developed in a series of steps. At the end of the sixth step, it was possible to keep in operation a system of well-wrought inspections which held down minor failures. Steps such as these enabled the creation of workplaces with no failures at all.

Specialized Maintenance Activities

Specialized maintenance activities were geared toward establishing a firmly-based maintenance system. They included after-the-fact maintenance, planned maintenance, predictive maintenance, and corrective maintenance activities. As seen in Figure 6, in order to create a systematic maintenance system that encompassed autonomous maintenance, the plant introduced a system that included the use of computers. This system was known as "COMET."

■ **After-the-fact maintenance**

This is more than simply fixing a machine when it breaks down. It also includes measures designed to prevent the same problem from occurring again.

Specialized Maintenance and Autonomous Maintenance in the Process Industries 127

Figure 6 Systematic Maintenance Flow

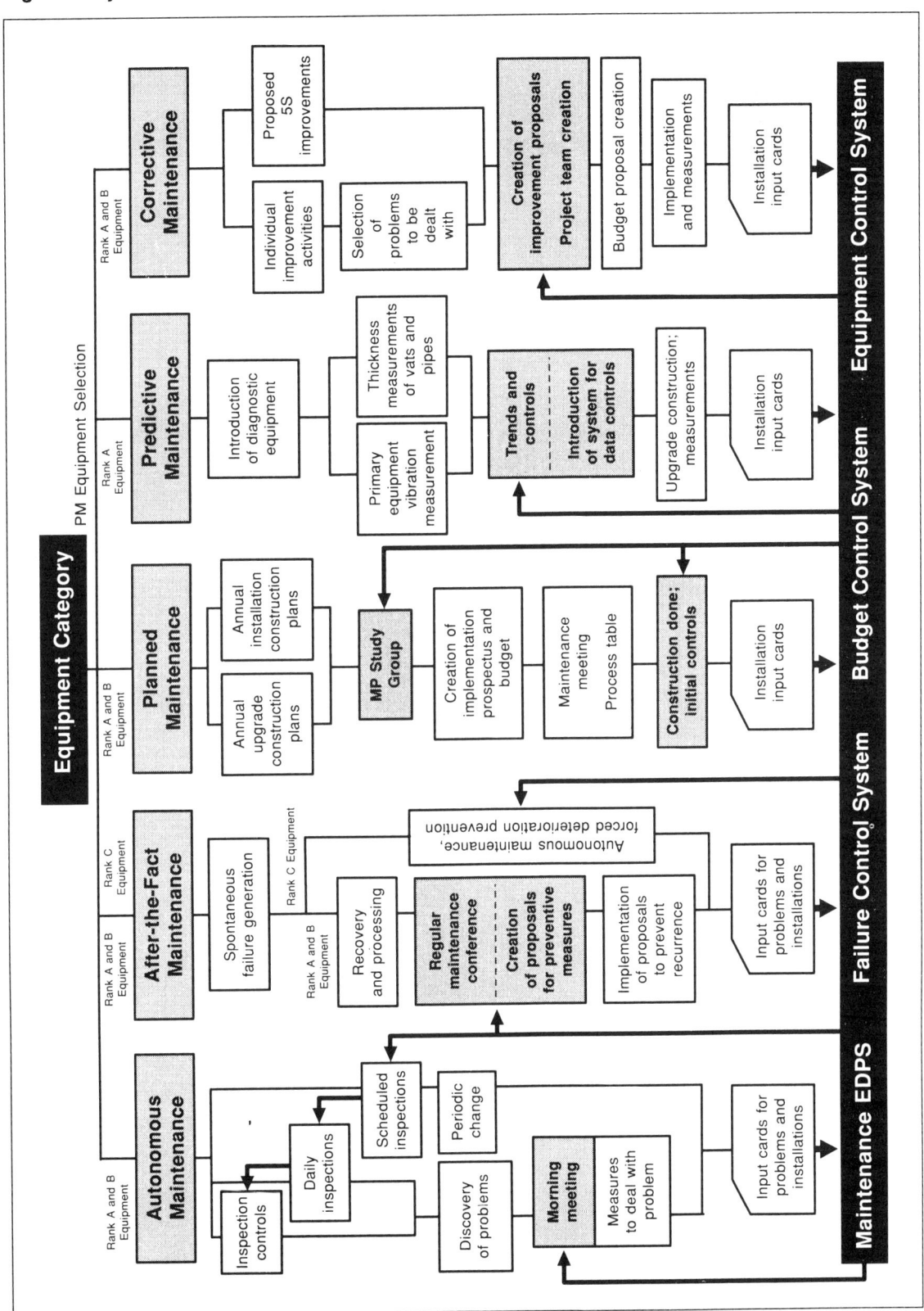

Figure 7 Reductions in Serious Failures

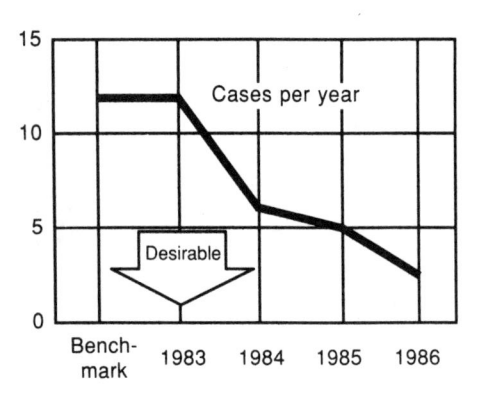

Figure 8 Reductions in Middle-Range Failures

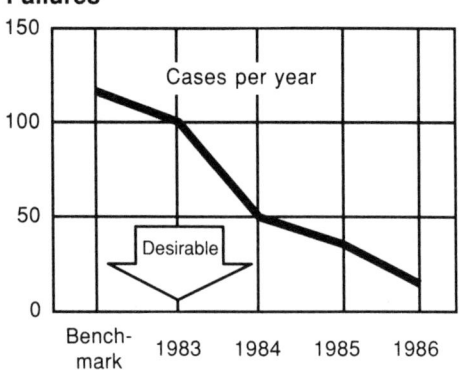

Further, this method involves carefully performed failure cause analyses, and the application of measures taken to other machines of the same type or model. As can be seen in Figures 7 and 8, these measures contributed significantly to the reduction of serious and medium-range failures.

■ Planned maintenance

Planned maintenance, or time-based maintenance, was expanded to cover a large number of machines (see Figure 9). Concurrently, the system of controls used for equipment installation work and modification installation work also was strengthened, and maintenance prevention (MP) activities were begun in the plant. These activities yielded

Figure 9 The Expansion of Equipment in the Planned Maintenance Area

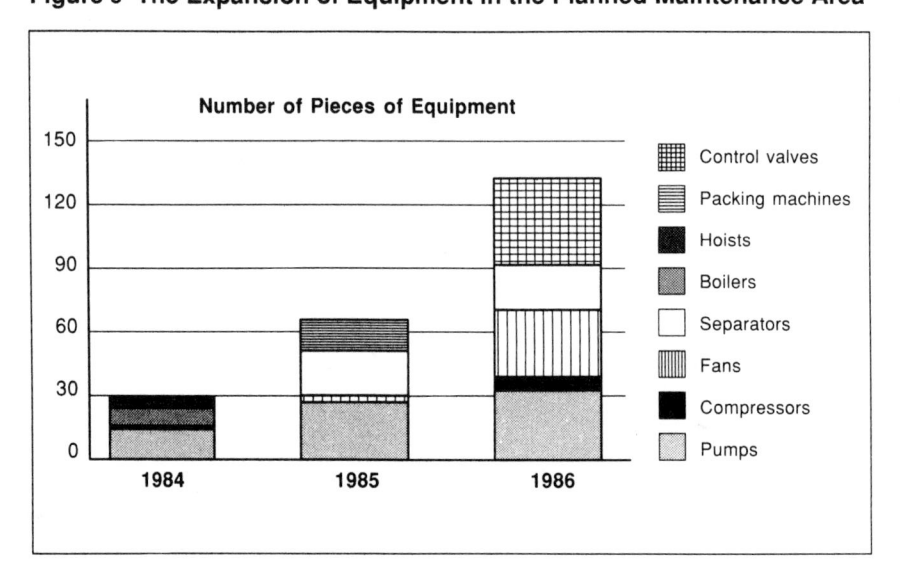

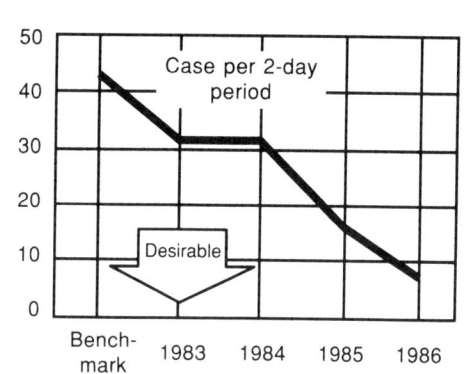

Figure 10 Initial Failures

significant results in the reduction of serious and medium-range failures. As shown in Figure 10, they also had a significant impact in the reduction of initial failures, in the first two days of the sugar making cycle.

■ Predictive maintenance

This program was applied in particular to large pumps and fans. A system was introduced to monitor carefully vibration trends data and PM data, and a condition-based maintenance program was added to the time-based maintenance discussed above. This predictive maintenance system was successful in blocking the increase of maintenance costs.

■ Corrective maintenance

Autonomous maintenance activities were supported by a system of difficult problem analysis. The production controls supervisors worked with the operators to perform individual improvements, which had considerable impact on improvements in the areas of energy conservation, conservation of resources, and conservation of labor.

Autonomous Maintenance Activities

Group-based autonomous maintenance activities were the central feature of the Nishi Nihon Sugar Manufacturing Co., Ltd. TPM program, which was developed on a number of different levels.

There were a number of different purposes and guidelines for this program development:

✓ To bring about a revolution in both personnel and corporate structure through the implementation of such activities

✓ To implement a thorough-going initial cleaning and flaw improvement program that would be instrumental in bring older equipment back to its initial specifications, and eliminate forced deterioration; to reduce failures and problems, and stabilize the manufacturing processes

✓ To thoroughly eliminate leaks and spills, and improve poor areas on the machine to minimize the need for manual work and the need for personnel

✓ To thoroughly implement visual maintenance controls and to create standards, thus creating a force of "human sensors" capable of spotting and understanding problems when they occur

✓ To implement a wide-ranging program of training on the machines to increase operator skills in the maintenance areas

✓ To create a system that would enable operators to inspect and control their machines on their own, in a reliable manner

✓ To create a system of autonomous controls for spare parts, auxiliary materials, tools, and documents

✓ To devise a way to review the system, from top management on down, that would lead to more vital group activities and the understanding of common problems

■ Overcoming obstacles posed by the process industries

When discussing step development, it should be remembered that modern TPM practices have been developed primarily around the machining and assembly industries, and there were very few case studies from the process industries when Nishi Nihon Sugar Manufacturing Co., Ltd. introduced its program in 1984. This caused major headaches in the compilation of the master plan. The characteristics of the process industries are themselves causes of obstacles to the successful implementation of autonomous maintenance activities. The problems that

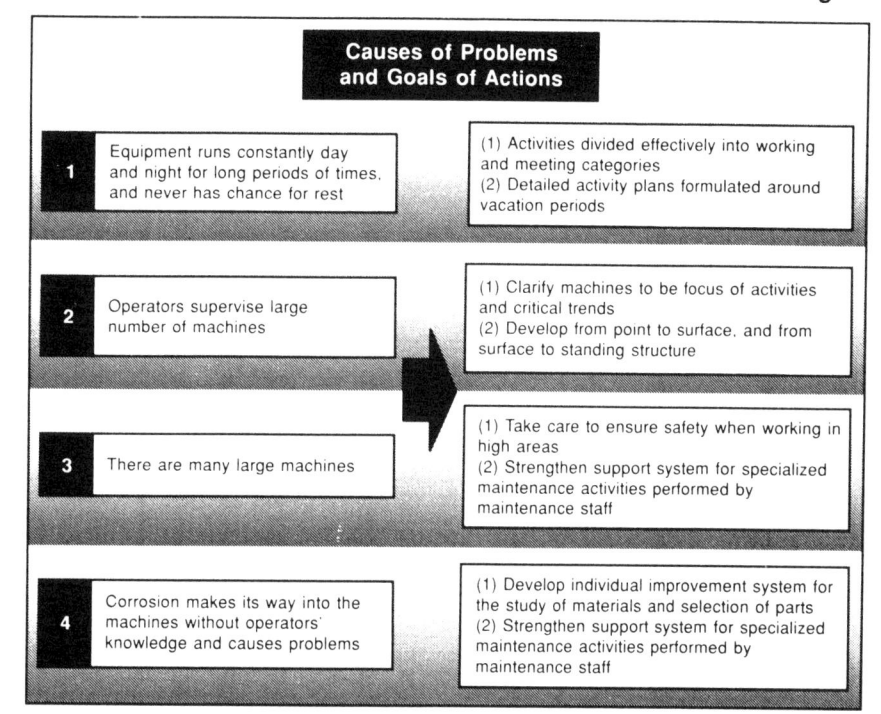

Figure 11 Problems Overcome in the Autonomous Maintenance Program

	Causes of Problems	and Goals of Actions
1	Equipment runs constantly day and night for long periods of times, and never has chance for rest	(1) Activities divided effectively into working and meeting categories (2) Detailed activity plans formulated around vacation periods
2	Operators supervise large number of machines	(1) Clarify machines to be focus of activities and critical trends (2) Develop from point to surface, and from surface to standing structure
3	There are many large machines	(1) Take care to ensure safety when working in high areas (2) Strengthen support system for specialized maintenance activities performed by maintenance staff
4	Corrosion makes its way into the machines without operators' knowledge and causes problems	(1) Develop individual improvement system for the study of materials and selection of parts (2) Strengthen support system for specialized maintenance activities performed by maintenance staff

were faced are outlined in Figure 11, along with the actions taken against these problems.

■ Characteristics of step development of autonomous maintenance

The method we have referred to as "step development" is characterized by the fact that it places considerable importance on encompassing a given number of machines within the program within a fixed time. It is based on the program devised by the Japan Plant Maintenance Association and develops, as shown in Figure 12, from "point" to "plane" to "cube."

■ Autonomous maintenance diagnosis

Diagnoses and evaluations at each stage of the process are extremely important in the development of an autonomous maintenance program.

The people in leadership positions within Nishi Nihon Sugar Manufacturing Co., Ltd. understood the necessity of both having a firm grip on what was going on in the workplace, as well as having a system for evaluation of the

Figure 12 From Point to Plane and Plane to Cube

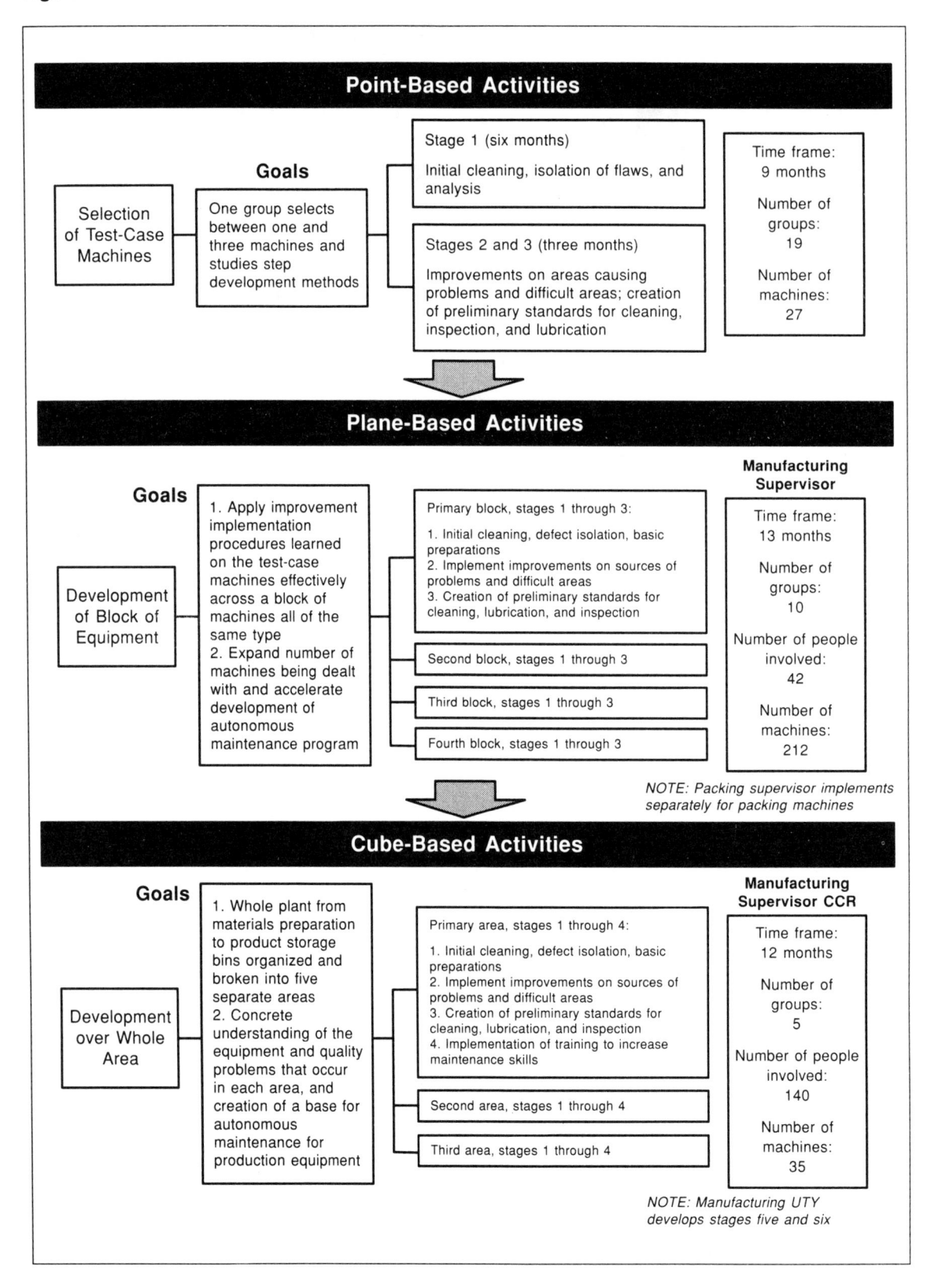

Point-Based Activities

Selection of Test-Case Machines

Goals: One group selects between one and three machines and studies step development methods

- Stage 1 (six months): Initial cleaning, isolation of flaws, and analysis
- Stages 2 and 3 (three months): Improvements on areas causing problems and difficult areas; creation of preliminary standards for cleaning, inspection, and lubrication

Time frame: 9 months
Number of groups: 19
Number of machines: 27

Plane-Based Activities

Development of Block of Equipment

Goals:
1. Apply improvement implementation procedures learned on the test-case machines effectively across a block of machines all of the same type
2. Expand number of machines being dealt with and accelerate development of autonomous maintenance program

- Primary block, stages 1 through 3:
  1. Initial cleaning, defect isolation, basic preparations
  2. Implement improvements on sources of problems and difficult areas
  3. Creation of preliminary standards for cleaning, lubrication, and inspection
- Second block, stages 1 through 3
- Third block, stages 1 through 3
- Fourth block, stages 1 through 3

Manufacturing Supervisor
Time frame: 13 months
Number of groups: 10
Number of people involved: 42
Number of machines: 212

NOTE: Packing supervisor implements separately for packing machines

Cube-Based Activities

Development over Whole Area

Goals:
1. Whole plant from materials preparation to product storage bins organized and broken into five separate areas
2. Concrete understanding of the equipment and quality problems that occur in each area, and creation of a base for autonomous maintenance for production equipment

- Primary area, stages 1 through 4:
  1. Initial cleaning, defect isolation, basic preparations
  2. Implement improvements on sources of problems and difficult areas
  3. Creation of preliminary standards for cleaning, lubrication, and inspection
  4. Implementation of training to increase maintenance skills
- Second area, stages 1 through 4
- Third area, stages 1 through 4

Manufacturing Supervisor CCR
Time frame: 12 months
Number of groups: 5
Number of people involved: 140
Number of machines: 35

NOTE: Manufacturing UTY develops stages five and six

programs that were under implementation. The goal was to create a vital form of group activities, and diagnoses were thus encouraged at all levels of the corporate structure—section, department, and top management. Particular emphasis was placed on the top management diagnostic sessions, which were carried out some 202 times. The activities of each group were diagnosed on the average of 13 times each.

Overall Evaluation and Future Goals of the Program

The Nishi Nihon Sugar Manufacturing Co., Ltd. TPM program was conducted on multiple levels, with particular emphasis on specialized maintenance and autonomous maintenance activities, as we have seen. The major facets of the program are evaluated in Figure 13, which shows how the efforts to conserve energy and natural resources through training and individual improvements, and the efforts to reduce manpower requirements through the streamlining of office work, ultimately yielded a large number of both tangible and intangible results. It should be remembered that the program was based on the implementation of a company-wide, full employee participation 5S campaign.

The intangible benefits—the confidence born in the workforce that they could do anything they put their minds to and their overall consciousness revolution—were among the most important aspects of the campaign. The knowledge and confidence that have been developed through the activities to date must now be put together to take TPM to its next logical development.

134   REDUCING THE SIX MAJOR LOSSES

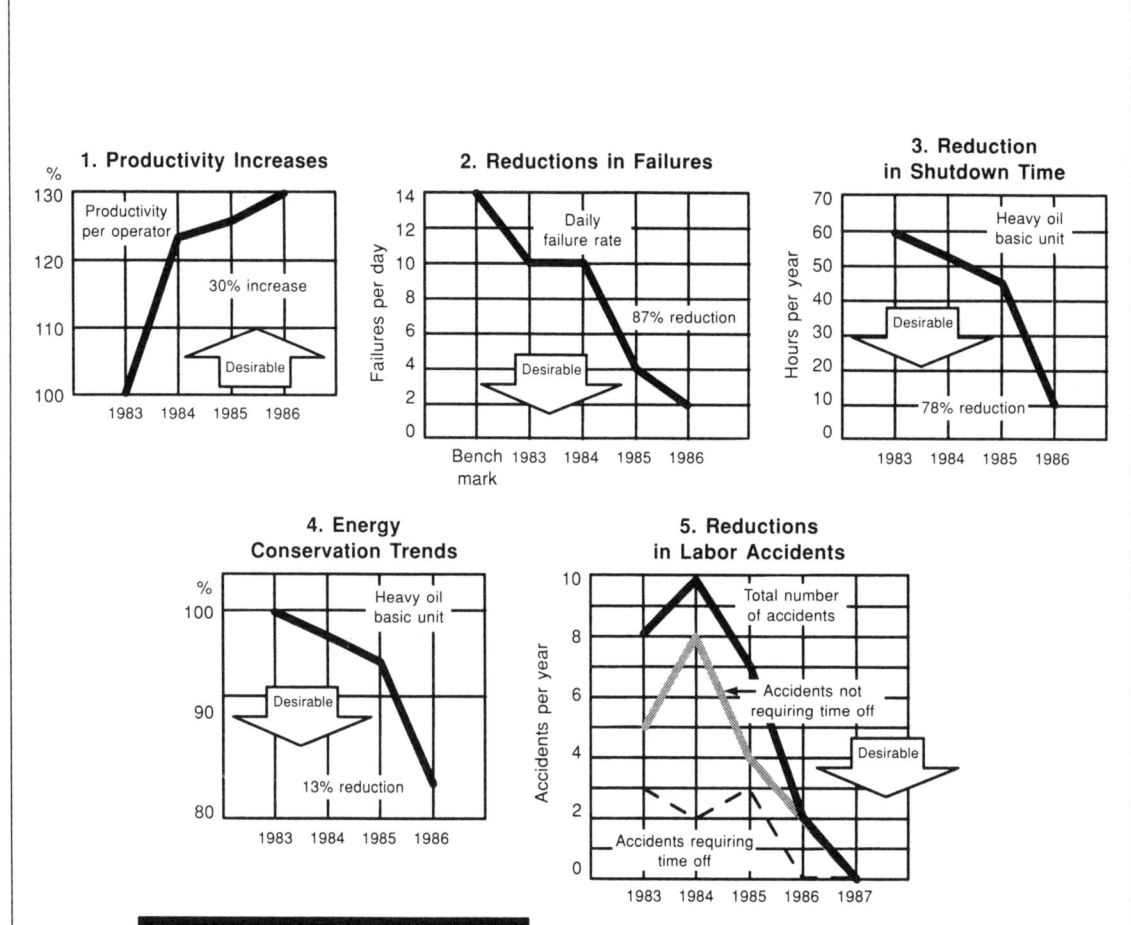

Figure 13 Overall Evaluation and Future Development

1. Productivity Increases — Productivity per operator, 30% increase (Desirable), 1983–1986

2. Reductions in Failures — Daily failure rate, 87% reduction (Desirable), Benchmark, 1983–1986

3. Reduction in Shutdown Time — Heavy oil basic unit, 78% reduction (Desirable), 1983–1986

4. Energy Conservation Trends — Heavy oil basic unit, 13% reduction (Desirable), 1983–1986

5. Reductions in Labor Accidents — Total number of accidents, Accidents not requiring time off, Accidents requiring time off (Desirable), 1983–1987

Future Topics for Development

Future work includes the full development of a TTM system through the formation of the steps remaining in the autonomous maintenance program. Three other major activities included in the second part of the TPM program, which is aimed at strengthening the corporate structure, also need development. These are: planning for minimal personnel needs, development of a total cost system, and corporate plans for new business activities.

	1988	1989	1990	1991
Completion of TPM activities				
Plans to minimize personnel	Plans and proposals	Kickoff		
Minimize total costs				
New business development plans				

Examples of Loss Reduction

Example 1 Test-Case Development

Test-case development is performed in stages 1 through 3. In Stage 1, operators are challenged to perform a thorough initial cleaning and become acquainted with their machines by disassembling them by themselves, so they can see what is involved in restoration of deteriorations. In Stage 2, emphasis is on measures to prevent spills and leaks, particularly of oil and sugar. In Stage 3, standards are created and the procedures which have worked to this point are made a part of the normal operation.

These activities continue for approximately nine months. Seven diagnostic sessions are conducted for each group, and the teams and their supervisors work together to learn implementation procedures. This period could be called the formulation of the basic foundation for autonomous maintenance activities.

Example 2 Block Development

In this step, a block is defined from a number of machines that are the same model and type, and stages 1 through 3 are implemented. At the same time, four different diagnostic sessions are held. The equipment is broken into blocks and supervised by seven groups headed by the manufacturing staff. A total of 212 machines (30 per block) were dealt with over a 13-month span, and the activities resulted in a significant reduction of machine problems and in the need for manual operations.

Example 3 Area Development

The area development step consists of the identification of five different areas within the manufacturing processes. Each area is supervised by one group, and was headed by a supervisor from the equipment department. These teams work with the specialized maintenance staff for problem analysis, and to implement Stage 4, an eight-course training program designed to increase operators' maintenance skills at the same time that stages 1 through 4 are implemented.

The result was a reduction in problems and in manual work, in addition to the elimination of one operator from each shift.

Area development includes a standing body of machines, consisting of both previous and subsequent processes, which is more effective in instituting quality improvements, conserving energy, and the like.

Example 4 Stage 5 and Stage 6 Development

After all PM equipment had been determined as part of stages 1 through 3 in the Utility (UTY) workplace, stages 5 and 6 were entered, in which activity frameworks for the other workplaces were created.

In Stage 5, activities begin with the creation of a set of periodic inspection standards by specific item for skills training. The stage also includes inspection patrol standards, test operation standards, and the creation of an annual maintenance calendar by the operators themselves. In Stage 6, the autonomous maintenance system is solidified by the development of workplace controls and storage standards for auxiliary materials, tools, spare parts, technical references, and the like.

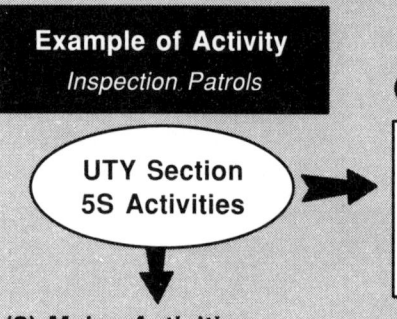

Example of Activity
Inspection Patrols

UTY Section 5S Activities

(1) Goals and Purposes

Patrol operations simplified so that anyone could perform inspections easily and accurately, without the need for basic documents while doing so, in order to implement MM controls and preventive measures through the development of 5S activities.

(2) Major Activities

1. Creation of Patrol Inspection Standards
   (a) Create a standards panel and mount in workplace
   (b) Record and display inspection areas and what is being looked for
   (c) Color code patrol cycles:
      Red: 2 hrs.
      Green: once per shift
      White: once per day
2. Patrol Path
   (a) Establish a path that anyone could follow efficiently
   (b) Indicate path with numbers and arrows on floors and walls
3. Thorough MM Implementation
   (a) Color-coded displays for correct ranges for pressure gages, fluid gages, and power gages
   (b) Color-code types of oil at openings where oil is added on machines
   (c) Thorough implementation of MM temperature controls for motors and bearings

(3) Features Implemented

1. Patrol inspection paths are established and MM procedures taken
2. Inspection standards posted

(4) Results

1. Unmanned Operation Implemented for UTY Section
Inspection patrols simplified and made more efficient to support further work on automation; unmanned operations made possible
2. Scope Enlarged
CCR members trained to be able to undertake UTY patrol operations

Part III

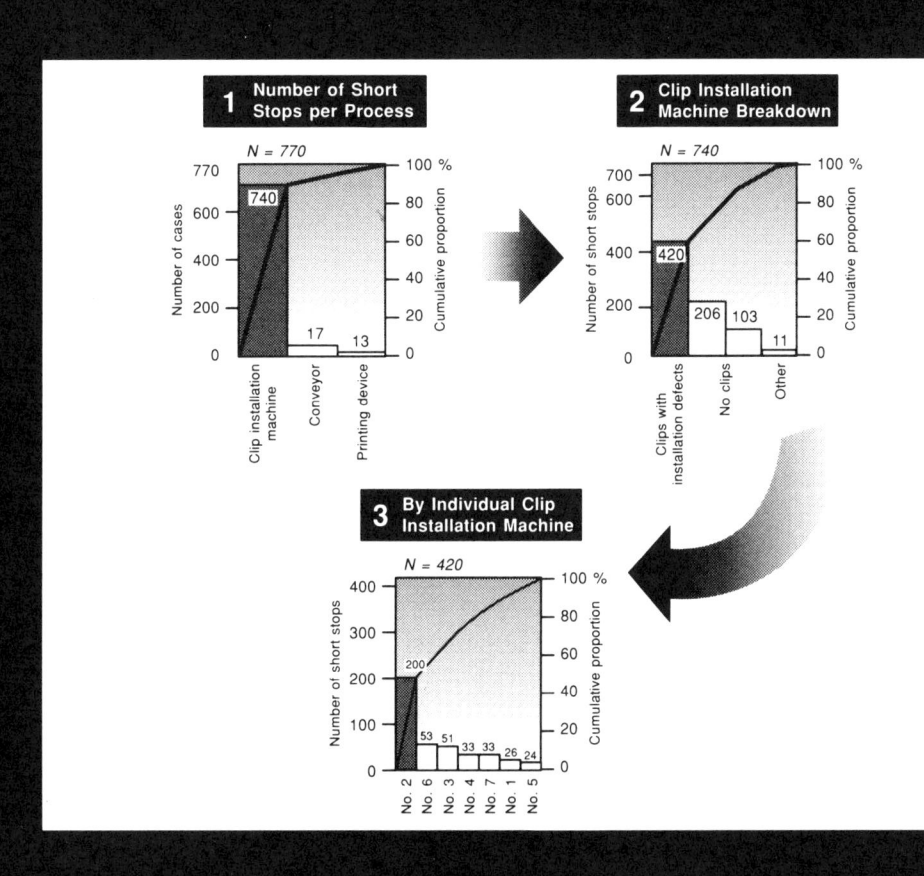

TPM Case Studies

TPM Case Studies

Overcoming the Six Major Losses

The "six major losses" in TPM are loss due to failures, loss due to setups, loss due to brief stops, loss due to speed drops, loss due to defects, and loss due to startups. Each of these losses must be addressed individually to keep a factory running at top capacity, although workplaces will tend to prioritize them in different ways.

The twelve examples which follow show improvements made on the shop floor to reduce losses from each of the six categories. The problems are unique to each plant that has shared its experiences here; the need for solutions, on the other hand, is universal.

Each of the case studies that follow is presented according to the same format: the improvement project is summarized in words, and the process involved is shown in pictures; then the problem is diagrammed, and the solution is depicted. The message is clear: successful solutions grow from accurate understandings of the problem.

We would like to thank the corporations that cooperated with the publication of this volume, sharing the steps in their acquisition of knowledge and the way they then acted on this knowledge.

Loss due to Failures

Improvements to Stop Breakage of Welding Robot Cable

The Project Because the operating range of welding robots is large, breaks began to occur in the auxiliary cable, especially that centered around the main unit. This cable was put under a good deal of excessive stress at the connections between the cable and the welding gun, due primarily to the movements of the robot when operating. The idea behind the improvement project was to slacken the bending angle of the cable at the terminal areas, where the most bending force was concentrated. Other improvement targets included reducing the time required to replace the cable itself, which was considered to be a consumable item. The net result of these improvements was that cable replacement time went from 495 to 135 minutes per month, and the volume of cable used dropped dramatically, from eleven to three separate units per month.

The Process   This was a welding robot process.

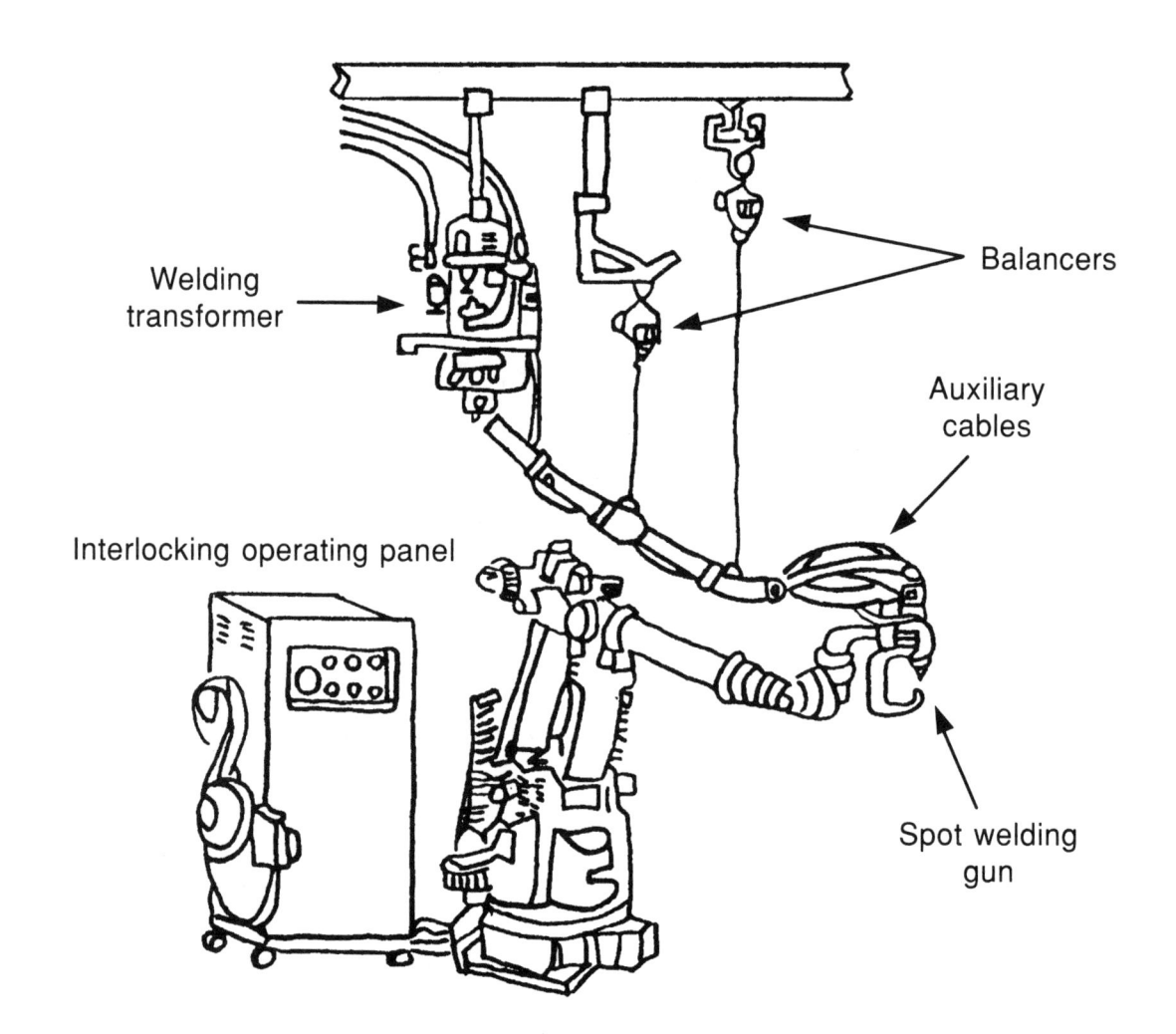

Improvements to Stop Breakage of Welding Robot Cable 143

The Problem   Each time a welding cable broke while the production line was in operation, the replacement operation would bring the line to a halt for between 40 and 50 minutes—no production was going on during this time. Cable breakage amounted to a loss of 495 minutes a month in production time, and to eleven cables a month in materials.

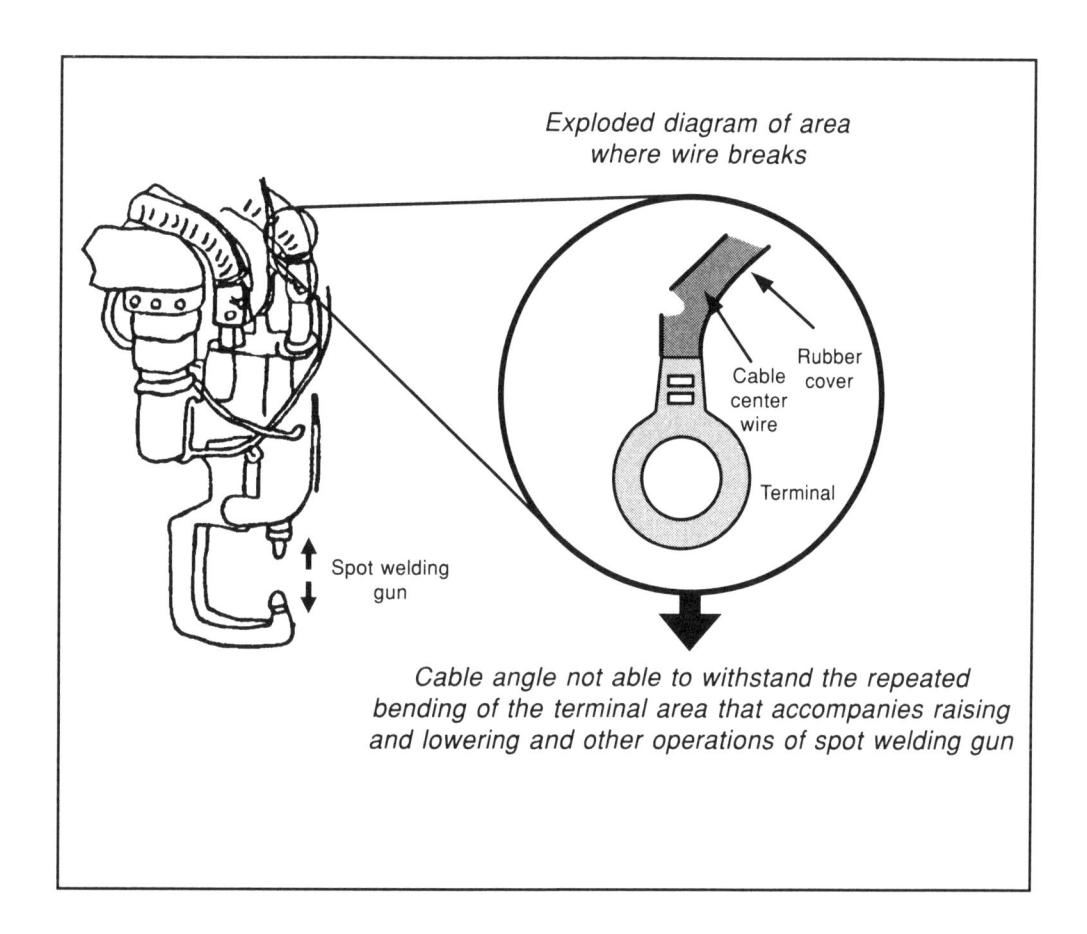

Exploded diagram of area where wire breaks

Rubber cover
Cable center wire
Terminal

Spot welding gun

Cable angle not able to withstand the repeated bending of the terminal area that accompanies raising and lowering and other operations of spot welding gun

The Solution

A protective collar was installed at the cable terminal area where connections were made. The results were an improvement over the previous situation, but not 100 percent acceptable, because breakage continued. An angle was thus added to the protective collar, so that it would not come into direct contact with the portion of the cable which bent. Four other improvements also were made:

- ✓ Improvements were made in the way the cable was bundled
- ✓ A butterfly screw was added to drain coolant
- ✓ Standard, special-use bolts were designed for the tools
- ✓ Improvements were made in the positions of the power supply and the welding gun

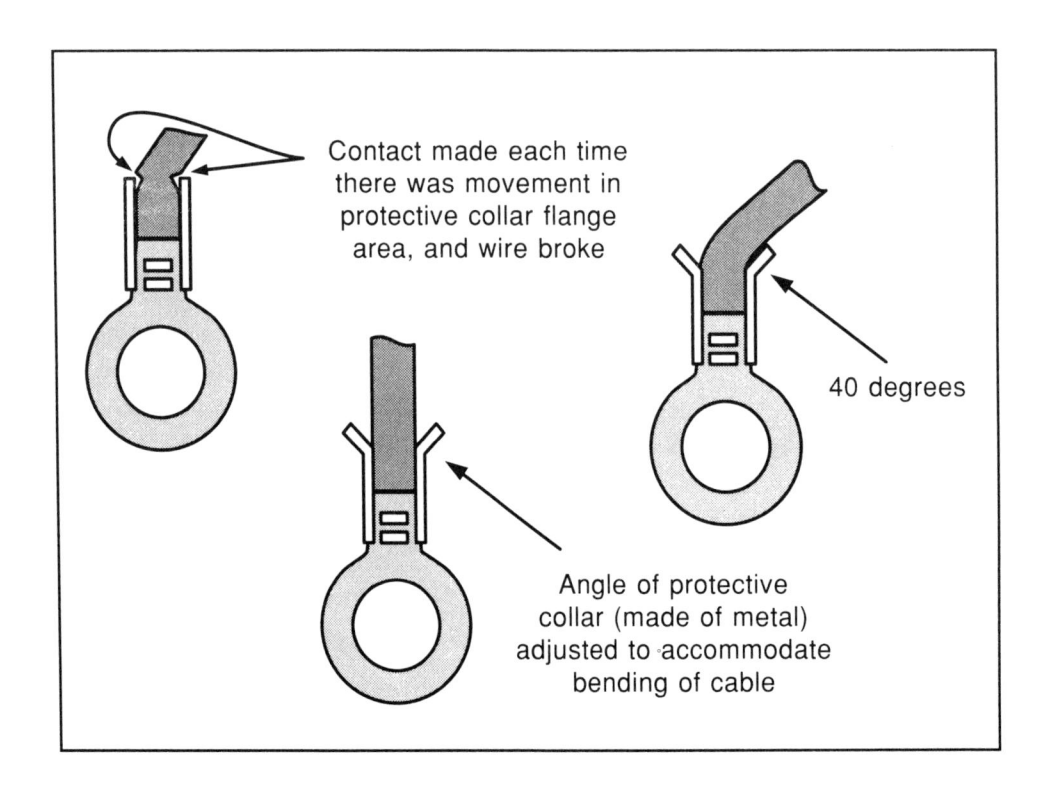

Contact made each time there was movement in protective collar flange area, and wire broke

40 degrees

Angle of protective collar (made of metal) adjusted to accommodate bending of cable

Lead Co., Ltd.

Loss due to Setups

One-Touch Setups Using Common Fixtures for Sharpening Cutting Tools

The Project

The loss due to setup adjustments was serious, and caused by a number of different factors: there were many auxiliary fixtures; they were heavy and difficult to carry; it was difficult to position the fixtures; the notches made for alignment were hard to see and harder to use; it was difficult to position the grinding wheel cover; and the grinding wheel head's basic structure was overly complex. The loss stemming from changing the wheels was 3.88 hours per month, and the adjustment operation loss was 18.82 hours per month.

A number of different improvements were implemented to correct this situation, resulting in a reduction of time amounting to approximately 20 percent. The next step is to use a smaller indexing fixture that can be put in horizontally. Two other goals:

✓ Gaining multifunctionality by using an automatic indexing device

✓ The fabrication of a grinding wheel forming fixture using a reamer with a specially designed cutting tool

The Process   The operation involved was the sharpening of cutting tools. The system involved the collection of cutting tools after they had been used, sharpening them, and then providing each process with sharpened tools.

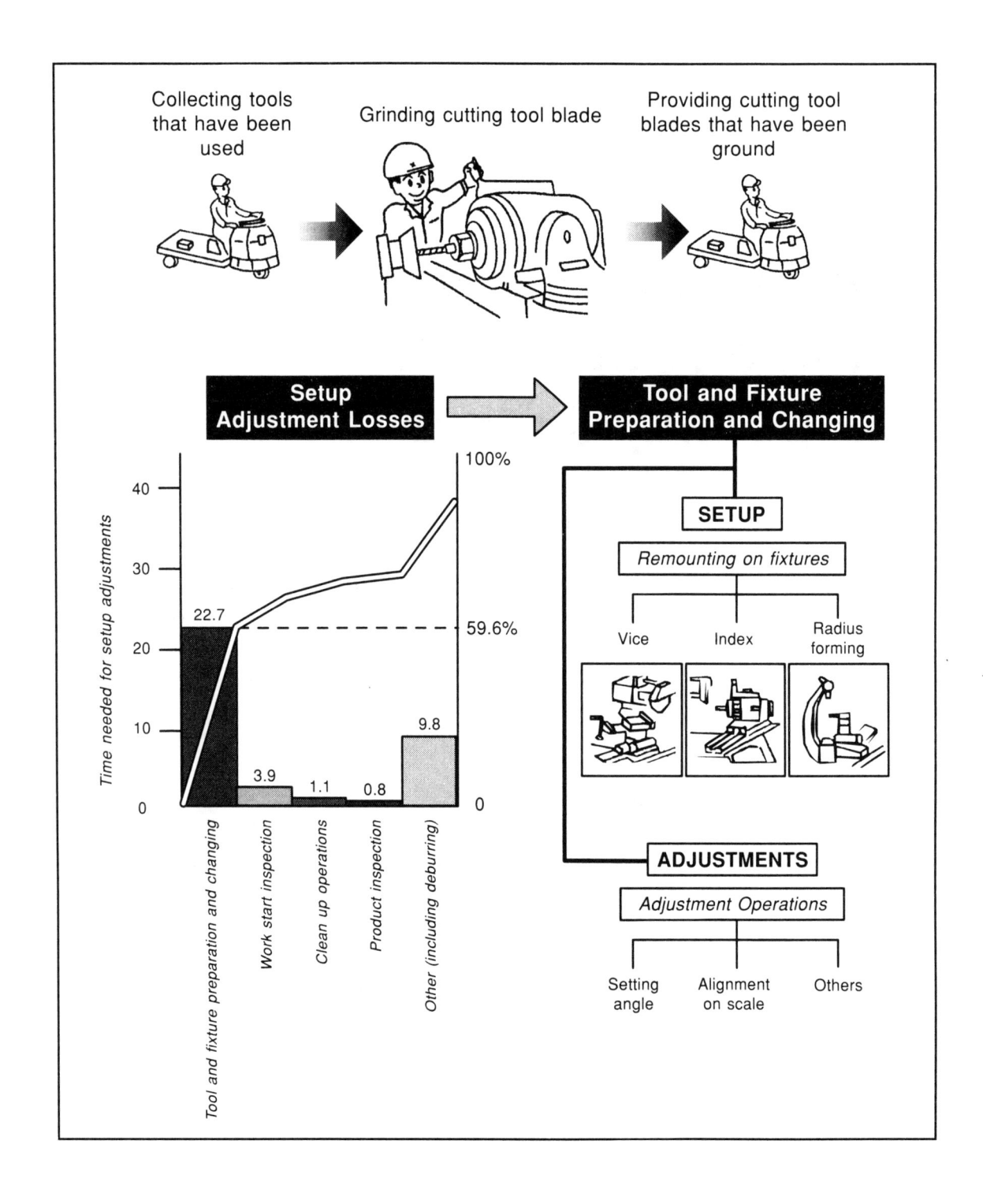

Collecting tools that have been used → Grinding cutting tool blade → Providing cutting tool blades that have been ground

Setup Adjustment Losses ⇒ **Tool and Fixture Preparation and Changing**

Time needed for setup adjustments:
- Tool and fixture preparation and changing: 22.7 (59.6%)
- Work start inspection: 3.9
- Clean up operations: 1.1
- Product inspection: 0.8
- Other (including deburring): 9.8

SETUP
Remounting on fixtures
- Vice
- Index
- Radius forming

ADJUSTMENTS
Adjustment Operations
- Setting angle
- Alignment on scale
- Others

One-Touch Setups Using Common Fixtures for Sharpening Cutting Tools 147

The Problem   There were two basic problems:

- ✓ There were too many cutting tool changes to be made at the index area
- ✓ The grinding wheel cover was difficult to position properly

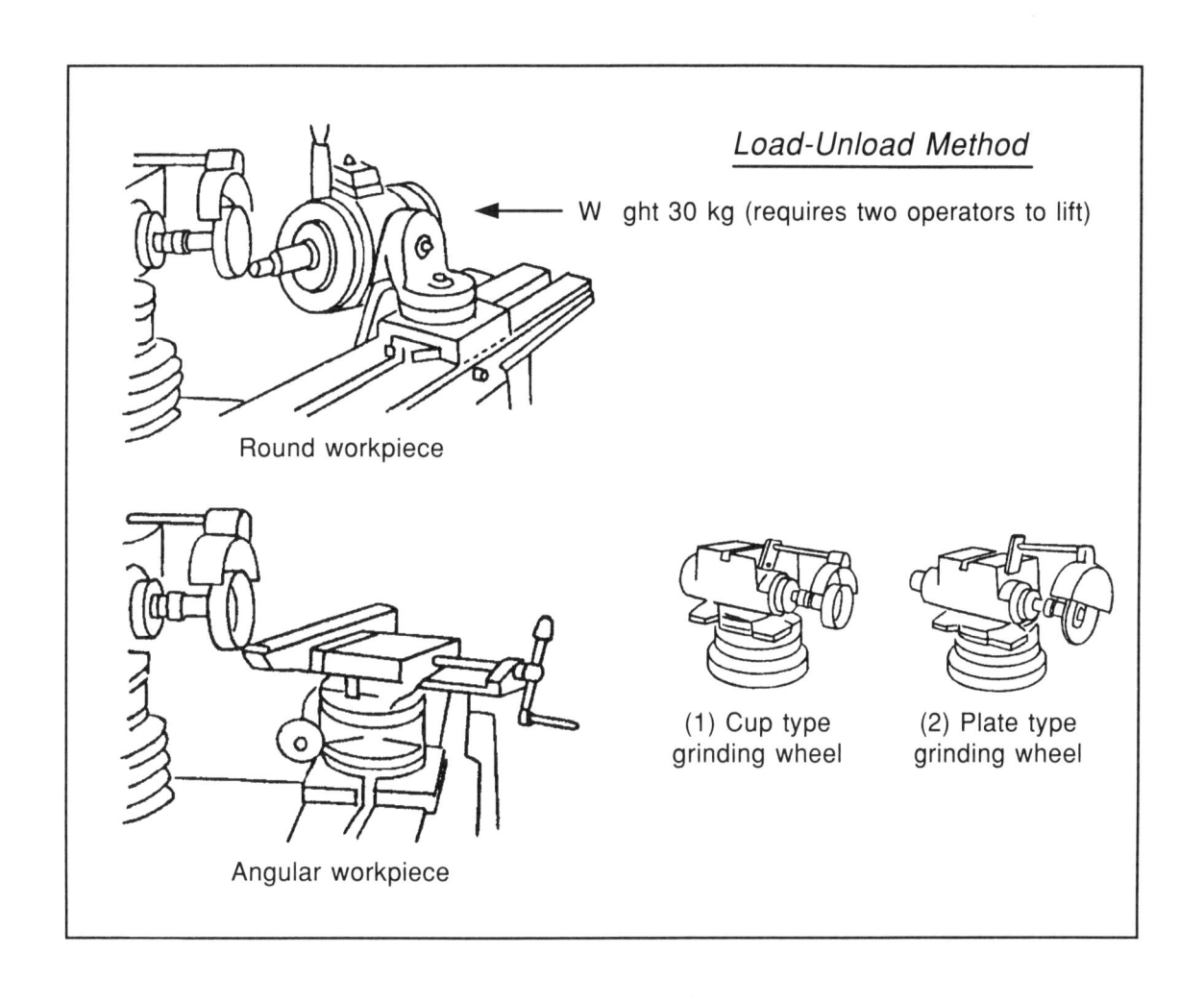

Load-Unload Method

← Weight 30 kg (requires two operators to lift)

Round workpiece

Angular workpiece

(1) Cup type grinding wheel

(2) Plate type grinding wheel

The Solution

These problems were approached as follows:

✓ A small-sized indexing fixture was developed; this was both lighter than the previous fixture and also could be used with angular cutting tools as well as round ones

✓ The load-unload type of cover for cup type grinding wheels and plate type grinding wheels was changed to a magazine storage type cover

The net result of these changes was the reduction of preparation exchange time from 22.7 hours to 18.1 hours.

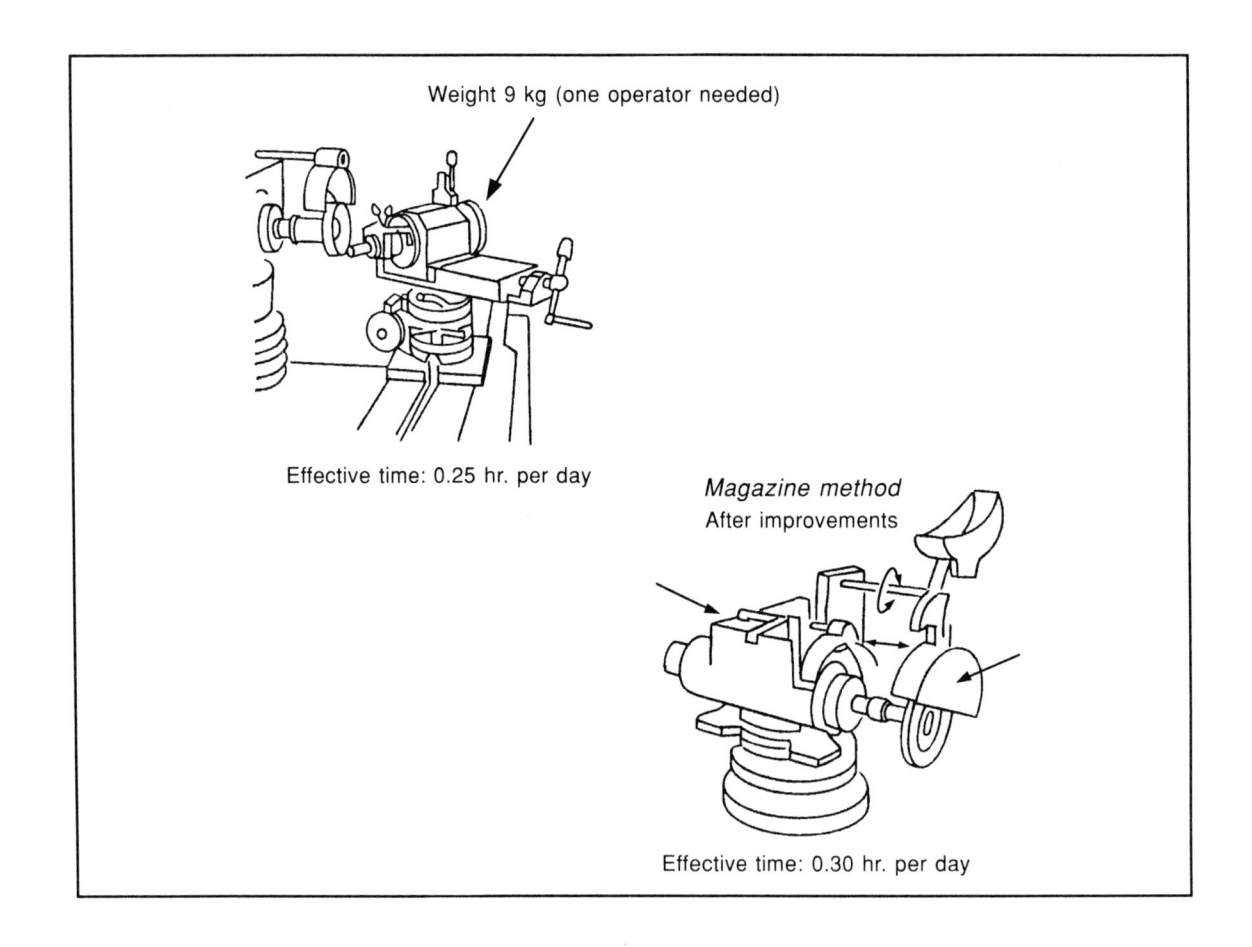

Weight 9 kg (one operator needed)

Effective time: 0.25 hr. per day

Magazine method
After improvements

Effective time: 0.30 hr. per day

Zexel Co., Ltd., Higashi Matsuyama Plant

Loss due to Setups

Shortening Setup Adjustment Time for Bend Reinforced Glass

The Project

There are seventeen model changeovers each month, and a good deal of time is required for each of the setup adjustments in each of these cases. Approximately 10 percent of the time was loss. The setup adjustment operation was broken into the two categories of setup change (replacing the forming machine), and quality checks and adjustments. It was discovered that the major source of loss was in putting on and taking off the air hose for the cooling machine (a setup change operation) on the one hand, and adjustments to the forming die (adjustment) on the other. A total of 43 improvement suggestions were implemented to deal with these problems. As a result of the accumulated effect of these improvements, the 100 hours that had been required for setup adjustments were cut by one-fifth, and quality products were output from the first run of the machine after the setup. The overall result was an increase of eight percent in production volume. The current goals are to eliminate totally the need for quality checks, to cut setup adjustment time to zero, and to achieve acceptable quality straight from the setup.

The Process The plant has a multi-model production system specializing in the manufacture of bend reinforced glass. The processes involved are shown below.

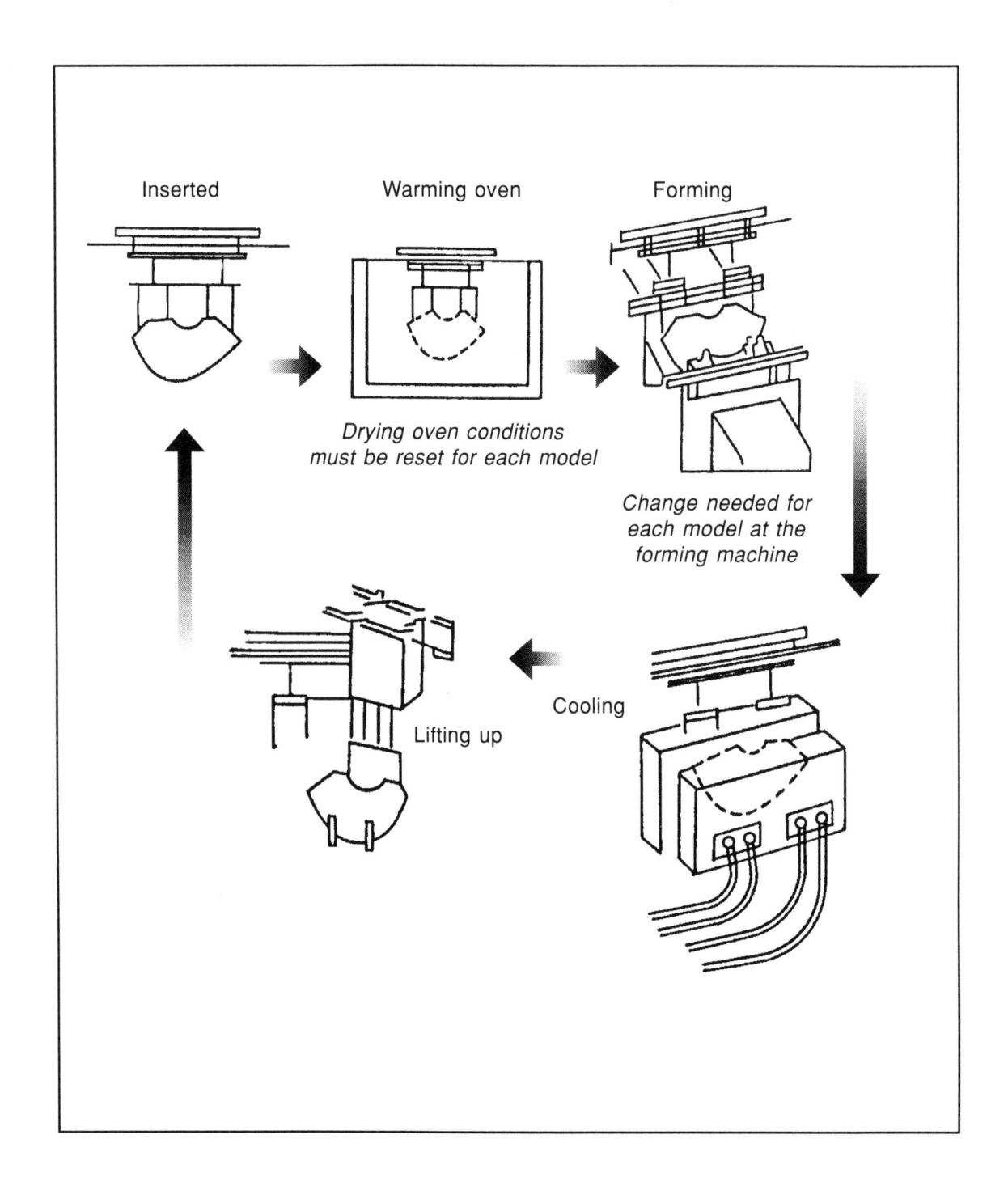

- Inserted
- Warming oven — *Drying oven conditions must be reset for each model*
- Forming — *Change needed for each model at the forming machine*
- Cooling
- Lifting up

Shortening Setup Adjustment Time for Bend Reinforced Glass

The Problem The two major problems isolated were the adjustments required for the forming die (an adjustment problem) and putting on and taking off the air hose for the cooling machine (a setup problem). Concerning the forming die, the areas where the glass comes into strong contact suffered fast wear from the heat. The air hose problem was centered around the fact that it was necessary to actually climb into the machine to take the hose off or put it on.

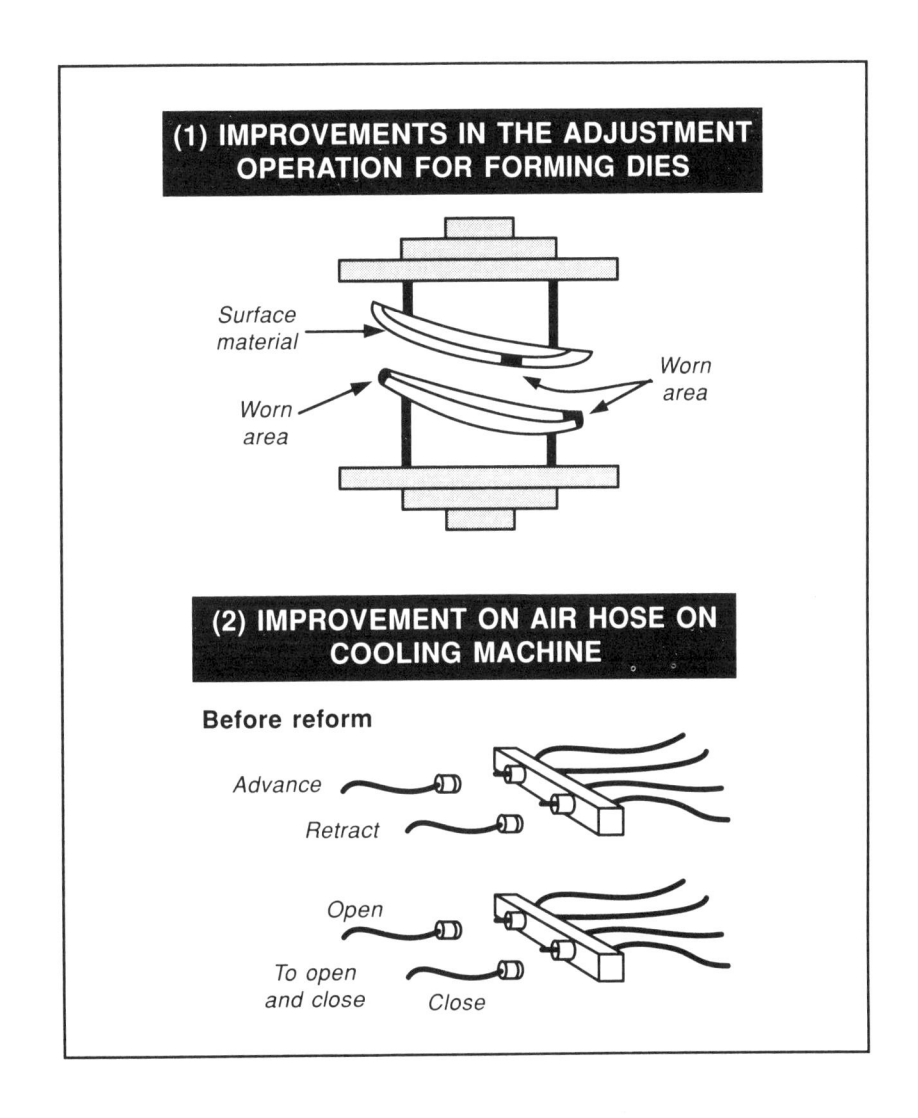

(1) IMPROVEMENTS IN THE ADJUSTMENT OPERATION FOR FORMING DIES

Surface material
Worn area
Worn area

(2) IMPROVEMENT ON AIR HOSE ON COOLING MACHINE

Before reform

Advance
Retract

Open
To open and close
Close

The Solution   The two problems were dealt with as follows:

- ✓ Distribution was changed, decreasing the distortion of the die. This dropped adjustment time from 34 to seven minutes.

- ✓ The connection portion of the unit was brought outside the main unit, the hose was bundled, color-coding was employed, and the shapes of the couplers were changed. This provision of better visual guides reduced the time needed to take the hose off or put it on from five minutes to almost nothing.

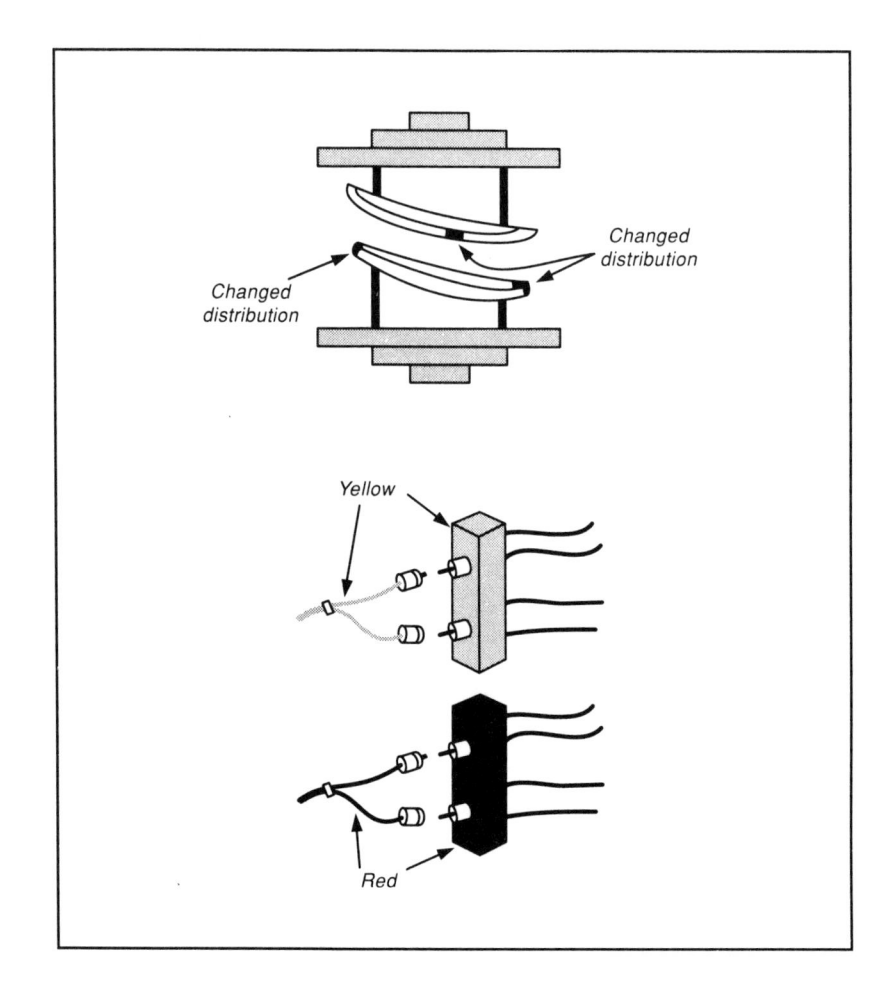

Nipponzaka Glass, Tsurumai Plant

Loss due to Brief Stops

Cutting Clip Attachment Defects to 1/37th the Former Level

The Project

All of the basic conditions had been implemented before the adoption of any countermeasures, but this had resulted in no effects, and a PM analysis was conducted on the attachment defects. This revealed that there were two basic problems. The first was positioning gaps caused by interference between the case clip seat position and arm clip on the one hand, and the cover on the other; and the second was a variety of installation defects caused by deviations in precision in the clips themselves. A number of improvements were implemented to deal with these problems. Technical guidance also was provided to a cooperating plant which manufactured the dies used, thus correcting problems and resulting in a higher level of quality in the clips. This resulted in major drops in brief stop loss, of course, and the overall effect of the project was significant.

The Process The following tables show the breakdown of the processes involved in terms of the number and types of brief stops experienced.

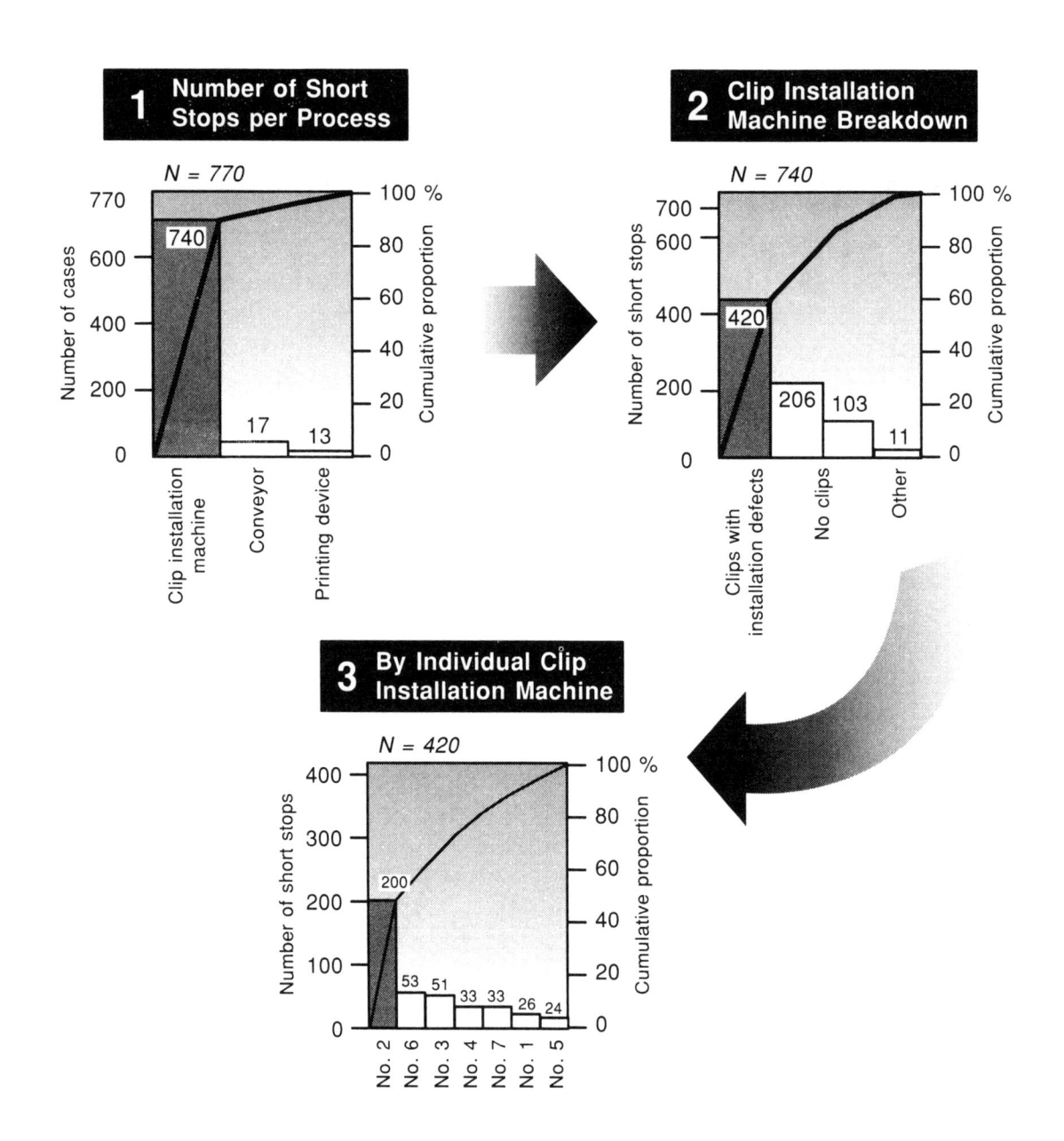

1. Number of Short Stops per Process (N = 770)

Process	Number of cases
Clip installation machine	740
Conveyor	17
Printing device	13

2. Clip Installation Machine Breakdown (N = 740)

Cause	Number of short stops
Clips with installation defects	420
No clips	206
(unlabeled)	103
Other	11

3. By Individual Clip Installation Machine (N = 420)

Machine	Number of short stops
No. 2	200
No. 6	53
No. 3	51
No. 4	33
No. 7	33
No. 1	26
No. 5	24

Cutting Clip Attachment Defects to 1/37th the Former Level

The Problem The charts shown on the previous page revealed three major facts about the problem:

- ✓ The clip attachment machine was responsible for nearly all of the problems
- ✓ A full fifty percent of the attachment defects were at the No. 2 position
- ✓ The PM analysis conducted on the clip attachment defects showed that the major problems were defects in case shape and in the robot operation

The Solution Improvements were made on the robot arm and on the case clip seat. These cut the number of brief stops from 770 to 21, or 1/37th of the previous level.

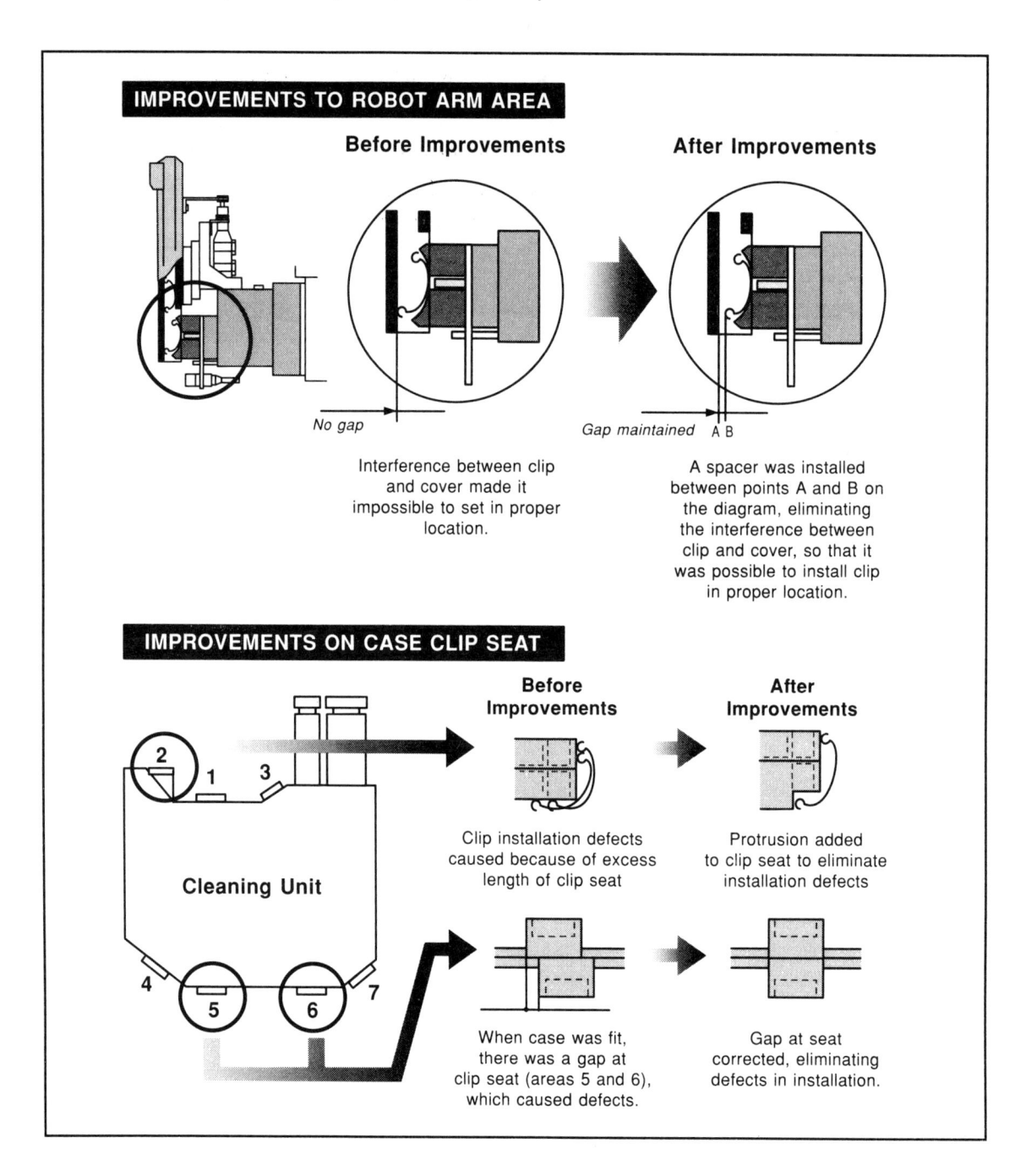

IMPROVEMENTS TO ROBOT ARM AREA

Before Improvements: Interference between clip and cover made it impossible to set in proper location. (No gap)

After Improvements: A spacer was installed between points A and B on the diagram, eliminating the interference between clip and cover, so that it was possible to install clip in proper location. (Gap maintained A B)

IMPROVEMENTS ON CASE CLIP SEAT

Cleaning Unit

Before Improvements: Clip installation defects caused because of excess length of clip seat

After Improvements: Protrusion added to clip seat to eliminate installation defects

Before Improvements: When case was fit, there was a gap at clip seat (areas 5 and 6), which caused defects.

After Improvements: Gap at seat corrected, eliminating defects in installation.

Zexel Co., Ltd., Higashi Matsuyama Plant

Loss due to Brief Stops

Overcoming Problems with Clogged Screws

The Project Simple observation showed that the most common place for screws to become clogged was in the area where the hose began its bend. The hose connects the narrow space between the parts feeder and screwdriver tip as though it were a suture, and receives force each time a screw is tightened. For this reason, it is not fixed in place, but rather is kept slack. The bending portion of this slack area was kept as short as possible, and the hose was held in place by a flexible spring. This was then changed on a periodically scheduled basis, even if screws did not get clogged inside the hose; this resulted in an overall reduction in the number of instances of screw clogging, reduced wear inside the hose, and lengthened the overall service life of the hose.

The Process The process involved is the automatic screw tightening in the external mounting process for video cassette recorders.

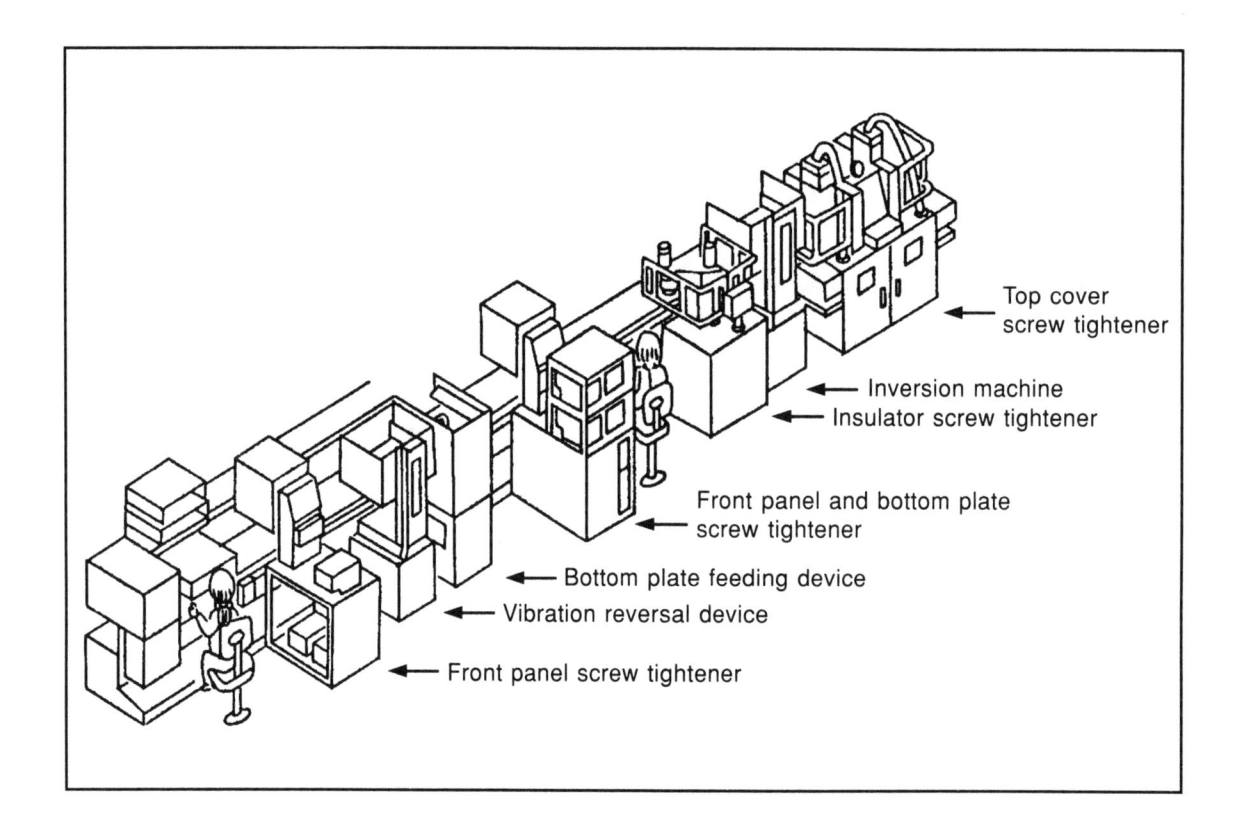

- Top cover screw tightener
- Inversion machine
- Insulator screw tightener
- Front panel and bottom plate screw tightener
- Bottom plate feeding device
- Vibration reversal device
- Front panel screw tightener

Overcoming Problems with Clogged Screws

The Problem Screws would frequently get caught inside the hose to the automatic screw tightener. When this happened, no screw would be fed to the tightener, and the hose had to be changed. Sometimes, a screw would clog inside a hose that had just been changed, making it apparent that a close look at the problem was needed.

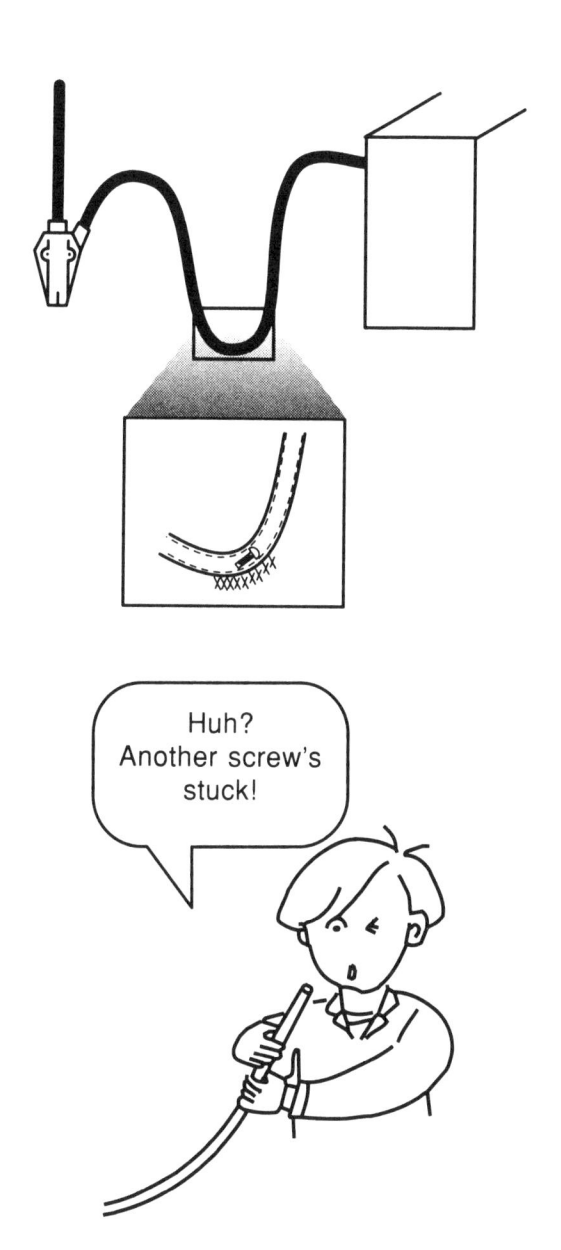

Huh? Another screw's stuck!

The Solution   There was slack in the hose, and it was this area where the problems occurred. The hose was thus shortened, and the bend made less pronounced. This cut the number of screws being clogged inside the hose, and lengthened the period between hose changes.

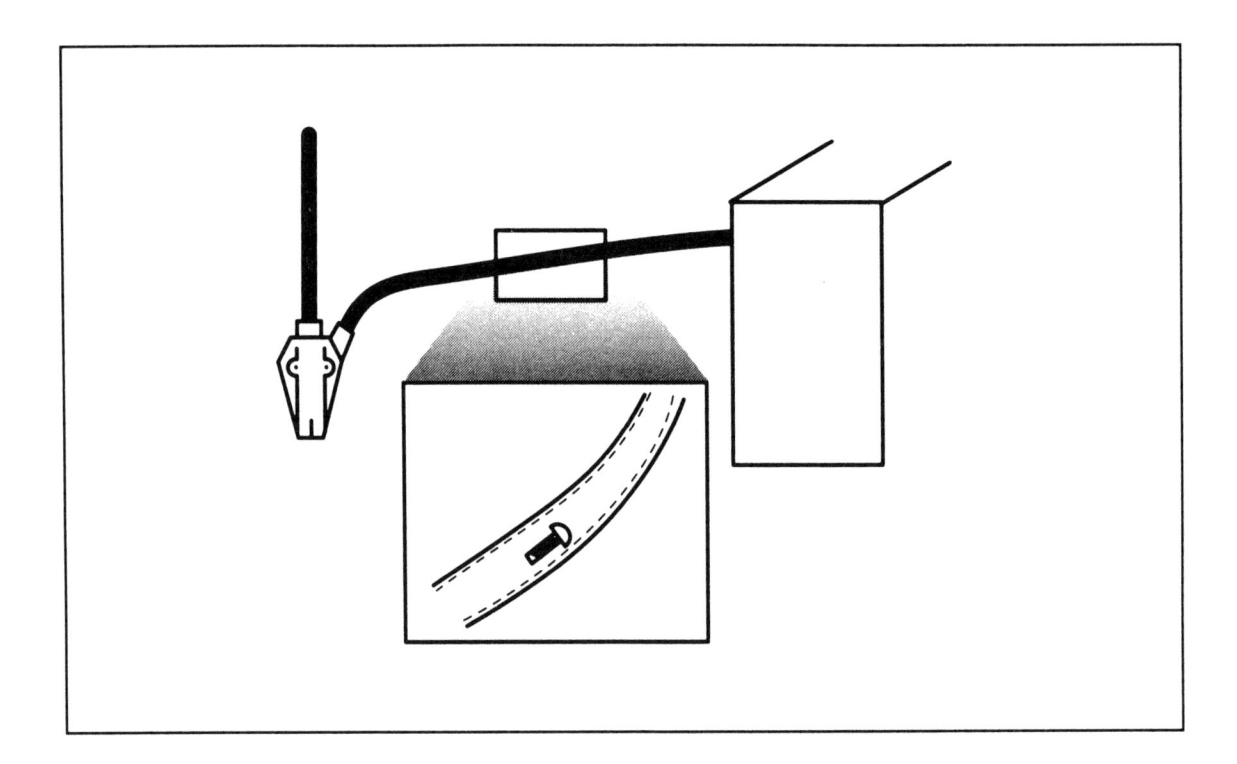

NEC Home Electronics, Ltd., Gotenba Plant

Loss due to Brief Stops

Eliminating Brief Stops at the Transfer Machine

The Project Initially, improvement activities undertaken by the operators resulted in a fifty percent drop in brief stops, but this was nowhere close to the goal of the project, which was to cut such stops to 1/10th their former level. To attain this goal, members of the workforce studied the principles of PM analysis, and began applying what they learned to the problems that appeared on their machines. The results they attained were a testimony to their skills, and this gave them renewed confidence to continue working toward the goal of brief stop reduction. With their renewed efforts, they were able to greatly exceed the original goal, bringing brief stops to 1/20th their former level.

The Process   The process involved was a transfer machine used for the machining of hydraulic cutoff valve bodies such as the one shown in the figure below. After the material is brought in and set in the upper magazine, it is automatically transported, milled, drilled, bored, and tapped, passing in all through 30 different processes before being automatically offloaded to the completed work magazine.

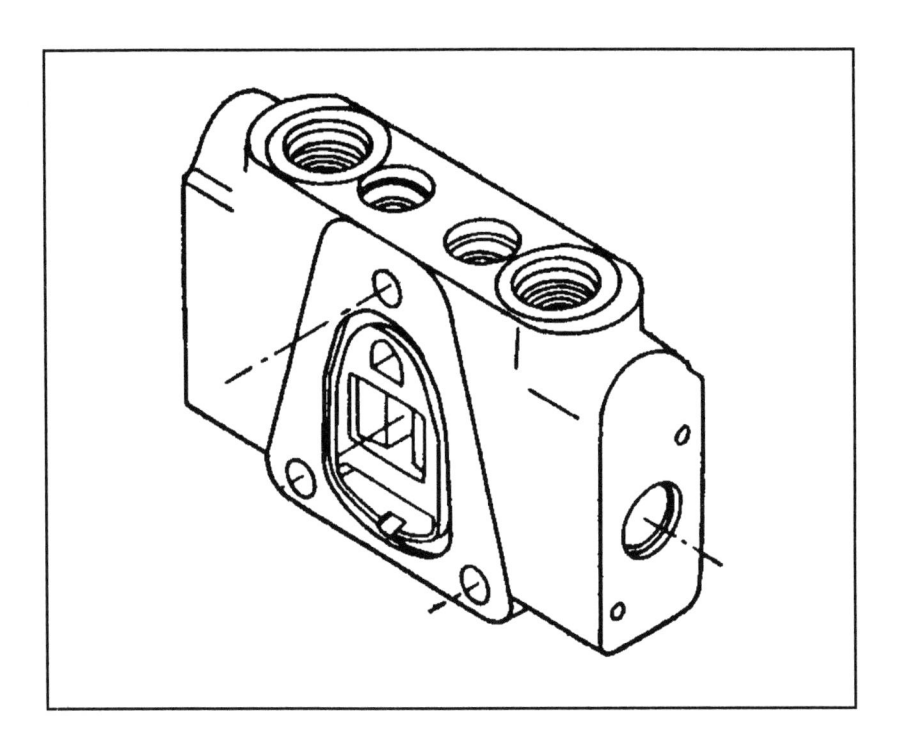

Eliminating Brief Stops at the Transfer Machine

The Problem There were as many as 1000 brief stops each month, resulting in deviations in the completed work and the inability to achieve anticipated output figures. The machine incorporates a total of 50 different stations, including posture change, washing, foolproofing, and idling; no matter where a brief stop occurred, the net result was the same: the entire line would have to stop.

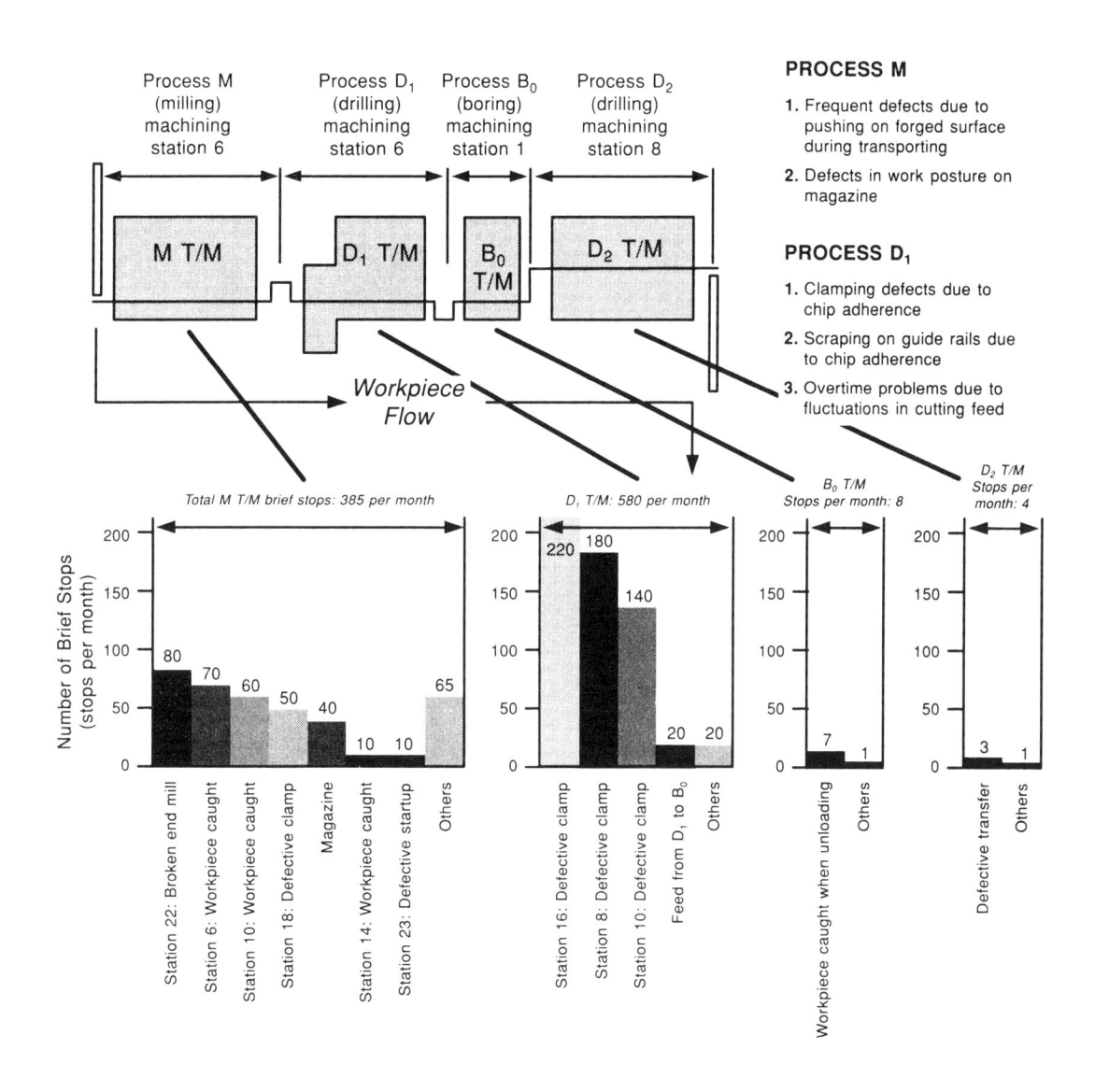

Process M (milling) machining station 6
Process D₁ (drilling) machining station 6
Process B₀ (boring) machining station 1
Process D₂ (drilling) machining station 8

PROCESS M
1. Frequent defects due to pushing on forged surface during transporting
2. Defects in work posture on magazine

PROCESS D₁
1. Clamping defects due to chip adherence
2. Scraping on guide rails due to chip adherence
3. Overtime problems due to fluctuations in cutting feed

Total M T/M brief stops: 385 per month

Station	Stops
Station 22: Broken end mill	80
Station 6: Workpiece caught	70
Station 10: Workpiece caught	60
Station 18: Defective clamp	50
Magazine	40
Station 14: Workpiece caught	10
Station 23: Defective startup	10
Others	65

D₁ T/M: 580 per month

Station	Stops
Station 16: Defective clamp	220
Station 8: Defective clamp	180
Station 10: Defective clamp	140
Feed from D₁ to B₀	20
Others	20

B₀ T/M Stops per month: 8

	Stops
Workpiece caught when unloading	7
Others	1

D₂ T/M Stops per month: 4

	Stops
Defective transfer	3
Others	1

The Solution   A number of improvements were made on the machines:

✓ A plate was fixed to the finger, which presses against workpieces to push them out of the machine, so that the pressing area is a flat surface rather than a line (to prevent workpieces from being caught in the machine)

✓ The height of the magazine hand was adjusted (to prevent workpieces from falling)

✓ Recesses were added to the guide rail (to prevent workpieces from being caught in the machine)

Additionally, a PM analysis was conducted on the clamping defects.

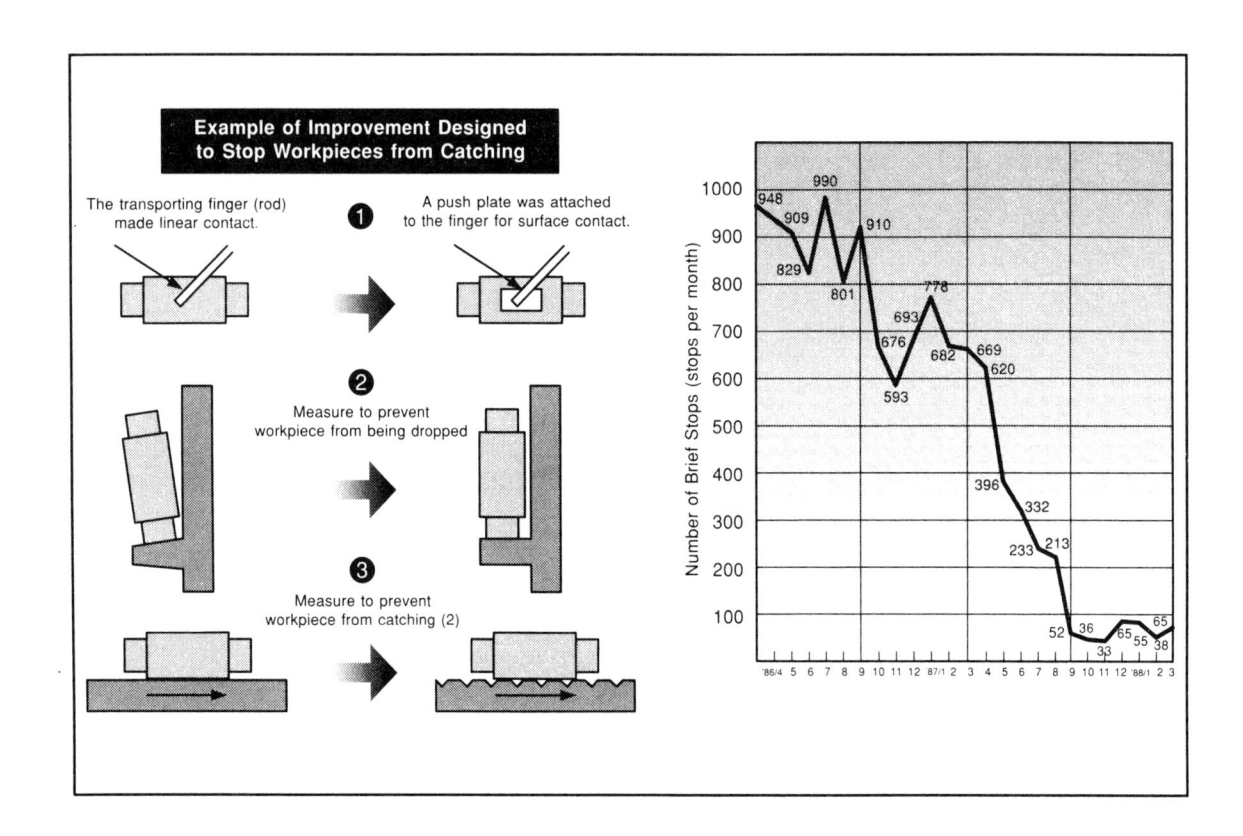

Example of Improvement Designed to Stop Workpieces from Catching

① The transporting finger (rod) made linear contact. → A push plate was attached to the finger for surface contact.

② Measure to prevent workpiece from being dropped

③ Measure to prevent workpiece from catching (2)

Number of Brief Stops (stops per month):
86/4: 948; 5: 909; 6: 829; 7: 990; 8: 910; 9: 801; 10: 676; 11: 593; 12: 693; 87/1: 778; 2: 682; 3: 669; 4: 620; 5: 396; 6: 332; 7: 233; 8: 213; 9: 52; 10: 36; 11: 33; 12: 65; 88/1: 55; 2: 38; 3: 65

Nihon Spindle Mfg. Co., Ltd., Kameoka Manufacturing Plant

Loss due to Speed Drops

A 13 Percent Improvement by Upgrading the Machining Program

The Project

Using automated transporting to link all machining processes together for a given product pays dividends in terms of reduction of manpower requirements (it can even lead to fully unmanned machining) and the reduction of work-in-process inventory, but this measure also can cause loss. Briefly stated, if there are differences in cycle times among the machining processes, the process with the longest cycle time comes to define machining capacity for the entire line, which means speed losses will occur throughout the remaining processes. In this particular project, the bottleneck was in the first process, drilling and tapping. An upgrading of the machining program for this process, though, changed the order of movement for the loading unit, thus shortening cycle time and improving speed throughout the line by thirteen percent.

The Process This project was carried out on the machining line, a line which handles all the machining processes for one product. These processes were put together in a line format by using several automated machines, as well as the automation of the transporting operation that carries the product from machine to machine for automated machining.

A 13 Percent Improvement by Upgrading the Machining Program 167

The Problem The speed drops in the first process were a major factor in increasing costs and in lowering the machining output per hour, as can be seen in the table below.

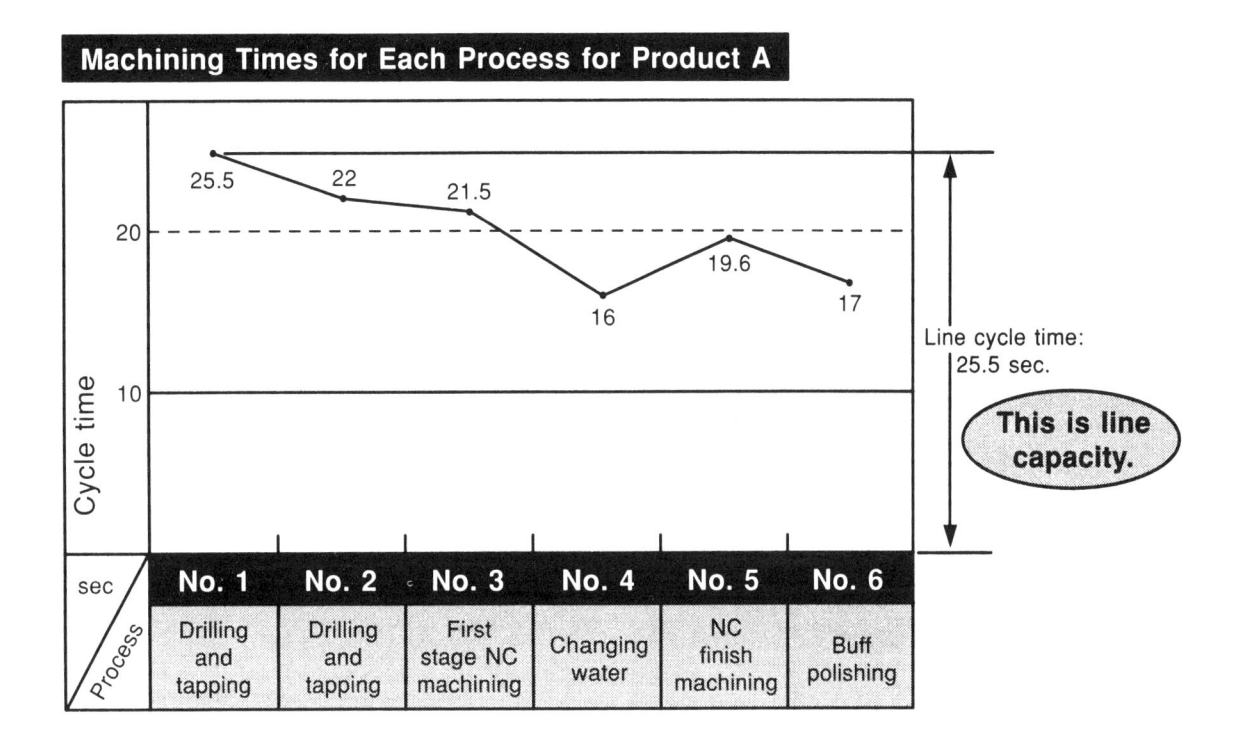

Machining Times for Each Process for Product A

Process	No. 1 Drilling and tapping	No. 2 Drilling and tapping	No. 3 First stage NC machining	No. 4 Changing water	No. 5 NC finish machining	No. 6 Buff polishing
Cycle time (sec)	25.5	22	21.5	16	19.6	17

Line cycle time: 25.5 sec.

This is line capacity.

The Solution The machining program was upgraded to handle the order of movement for the loading unit, as shown below. This shortened cycle time and inproved overall line speed by 13 percent.

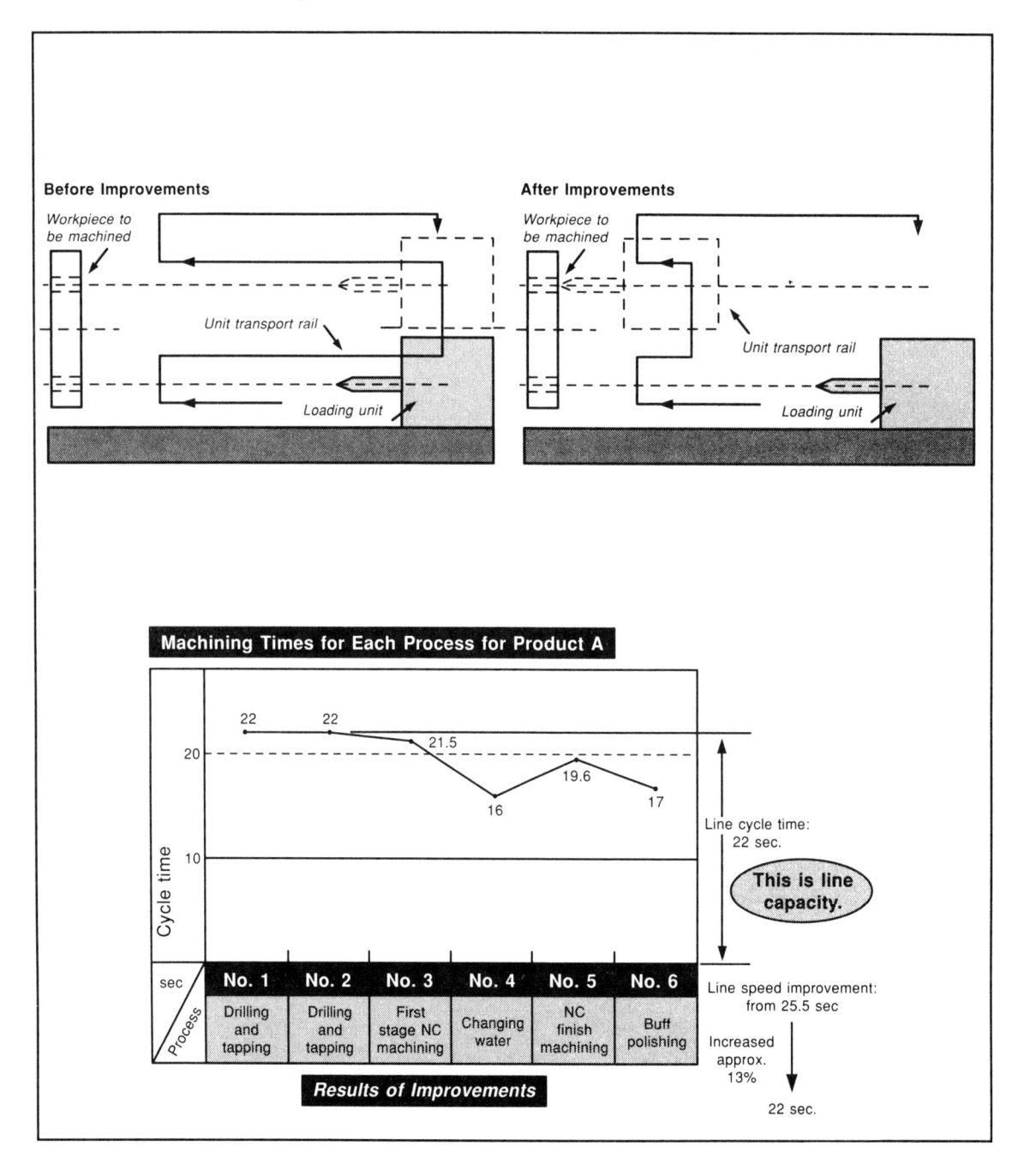

Before Improvements / After Improvements

Diagrams showing workpiece to be machined, unit transport rail, and loading unit before and after improvements.

Machining Times for Each Process for Product A

Process	No. 1 Drilling and tapping	No. 2 Drilling and tapping	No. 3 First stage NC machining	No. 4 Changing water	No. 5 NC finish machining	No. 6 Buff polishing
Cycle time (sec)	22	22	21.5	16	19.6	17

Line cycle time: 22 sec.
This is line capacity.

Line speed improvement: from 25.5 sec
Increased approx. 13%
↓
22 sec.

Results of Improvements

NEC Home Electronics, Ltd., Gotenba Plant

Loss due to Speed Drops

Maximizing Speed Efficiency for a Hydraulic Press

The Project

A time analysis was made of machine operations through a single cycle, revealing the core areas at which the machine was idle. It was discovered that there were a number of slowdowns and idle operations because those who made the operation time settings judged all operations in terms of safety, using as their criteria only the intuition and experience they had built up with conventional ways of operating. Tests were performed with overlapping operations concerned with quality and safety, and a number of small improvements were made that resulted in a reduction of cycle time by one-fourth.

This reduction resulted in a 137 percent increase in productivity, which translated into an additional $3,300-plus output per month—not an inconsiderable amount.

The Process The processes take place on a hydraulic die press, shown at the bottom of the following diagram. A number of discrete steps were required, as shown.

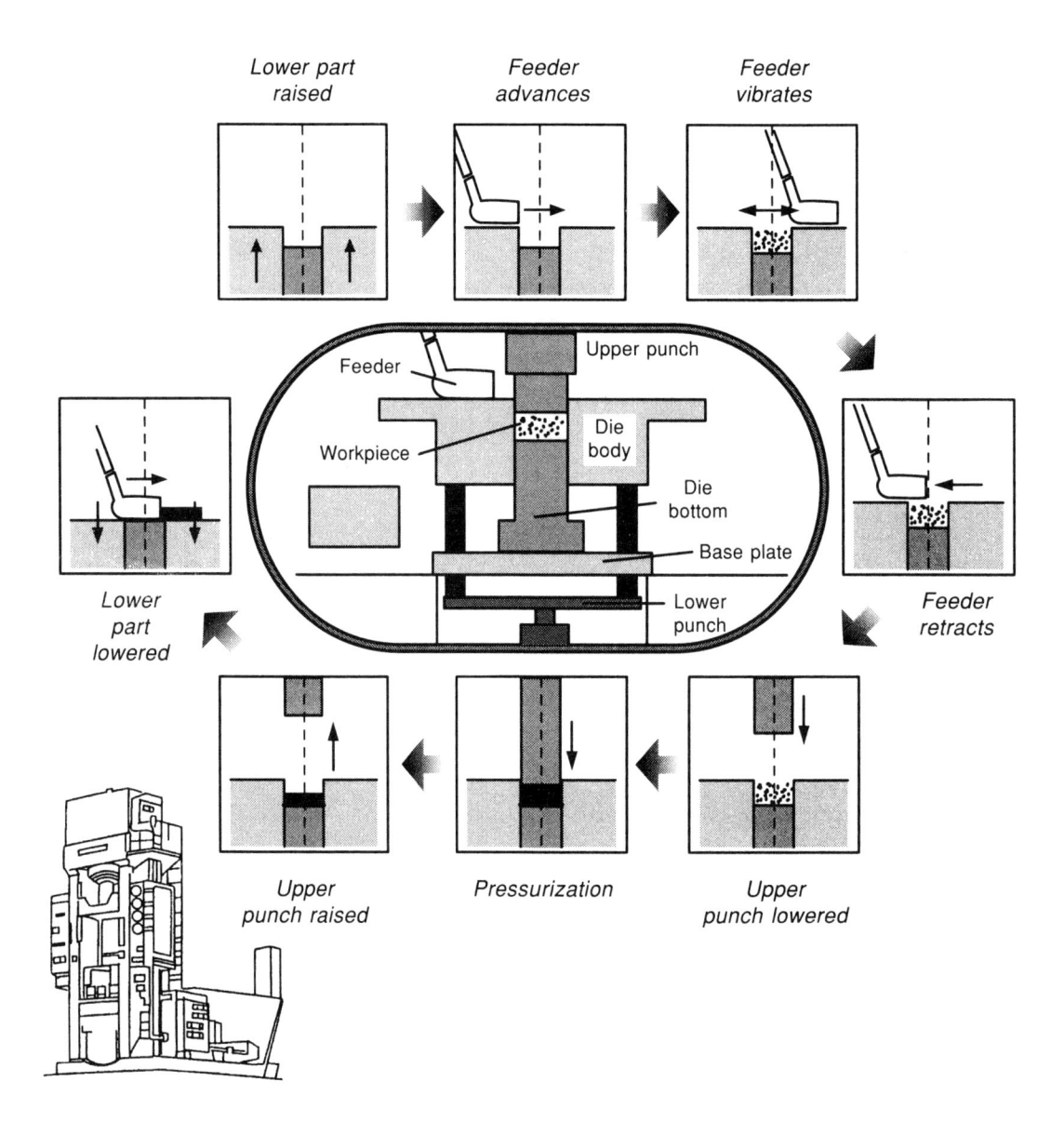

Maximizing Speed Efficiency for a Hydraulic Press 171

The Problem In each 18.1 second cycle, there were a number of places where time was lost:

✓ Feeder vibration

✓ Lowering upper ram at low speed

✓ Raising upper ram

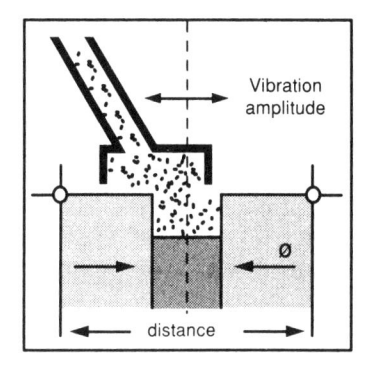

(1) Feeder vibration

Distance of vibration amplitude is great, compared to shape (circumference) of workpiece in die. Number of amplitudes is great.

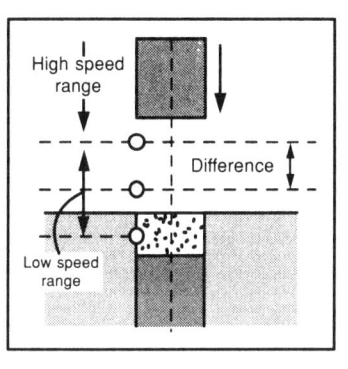

(1) Upper ram lowered at low speed

The point at which upper punch was changed to low speed was too soon, using too much time prior to start of cutting. There were individual differences in setting of this changeover point.

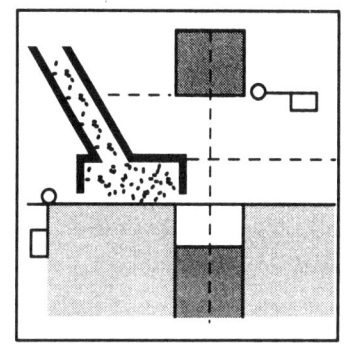

(3) Upper ram raised

The upper punch stroke was too long. The timing was not good between the upper punch and the feeder movement.

The Solution   Feeder vibration was lowered from 4 to 2.1 seconds. Additional improvements were made in the pressure extraction of the lower ram, feeder advance and retraction, high-speed lowering of the upper punch, low-speed lowering of the upper punch, and raising of the upper punch. The net result was to change the cycle time from 18.1 to 13.2 seconds.

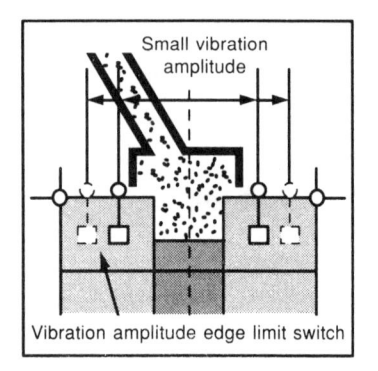

Limit switch positions were established on the inside so that the feeder would vibrate within the workpiece shape area (circumference).

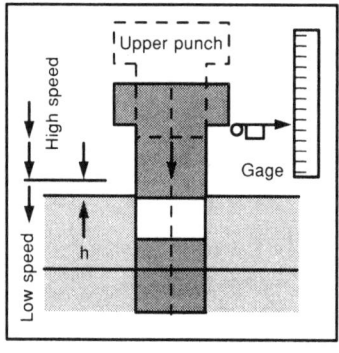

A gage was added to hold the movement of the upper punch (from high to low speed) in the minimum amount of time; dimensions of h were standardized at 10 mm.

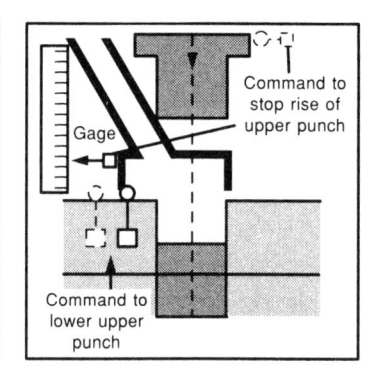

A gage was added to hold stroke movement of upper punch to minimum movement distance. Also, changes were made to ensure that the upper punch lowering command was issued quickly, so that upper punch and feeder operations would overlap.

Japan Powder Metallurgy Co., Ltd., Yamashina Office

Loss due to Speed Drops

Reducing Machining Cycle Time for Special Pulleys

The Project The line in question is made up of two numerically controlled lathes and one machining center, but it had a low daily output and high costs. Time studies were taken of operator motions, walk time, machining time, and the like, a man-machine chart was compiled, and improvement projects were brought into focus. The man-machine chart showed that the lack of balance in machining times between the machining center and the NC lathes had given rise to long period of times spent waiting. The movement of the operators was also overly complex. The major improvements included changes in the layout and the creation of special fixtures to reduce the machining time of the machining center.

The Process Six different processes were involved, as shown in the diagram below.

Man-Machine Chart Diagram

EQUIPMENT	PROCESS	DIAGRAM OF PROCESS	MACHINING TIME
	Forged materials		148 sec.
① NC lathe 1	Finish machining of ID		
② Hydraulic pressure insertion machine	Insertion of mandrel		168 sec.
③ NC lathe 2	Finish machining of OD		
④	Air feed		
⑤ Machining center	Milling and chamfering at three locations / R-groove machining at eight locations	Milling and chamfering at three locations	230 sec.
⑥	Inspection		

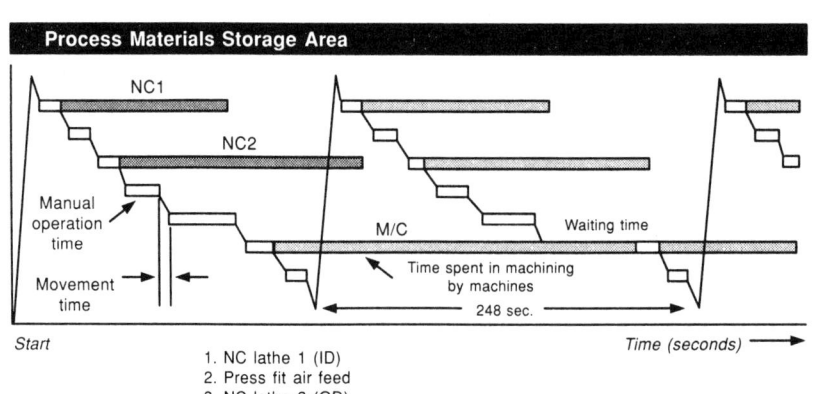

Process Materials Storage Area

- NC1
- NC2
- Manual operation time
- Movement time
- M/C
- Waiting time
- Time spent in machining by machines
- 248 sec.
- Start
- Time (seconds) →

1. NC lathe 1 (ID)
2. Press fit air feed
3. NC lathe 2 (OD)
4. Press fit air feed, OD inspection
5. Machining
6. Storage of parts passing milling inspection

Reducing Machining Cycle Time for Special Pulleys

The Problem The lack of machining time balance between the NC lathes and the machining center forced operators to wait for long periods of time. A study of basic turning conditions also resulted in the discovery of a number of other problems:

- ✓ Machine directions were wrong
- ✓ There was too much distance between the lathes and the machining center
- ✓ Material was stacked in a way that made it difficult to handle
- ✓ Too much time was required for bleeding air
- ✓ Too much time was required for tool changes
- ✓ Time was wasted in making air cuts
- ✓ Too much time was used in returning tools to their zero positions
- ✓ Many movements were simply wasted
- ✓ The materials storage area was in the wrong place
- ✓ The inspection table was in the wrong place
- ✓ The cutting tank was underground
- ✓ Too much time was spent in oil replenishment
- ✓ There were deviations in cycle time for the different processes
- ✓ Too much time was spent in indexing workpieces

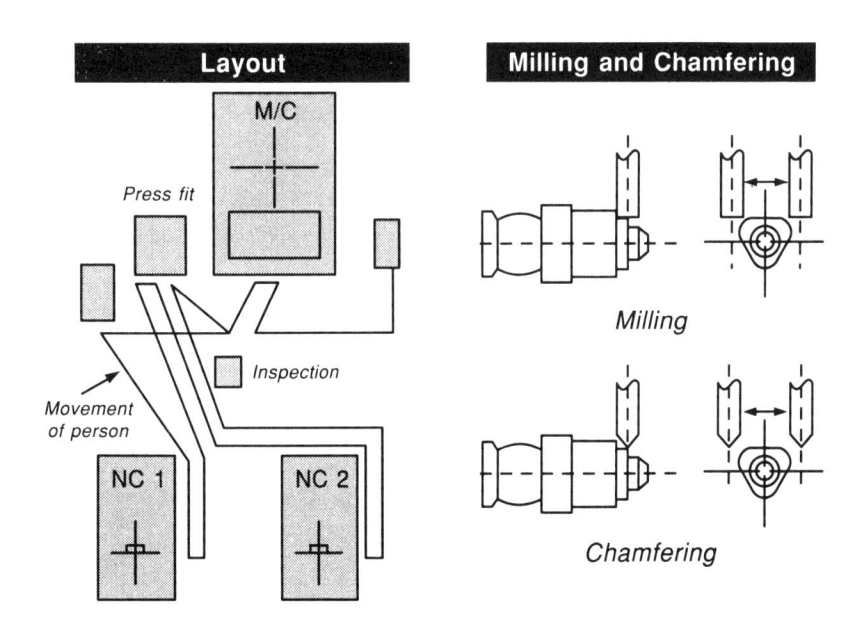

The Solution   Three major improvements were made:

- ✓ The layout was changed
- ✓ Milling and chamfering were performed at the same time
- ✓ Tools were designed for common use on the machining center

These improvements enabled a cycle time reduction from 248 to 190 seconds.

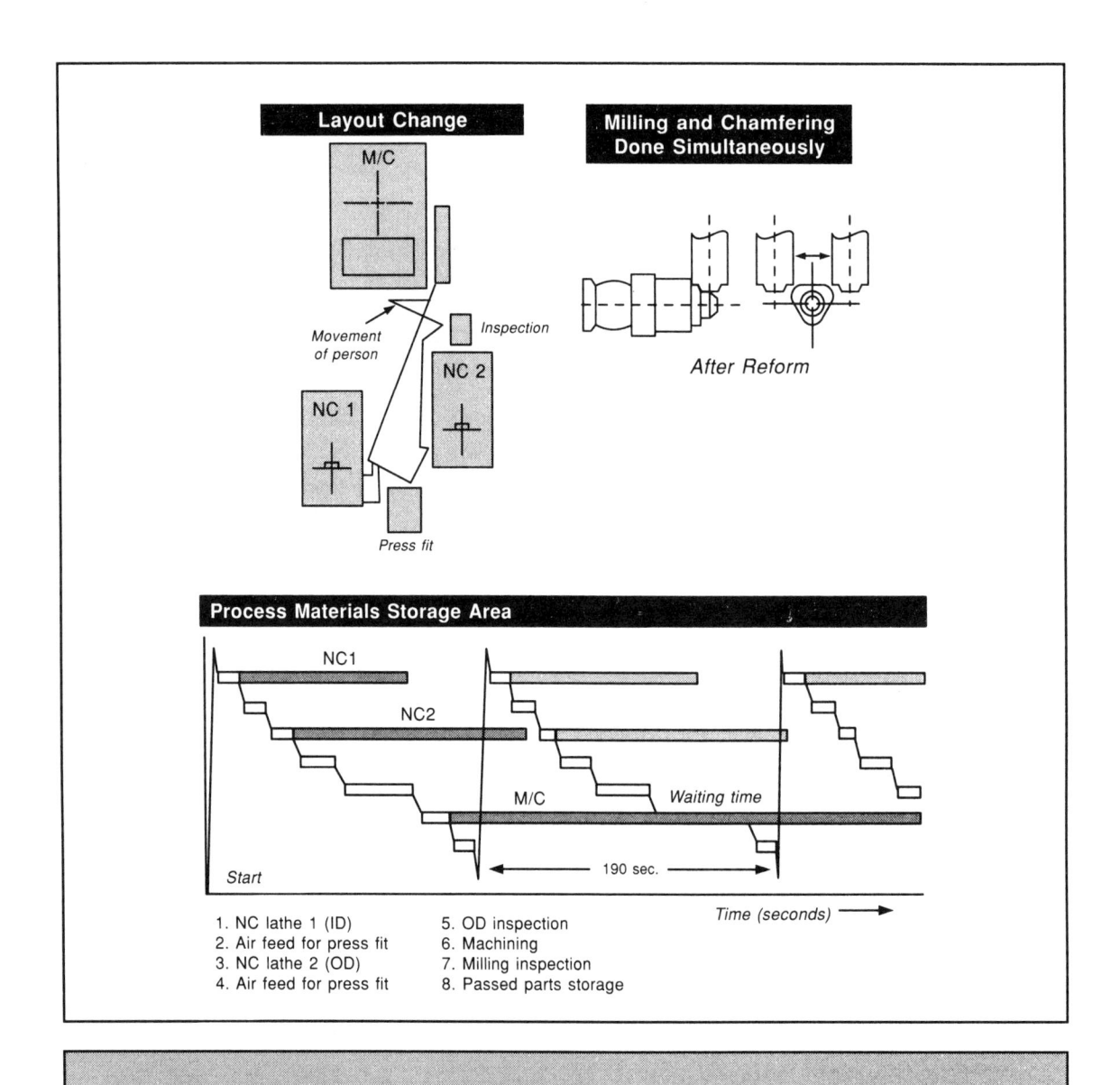

Layout Change

Milling and Chamfering Done Simultaneously

After Reform

Process Materials Storage Area

190 sec.

Time (seconds)

1. NC lathe 1 (ID)
2. Air feed for press fit
3. николи lathe 2 (OD)
4. Air feed for press fit
5. OD inspection
6. Machining
7. Milling inspection
8. Passed parts storage

Nihon Spindle Mfg. Co., Ltd., Main plant

Loss due to Defects

Countermeasures against Defects in Circularity with Cylindrical Grinding Machines

The Project

The basic conditions were established through an initial round of improvements, but this met with no appreciable results, so a PM analysis was made of the defects being produced. One problem was workpiece center runout in response to the grinding wheel. As a result of the application of PM analysis to this problem, the relationship between the center pushing side clamping force and abnormal wear was clarified, and improvements were made to reduce the problem. Attention then was given to improvements designed to maintain product quality at the machine. One measure adopted in this regard was the use of an 8μ coating that would make the wear threshold (time when change is needed) visibly evident. This enabled the operator to perform autonomous controls (done every morning during the autonomous checks) and thus eliminate quality defects.

The Process The processes involved are shown below. Special attention was paid to the grinding of the outer diameter of the shaft.

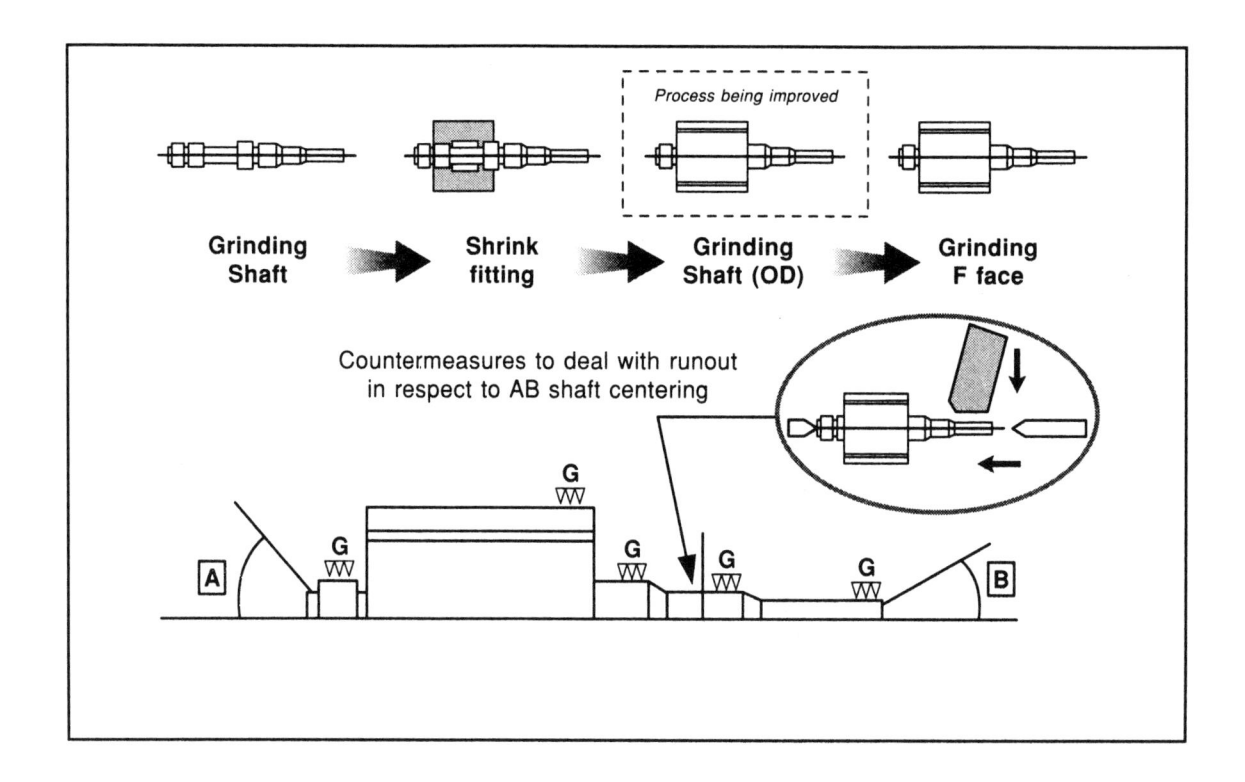

Countermeasures against Defects in Circularity with Cylindrical Grinding Machines 179

The Problem   The trends which emerged as a result of measuring each individual defect in all points are shown on the graph below. A PM analysis was conducted, then a machining point analysis, and it was hypothesized that the problem was runout between the center of the grinding wheel and the center of the workpiece. The locations of the defects and the conditions under which defects arose were tabulated, and the conclusion was that there was a problem on the center pushing side.

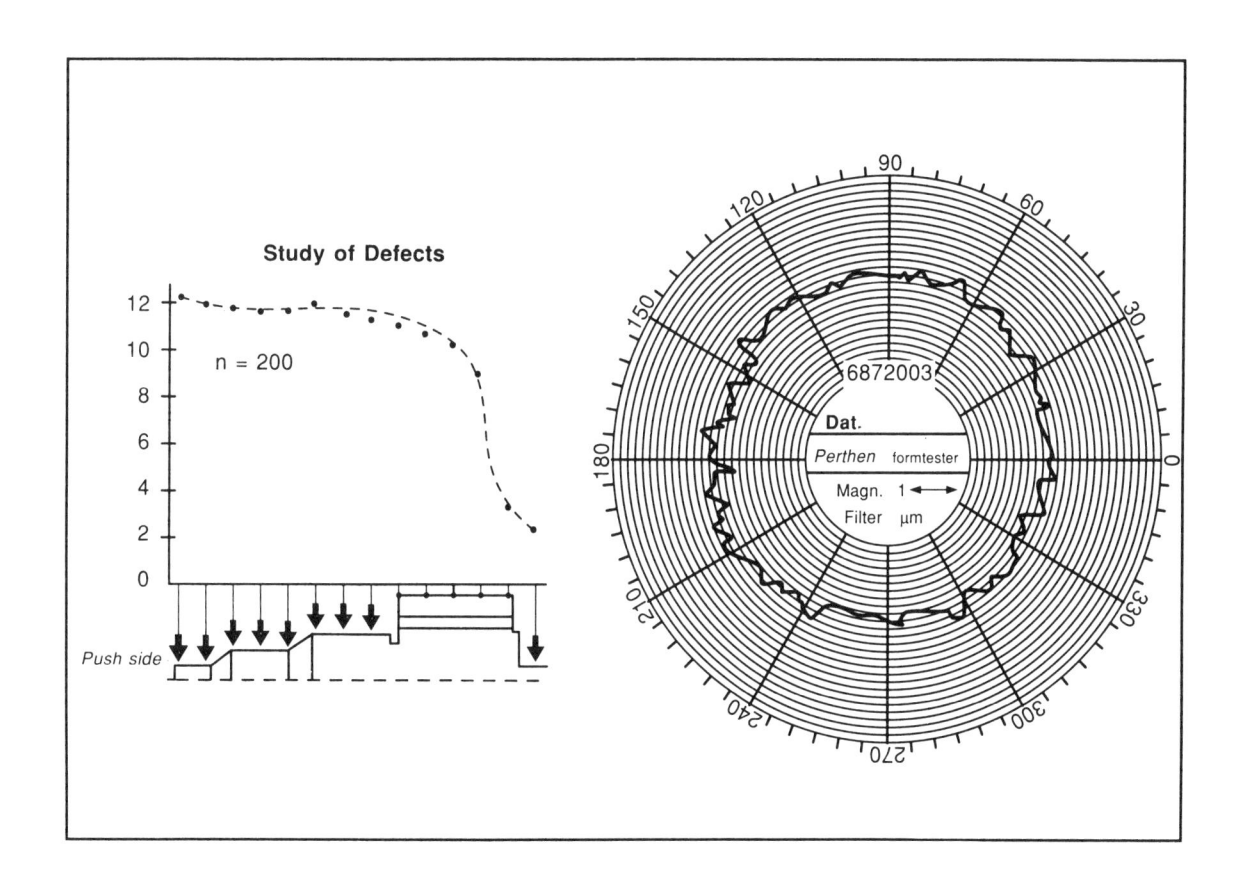

The Solution

In order to improve the wiper effect, which was used to eliminate foreign matter from the center, the cutting tool was notched. As a wear-resistant measure designed to stop the use of centers that had worn beyond a threshold of 9μ, a titan coating was added. Thus operators could see when the coating was worn through and tell visually when the tool needed to be changed. This measure enabled the operators to perform visual checks during their morning autonomous inspections, and it brought defects to zero. The elimination of the need for quality checks made a significant impact on the increase of productivity.

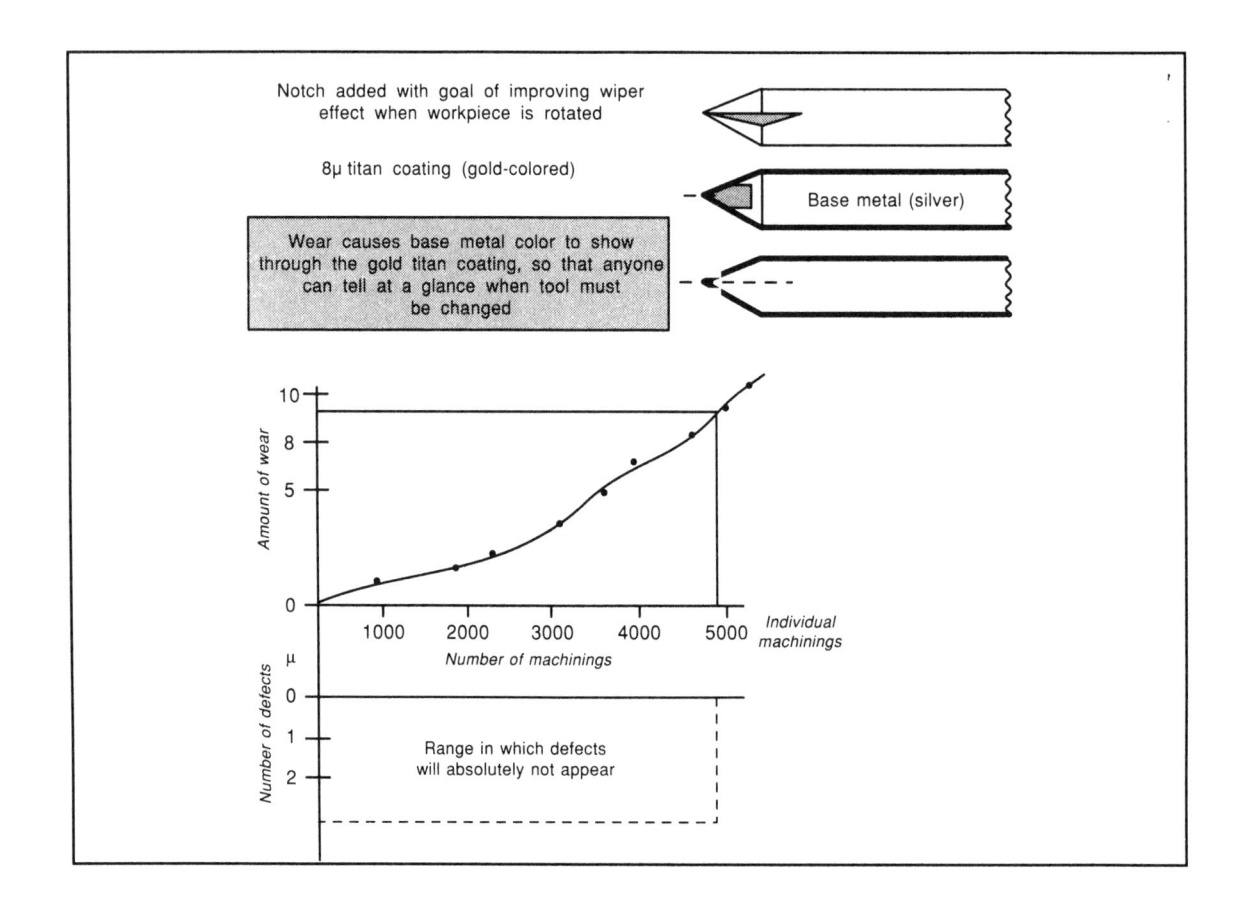

Notch added with goal of improving wiper effect when workpiece is rotated

8μ titan coating (gold-colored)

Base metal (silver)

Wear causes base metal color to show through the gold titan coating, so that anyone can tell at a glance when tool must be changed

Range in which defects will absolutely not appear

Amount of wear (μ) vs *Number of machinings* / *Individual machinings*

Number of defects

Zexel Co., Ltd., Konan Plant

Loss due to Defects

Reducing Defects in Welding

The Project   The processes for this product involve the use of a welding robot to perform CO_2 welding on four types of brackets on to a column pipe. Defects experienced include off-center welding, pinholes, holes, and the like, and nearly all defects required manual reworking. The improvement project first identified the causes of defects, finding them in a wide range of factors, including workpiece, welding robot, welding fixture, and welding method. Some 38 main improvements were implemented, over a period of five months. The result was that the monthly defect rate went from 14.2 percent to 1.3 percent, and the manual reworking time dropped from 1730 to 154 minutes per month.

The Process   The machining process flow is shown below, and the product made is pictured to the right.

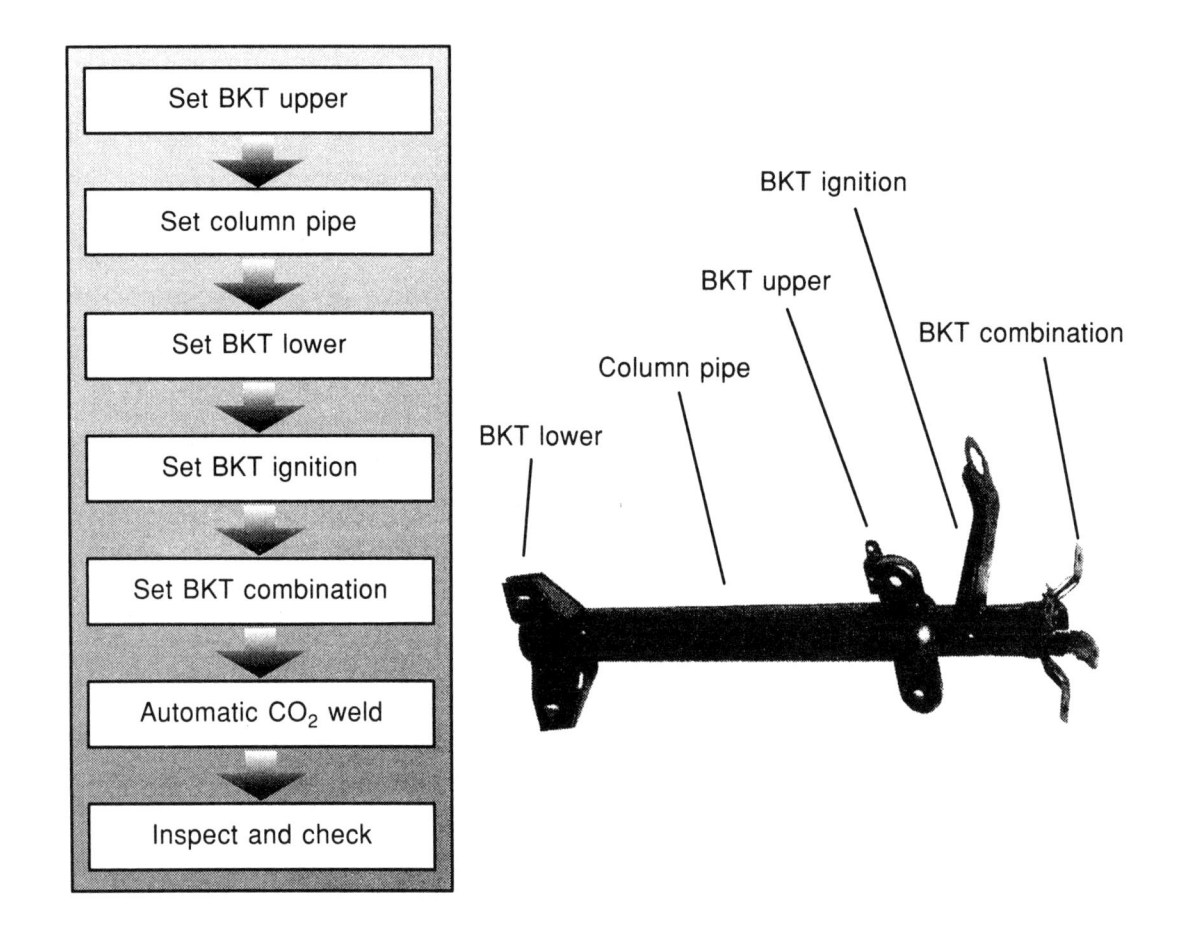

```
Set BKT upper
     ↓
Set column pipe
     ↓
Set BKT lower
     ↓
Set BKT ignition
     ↓
Set BKT combination
     ↓
Automatic CO₂ weld
     ↓
Inspect and check
```

Labeled product parts: BKT lower, Column pipe, BKT upper, BKT ignition, BKT combination.

Reducing Defects in Welding 183

The Problem   Manual reworking required 1730 minutes per month. A total of 47 products were thrown away each month because of unrepairable defects. These problems are broken down in the following table.

Problems / Location	Off center	Pin holes	Holes	**TOTAL**
BKT upper	232	14	5	252
BKT lower	15	10	10	35
BKT ignition	218	81	106	405
TOTAL	466	105	122	692

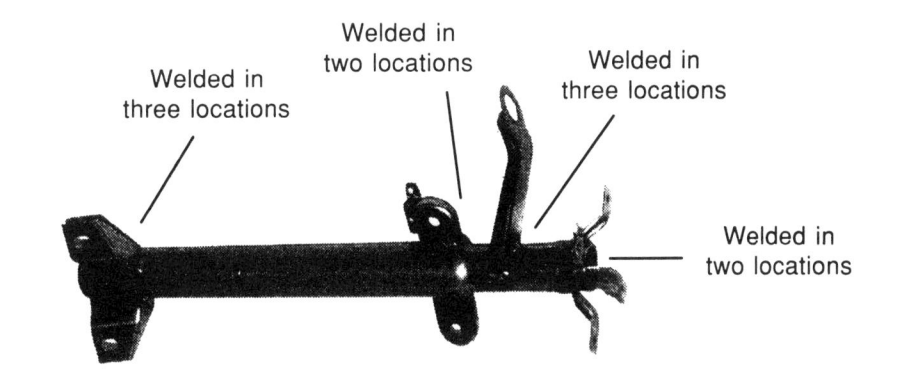

Welded in three locations

Welded in two locations

Welded in three locations

Welded in two locations

184   TPM CASE STUDIES

The Solution   The improvements to the workpiece are shown in the figure below. Improvements to the equipment include the following:

- ✓ Changes were made in the teaching process for the robot (from linearity to arc)
- ✓ Welding wire torsion was improved by changing the conduit tube from 3^M to 2^M
- ✓ Wiping cycle was upgraded
- ✓ Welding current was stabilized
- ✓ Welding contact tip was improved
- ✓ Welding torch angle and distance were revaluated
- ✓ Welding fixture was improved

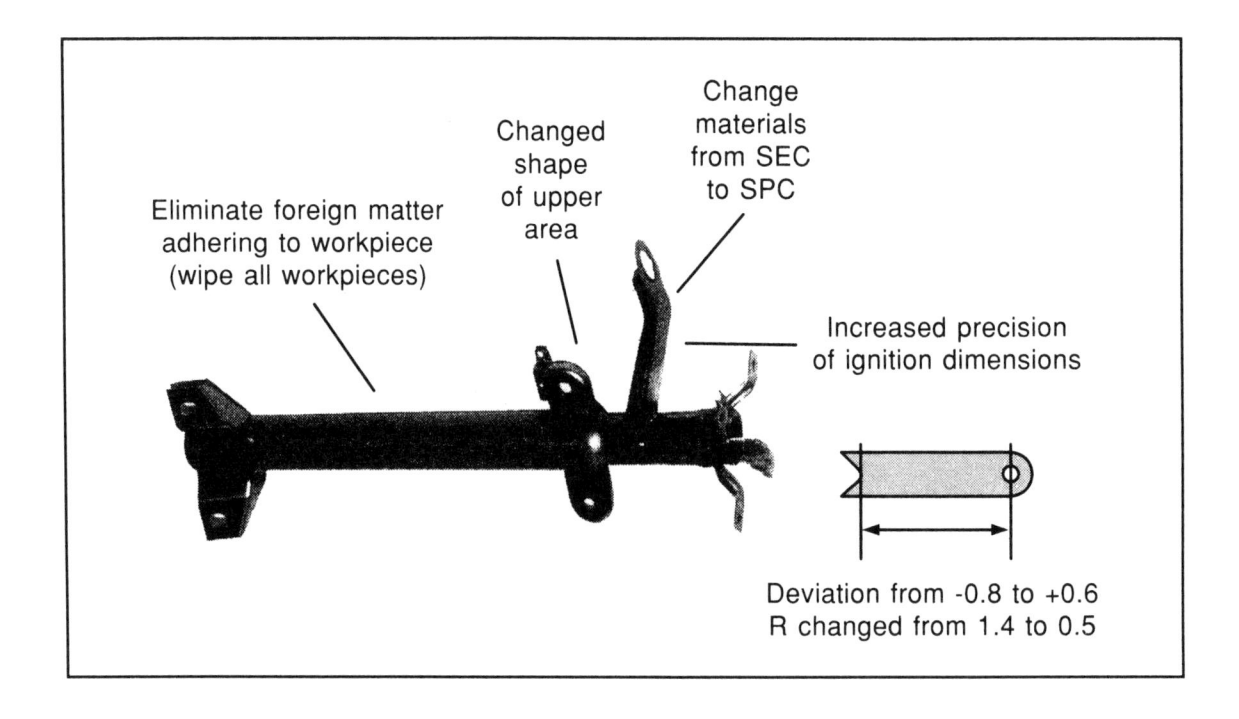

Eliminate foreign matter adhering to workpiece (wipe all workpieces)

Changed shape of upper area

Change materials from SEC to SPC

Increased precision of ignition dimensions

Deviation from -0.8 to +0.6
R changed from 1.4 to 0.5

Lead Co., Ltd.

Loss due to Startups

Immediately Acceptable Quality for Machine Pressed Powder Molded Products

The Project Many operations in the powder molding processes require a good deal of experience and intuition, and it has always been considered virtually impossible to produce acceptable quality immediately from startup because of the many adjustments required. This has long been recognized as a source of loss, but one that could not be helped. The problems in the so-called "intuitive" jobs became evident when these jobs were quantified, and this enabled the performance of a number of experiments to determine what improvement proposals would work. For example, adjustments in the amount of fill were linked to the operator's handle adjustments through the use of visible dividing rings.

This reduced the number of trial formings from 50 to four, cut the time to one-fifth the original level, and made it possible to achieve acceptable quality virtually from the start.

The Process   There are six main manufacturing processes: mixing, forming, sintering, machine processing, inspection, and shipping. Principle set procedures are as follows:

- ✓ Die body and lower punch surfaces aligned. By keeping die body and upper surface of lower punch as the same surface, the extrusion adjustment nut (see diagram below) is adjusted.
- ✓ Fill depth set. The setting for the fill depth for the powder (input allowance) is made by adjusting the fill adjustment nut to the depth of fill.
- ✓ Thickness adjustment. The stroke volume for the upper punch is adjusted by the use of the upper ram adjustment nut.

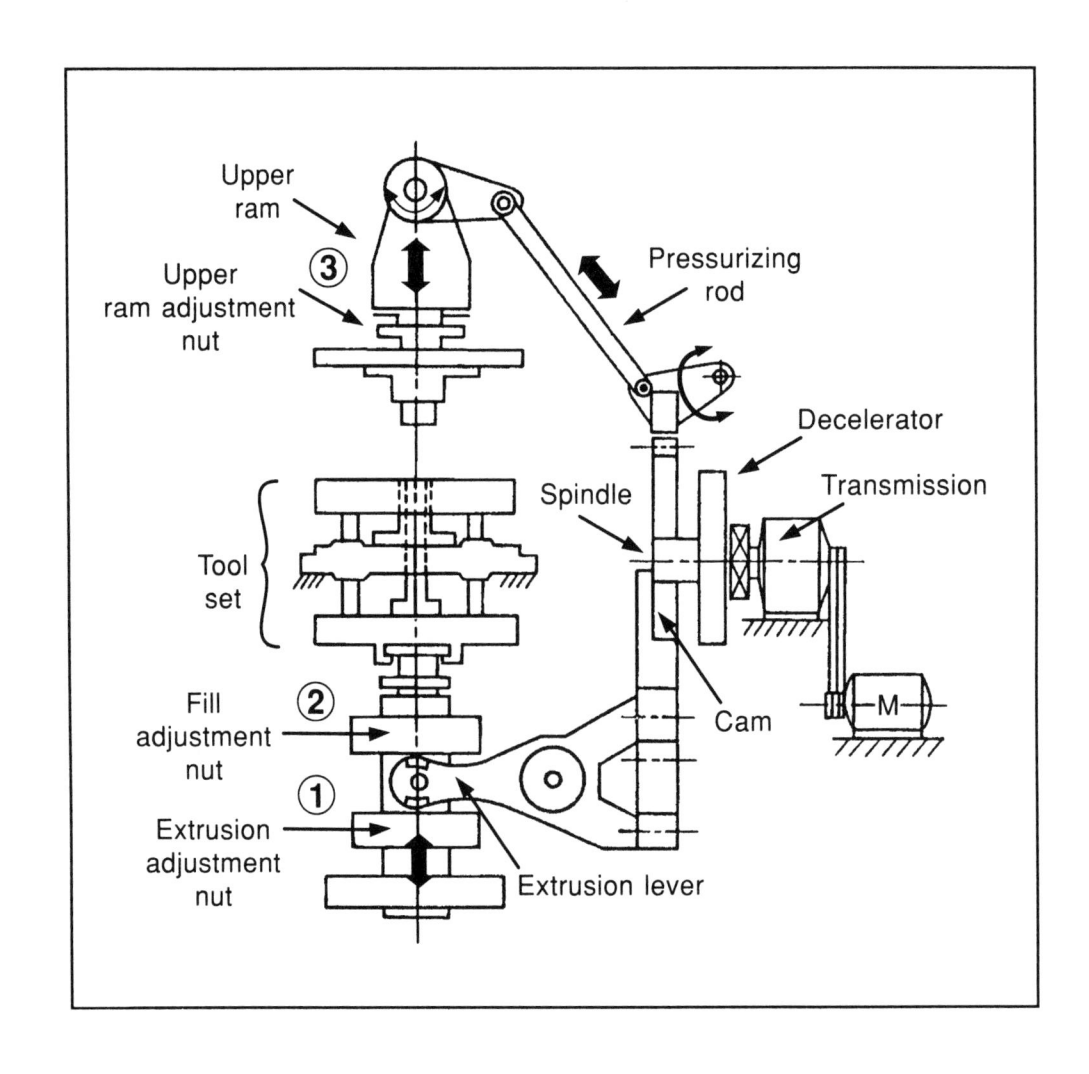

The Problem

There were three major problems, as described below.

First, the indicators on scale B, used to align the surfaces of the die body and the upper punch, were 1mm apart. This was not fine enough, thus requiring more time for the adjustment operation. Because of changes in the reference value when the die end surface was corrected, adjustment time was 3 min. 40 sec., and two trial runs were required.

Second, weight was determined by the fill height (H), and scale A was used to adjust to the reference point. Because model differences and unclear dimensions for H made this an intuitive operation, it required about 5 min. 5 sec. for adjustments to be completed. Up to 20 trial runs were required.

Third, because the dead point position (reference face) was unclear, scale C—used for positioning for H_1—was of no use. Adjustment time was 6 min. 25 sec., and 30 trial runs were required.

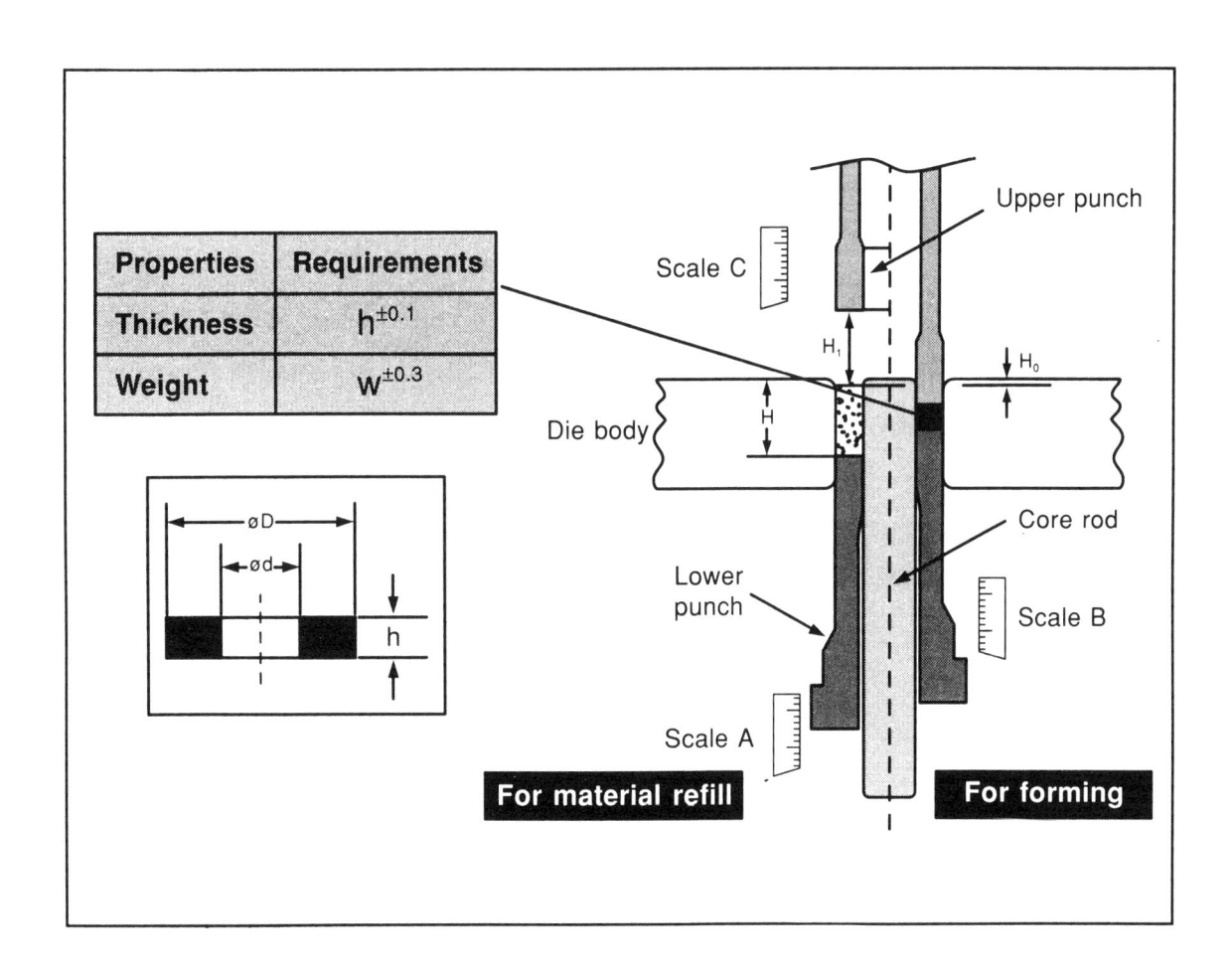

Properties	Requirements
Thickness	$h^{\pm 0.1}$
Weight	$w^{\pm 0.3}$

The Solution

The problems were addressed as follows.

First, a micrometer was used to align the die body and the lower punch surface. After dimension B has been taken, split ring B can be moved by a single touch (through the use of a base metal with a slide for positioning) to the proper position.

Second, the setting of fill height dimension A is done by the use of a block gage, and the setting is made by turning split ring A. One notch on the ring represents a fill of 0.06 grams for minute adjustments, and the final positioning is set by the use of a base metal with a slide.

Third, the reference value that could be used to stop the upper punch at the dead point position was ascertained, and stroke C is now positioned by the upper ram adjustment nut, with a block gage.

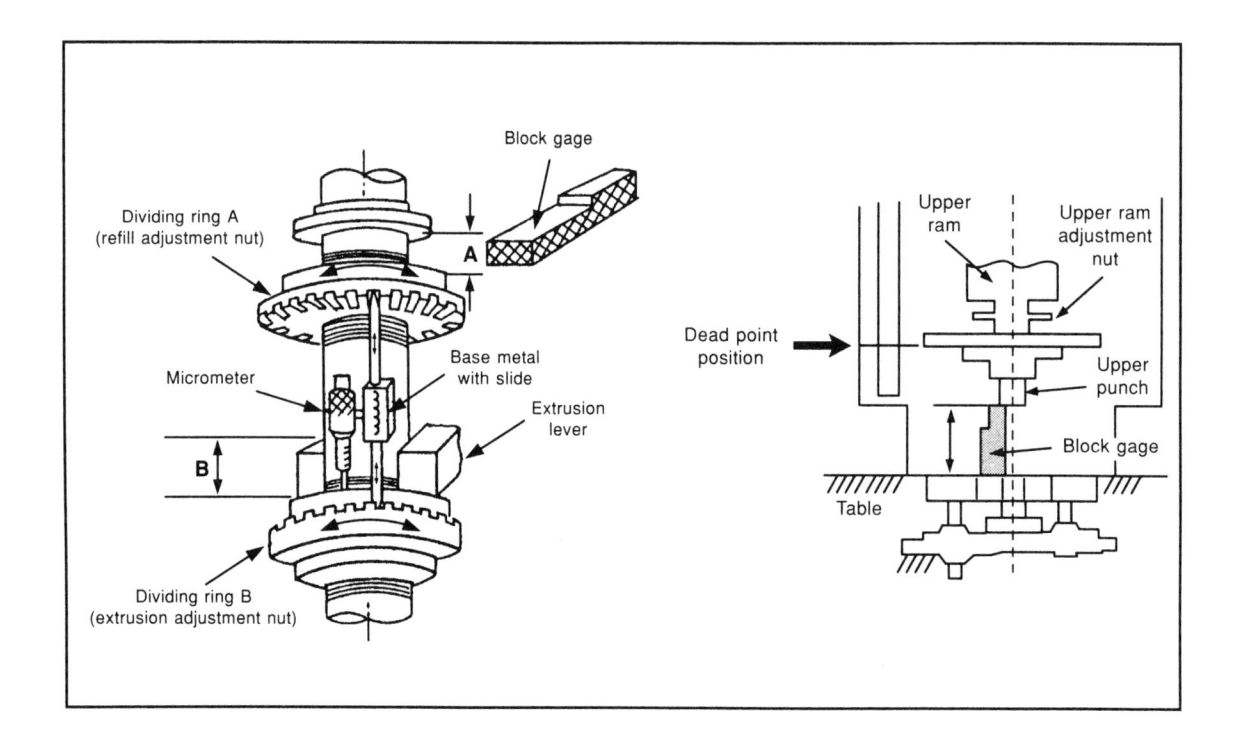

Japan Powder Metallurgy Co., Ltd., Yamashina Office

BOOKS FROM PRODUCTIVITY PRESS

Productivity Press publishes and distributes materials on continuous improvement in productivity, quality, and the creative involvement of all employees. Many of our products are direct source materials from Japan that have been translated into English for the first time and are available exclusively from Productivity. Supplemental products and services include membership groups, conferences, seminars, in-house training and consulting, audio-visual training programs, and industrial study missions. Call toll-free 1-800-394-6868 for our free catalog.

Uptime
Strategies for Excellence in Maintenance Management
John Dixon Campbell

Campbell outlines a blueprint for a world class maintenance a program by examining, piece by piece, its essential elements—leadership (strategy and management), control (data management, measures, tactics, planning and scheduling), continuous improvement (RCM and TPM), and quantum leaps (process reengineering). He explains each element in detail, using simple language and practical examples from a side range of industries. This book is for every manager who needs to see the "big picture" of maintenance management. In addition to maintenance, engineering, and manufacturing managers, all business managers will benefit from this comprehensive yet realistic approach to improving asset performance.
ISBN 1-56327-053-6 / 180 pages / $35.00 / Order UP-B239

Fast Focus on TQM
A Concise Guide to Companywide Learning
Derm Barrett

Finally, here's one source for all your TQM questions. Compiled in this concise, easy-to-read handbook are definitions and detailed explanations of over 160 key terms used in TQM. Organized in a simple alphabetical glossary form, the book can be used as a primer for anyone being introduced to TQM or as a complete reference guide. It helps align teams, departments, or entire organizations in a common understanding and use of TQM terminology. For anyone entering or currently involved in TQM, this is one resource you must have.
ISBN 1-56327-049-8 / 186 pages / $19.95 / Order FAST-B239

Handbook for Productivity Measurement and Improvement
William F. Christopher and Carl G. Thor, eds.

An unparalleled resource! In over 100 chapters, nearly 80 front-runners in the quality movement reveal the evolving theory and specific practices of world-class organizations. Spanning a wide variety of industries and business sectors, they discuss quality and productivity in manufacturing, service industries, profit centers, administration, nonprofit and government institutions, health care and education. Contributors include Robert C. Camp, Peter F. Drucker, Jay W. Forrester, Joseph M. Juran, Robert S. Kaplan, John W. Kendrick, Yasuhiro Monden, and Lester C. Thurow. Comprehensive in scope and organized for easy reference, this compendium belongs in every company and academic institution concerned with business and industrial viability.
ISBN 1-56327-007-2 / 1344 pages / $90.00 / Order HPM-B239

Productivity Press, Inc., Dept. BK, P.O. Box 13390, Portland, OR 97213-0390
Telephone: 1-800-394-6868   Fax: 1-800-394-6286

TPM Development Program
Implementing Total Productive Maintenance
Seiichi Nakajima (ed.)

This book outlines a three-year program for systematic TPM development and implementation. It describes in detail the five principal developmental activities of TPM:
- Systematic elimination of the six big equipment-related losses through small group activities
- Autonomous maintenance (by operators)
- Scheduled maintenance for the maintenance department
- Training in operation and maintenance skills
- Comprehensive equipment management from the design stage

Long considered the "bible" of TPM, this book provides critical guidance for anyone implementing TPM.
ISBN 0-915299-37-2 / 428 pages / $85.00 / Order DTPM-B239

TPM in Process Industries
Tokutaro Suzuki (ed.)

Process industries have a particularly urgent need for collaborative equipment management systems like TPM that can absolutely guarantee safe, stable operation. In *TPM in Process Industries*, top consultants from JIPM (Japan Institute of Plant Maintenance) document approaches to implementing TPM in process industries. They focus on the process environment and equipment issues such as process loss structure and calculation, autonomous maintenance, equipment and process improvement, and quality maintenance. Must reading for any manager in the process industry.
ISBN 1-56327-036-6 / 400 pages / $85.00 / Order TPMPI-B239

Training for TPM
A Manufacturing Success Story
Nachi-Fujikoshi (ed.)

A detailed case study of TPM implementation at a world-class manufacturer of bearings, precision machine tools, dies, industrial equipment, and robots. In just 2-1/2 years the company was awarded Japan's prestigious PM Prize for its program. Here's a detailed account of their improvement activities—and an impressive model for yours.
ISBN 0-915299-34-8 / 274 pages / $65.00 / Order CTPM-B239

TO ORDER: Write, phone, or fax Productivity Press, Dept. BK, P.O. Box 13390, Portland, OR 97213-0390, phone 1-800-394-6868, fax 1-800-394-6286. Send check or charge to your credit card (American Express, Visa, MasterCard accepted).

U.S. ORDERS: Add $5 shipping for first book, $2 each additional for UPS surface delivery. Add $5 for each AV program containing 1 or 2 tapes; add $12 for each AV program containing 3 or more tapes. We offer attractive quantity discounts for bulk purchases of individual titles; call for more information.

INTERNATIONAL ORDERS: Write, phone, or fax for quote and indicate shipping method desired. For international callers, telephone number is 503-235-0600 and fax number is 503-235-0909. Prepayment in U.S. dollars must accompany your order (checks must be drawn on U.S. banks). When quote is returned with payment, your order will be shipped promptly by the method requested.

NOTE: Prices are in U.S. dollars and are subject to change without notice.

Productivity Press, Inc., Dept. BK, P.O. Box 13390, Portland, OR 97213-0390
Telephone: 1-800-394-6868   Fax: 1-800-394-6286